CFO NITI

CFO NITI

CANDID CONVERSATIONS WITH INDIA'S FINEST FINANCE LEADERS | GET INSPIRED

PRAMOD BAGRI & SANDEEP KUMAR

KONARK

Konark Publishers Pvt Ltd
New Delhi • Seattle

Konark Publishers Pvt. Ltd
206, First Floor,
Peacock Lane, Shahpur Jat,
New Delhi 110 049
Phone: +91-11-41055065
Mob : +91-93552 93900, +91-93552 94900
e-mail: india@konarkpublishers.com
website: www.konarkpublishers.com

Konark Publishers International
8615, 13th Ave SW,
Seattle WA 98106
Phone: (415) 409-9988
e-mail: us@konarkpublishers.com

ISBN: 978-81-949286-9-0

Edited by Dipali Singh

Cover Design by Misha Oberoi

Book Design by Dushyant Parasher

Clipart Design by Vasu Agrawal

Typeset by Saanvi Graphics, Noida

Printed and bound at Thomson Press (India) Ltd

*Remembering **Maneesh Bhandari** whom we lost in 2020.*

Dear friend, this book is dedicated to you.

You remain in our thoughts.

Contents

Advance Praise

Great to see a book on some of India's finest CFOs. A Chief Financial Officer is a co-pilot to the business head, and is looked up to by the rest of the organization to ensure governance, manage risks, provide business solutions and drive strategy towards fulfilling the vision and mission for the team. Doing so requires integrity, backbone, functional excellence, business connect and leadership skills. Delighted to see this come through in the book.

—AMIT AGARWAL
Senior Vice President and Country Manager,
Amazon India

A very interesting read and must-have for all aspiring finance leaders. Six of India's best finance brains have opened up to give a bird's-eye view of how the CFO office operates and what it takes to run a successful finance organization. Young professionals would especially enjoy the life journeys and career growth of CFOs, and some practical advice on key skills needed to succeed in their careers. A great opportunity to learn from the insights of these personalities.

—KENICHI AYUKAWA
MD & CEO, Maruti Suzuki India Ltd

Good financial management can make a major difference to the success of any business organization. I would like to congratulate the authors for painstakingly capturing the financial wisdom of some of the best companies in this area and making it available to other business leaders to emulate and younger finance professionals to learn from. Of particular interest is the element how the CFO's role has evolved from being a controller to a partner at every step of business.

—R.C. BHARGAVA
Chairman, Maruti Suzuki India Ltd

In the fast-changing world, the role of a CFO is evolving much beyond finance. Today, the CFO is expected to be a catalyst for business transformation and a growth enabler. They bring the outside in, foster capabilities of the future and deal with ambiguous and uncertain situations to steer their company ahead.

Pramod Bagri and Sandeep Kumar's *CFO Niti* chronicles in an easy-to-read interview format, the learnings of leading CFOs in the country and how they have supported the journey of business excellence. I am sure each one of us—be it a student, an entrepreneur or a business leader—can learn from the experiences and wisdom of some of the finest finance professionals in the country.

—SANJIV MEHTA

CMD, Hindustan Unilever Limited
President, Unilever South Asia

The CFO is like a co-pilot for the organization. A good CFO can make an immense difference to how an organization is run. Not only should he or she possess the functional expertise that gets him or her into the job but also the business perspective that can make him or her an invaluable thought partner to the CEO. While authors have chosen well in featuring Koushik (Chatterjee, Executive Director and CFO, Tata Steel) in this book, I am sure all the other CFOs featured have also played a similarly important and pivotal role in their careers, and that makes this book a great treasure house of experiences that provides a lot of learning for future CFOs and business leaders.

—T. V. NARENDRAN

CEO & MD, Tata Steel

Life lessons are irreplaceable and impart the best learning. This book lucidly and very effectively summarizes for the benefit of the reader, practicing CFOs, aspiring CFOs, or for that matter all business or finance professionals, captivating lessons learned from the experiences of accomplished CFOs. Pramod and Sandeep have succeeded in getting the CFOs to open up and candidly share with the reader, about the people and events that shaped their lives.

—AMITABH CHAUDHRY
MD & CEO Axis Bank Ltd

The role of CFO has transformed from traditional financing and accounting focus to being a strategic partner to the CEO in shaping the vision plus growth of the organization and making crucial capital allocation decisions. Besides, they also are the conscience keepers for investors.

These world-class distinguished CFOs have played a pivotal role in driving their respective organizations to the top in their sector, together with a strong compliance and governance culture.

A must-read for all young professionals aspiring for a career in finance or indeed for existing management practitioners. Great to read how their personal journeys have guided their professional success.

—ASHU KHULLAR
Chief Executive Officer, Citi India
Region Head, South Asia

Through a series of engaging conversations with some exceptional CFOs, the authors have shone a light on the making of an outstanding CFO. The book also brings out the immense scope of the CFO's remit, which includes a key role in developing a company's strategy. As a consequence the CFO has to master a broad range of specializations. The book is a must-read for both aspiring CFOs as well as those wishing to hire dynamic and effective CFOs.

—ISHAAT HUSSAIN

Former Finance Director, Tata Sons

CFO Niti—as the title speaks—is an admirable anecdote of India's finest CFOs narrating their life journey, their ups and downs, the high stakes involved and the close calls that they took during their professional journey. It is a must-read not just for all finance professionals and young CFOs but for all corporate folks, especially those who occupy the C-Suites.

—JAYARAM EASWARAN

Author, Management Consultant and Independent Director – Jindal Stainless Ltd

I have always admired the role CFOs play as they are the real stewards of any firm. *CFO Niti* provides us insights into how six of India's finest CFOs have shaped their companies by following responsible growth strategy. These CFOs are leaders par excellence who have looked beyond numbers, accounting and audits, to build organizations of the 21st century. Positivity, sense of purpose, commitment, romancing with numbers, balancing risk—these are the attributes that define all six of them.

The book offers some interesting management nuggets and personal anecdotes of these iconic CFOs. The authors have done a commendable job in capturing the strong individualistic traits of each of these six leaders. These leaders have candidly shared their experiences and I am confident that the readers would be delighted to unlock this jewel box of learnings.

—KAKU NAKHATE

A very timely book. The role of CFO is evolving rapidly from holding final responsibility for accuracy and integrity of financial statements to becoming a conscience keeper of the firm to driving strategy and being a core partner to the CEO. The journey of six iconic CFOs captured with great insights and personal stories is a must-read, not only for budding finance professionals, but for all within the corporate world.

—KALPANA MORPARIA

Founder, KalMor Advisors

Good management comes from good judgement, and good judgement is acquired through lived experiences. This book provides readers with an insight into the lived experiences of some of India's top financial managements through in-depth interviews. The authors have done a great service in presenting the interview material in an engaging and organized way, whilst letting their protagonists' individual personalities shine through. The stories herein both inspire and provoke meaningful reflection.

—KARTHIK RAMANNA

Professor of Business & Public Policy, University of Oxford

I would like to congratulate the authors for bringing out the true colours of a CFO's life. *CFO Niti* is an apt title and corroborates with a strategic planning role that is expected of today's CFO. This book is a must-read for all finance professionals.

Readers will draw inspiration from the life lessons of India's six most accomplished CFOs. This book is about personal transformation, making career choices, of challenges confronting the CFO office and handling the C-Suite role.

—RAKESH CHOPRA

Chairman, Rajiv Gandhi Cancer Institute & Research Centre

This book certainly highlights the role of a CFO today, as he/she needs to be a visible leader in business, an excellent communicator and an influencer. The role has grown from a mere 'quarter to quarter' management, to ensuring that business operations are run efficiently and effectively to shape the organization's strategy for future growth and stability. Today's CFO certainly needs to be a true business partner to his/her CEO.

—S. RAMADORAI

Former CEO & MD, Tata Consultancy Services
Former Chairman, National Skill Development Agency & National Skill Development Corporation

CFO Niti is a book that fills a very large hole in an area that is a lot more significant than thought of. Actually, most people have never thought of how important the role of the CFO is in shaping the investment world—both good and bad. With some of the best Indian CFOs covered in this book, it will help demystify the CFO office and bring focus to the professional and personal lives of these leaders like never before.

—VALLABH BHANSALI

Co-Founder, ENAM Group

हरदीप एस पुरी
HARDEEP S PURI

सत्यमेव जयते

आवासन और शहरी कार्य राज्य मंत्री (स्वतंत्र प्रभार)
नागर विमानन राज्य मंत्री (स्वतंत्र प्रभार)
वाणिज्य एवं उद्योग राज्य मंत्री
भारत सरकार
Minister of State (I/C), Housing & Urban Affairs
Minister of State (I/C), Civil Aviation
Minister of State, Commerce & Industry
Government of India

With the 4th Industrial Revolution underway, Chief Financial Officers play an ever-critical role in the growth of our country's most prominent business organizations. The book CFO Niti fills a critical gap in these times of transition by bringing us in-depth stories from the career and personal lives of India's most influential CFOs. Lucidly written, the stories inspire, provoke and motivate the reader to be an exemplary leader and contributor. For young finance professionals, aspiring CFOs, and business leaders, this book is an insightful must-read.

(Hardeep S Puri)

New Delhi
15 June 2021

SURESH PRABHU
MEMBER OF PARLIAMENT
(RAJYA SABHA)

सत्यमेव जयते

7th April, 2021

MESSAGE

I wish to congratulate Mr. Pramod Bagri and Mr. Sandeep Kumar on completing this excellent book **"CFO NITI".** Chief Financial Officers play very crucial role in the success of business organizations. While a lot of literature is available about successful CEOs not much has been written about the CFOs and their contribution. This book makes an attempt to fill this gap.

The authors have made commendable effort of bringing together the view of six prominent CFOs of India who have shared their insight into the working of the best financial offices of the country. While it has been written about the CFOs its language is very lucid and I am confident that it will appeal both to the common people and the aspiring students who want to make their career in financial sector.

I wish all the best to the authors and publishers of the book.

With warm regards,

(Suresh Prabhu)

Mr. Pramod Bagri & Mr. Sandeep Kumar

ACKNOWLEDGEMENTS

We have two distinct sets of people to thank—those who helped make this book a reality, and those who had to suffer because of us while we tried to make this book a reality.

The biggest contribution to this book comes from our six Chief Financial Officers (CFOs). If they hadn't agreed to spare time from their packed calendars, taken an active interest to review all the content not once but multiple times, and provided us with support and encouragement throughout the rather difficult process of publishing, this book would not be a reality. When we sent out the first emails, we had asked the CFOs for a commitment of 180 minutes. We guess that each of them ended up spending at least between 20–30 hours of their time, even their weekends, for this book to take shape.

We want to thank Mr Abhishek Sanklecha, Mr Ankit Mundra and Mr Manish Kalghatgi for introducing us to the CFOs of Aditya Birla Group, Amazon India and Larsen & Toubro (L&T), respectively. Thank you, Mr Gaurav Jain (Mr Sushil Agarwal's office) and Mr Kushal Kumar (Mr Ajay Seth's office), for helping us enrich the contents for the respective CFOs.

Thank you, Ms Uma Iyer (Mr Srinivas Phatak's office), Mr Nagendra (Mr Raghava Rao's office) and Ms Ingrid Dgama (Mr Koushik Chatterjee's office) for arranging for us to get time on the CFOs' calendars and fielding our several calls for help and content.

We ended up recording hundreds of hours of content, almost 2000+ pages of rich content. But for the effort and perseverance of our team members, we would not have been able to transcribe and edit the text into a more palatable form. Thank you, Ms Sholi Muthukrishnan and Ms Praseeda Nirmal for transcribing and summarizing the contents and putting up with the tight timelines.

We are eternally grateful for the perseverance of our publisher and editors. Without Mr K.P.R. Nair's continuous encouragement (read reminders!), the book would never have been finished. Thank you, Ms Jiza Joy, our Project Manager, for bringing it all together and for bearing with us over the past 12 months. We want to thank our Editor Dipali Singh for making this book readable! Though a book is not 'judged' by its cover, we thank Misha Oberoi, our designer, for the excellent book cover.

Before these acknowledgements become longer than Greer Garson's Oscar acceptance speech, we want to end with the second group—the ones who had to accept our near absence while we travelled cross-country to conduct interviews and spent weekends transcribing and editing the material. When we took up this book, we didn't know how much work goes into writing even a half-decent book. Combined with our gruelling schedules, we went from being weekend husbands to being absent ones.

Like everything else in our lives, it was the patience and graciousness of our better halves—Sreedevi (Sandeep's wife) and Susheela (Pramod's wife)—that saw us through this project. We thank them from the bottom of our hearts for putting up with us.

Lastly, we want to thank our little ones—Niveditha (Sandeep's daughter), Rishit and Anikait (Pramod's sons)—who at their tender age helped their fathers out by not deleting the entire manuscript in anger, and for continuously reminding us to make the book more interesting as it was 'So boring, Papa.' Needless to say, they are negotiating claims for a Disney holiday to make up for all the missed hours over the past two years.

We are extremely grateful to our parents for their lifelong sacrifices, love and support that paved over all our mistakes and gave us the ability and confidence to pen a book like this one. This book is also inspired by constant encouragement from Vinod (Pramod's brother) and Sandeep's elder siblings (Vibha, Samir, Shishir, and Subir).

Our friends helped out by reading through the initial drafts and giving us valuable feedback. Thanks Nachappa Karthachira, Deepak Bhatter, Anand Balasubramanian and Rohit Choudhary for reading the first drafts.

No work is useful until it can be utilized. We thank you, readers, for taking the time to read this book. Many people have taken a lot of efforts and pain to bring this book in your hands. We hope you enjoy reading it as much as we did writing it. Heartfelt thanks!

INTRODUCTION

Don't ask yourself what the world needs. Ask yourself what makes you come alive, and go do that, because what the world needs is people who have come alive.

—HOWARD THURMAN

We have put together the life stories of six such leaders who have reached the pinnacle of their field by doing what makes them come alive. For the first time, they have opened up to share their stories publicly. They are India's most influential leaders in the Finance domain. Their organizations play a significant role in our country's overall Gross Domestic Product (GDP) and have some of the most sophisticated finance departments. They are the **Chief Financial Officers** (CFOs) of the most influential business organizations in India.

They are:

- Mr Ajay Seth, CFO and Member of Executive Board, Maruti Suzuki India Limited
- Mr Koushik Chatterjee, Executive Director and CFO, Tata Steel
- Mr Raghava Rao, CFO, Amazon India
- Mr R. Shankar Raman, Group CFO, L&T Group of Industries
- Mr Srinivas Phatak, CFO, Hindustan Unilever Limited
- Mr Sushil Agarwal, Group CFO and Director, Aditya Birla Group

CFO Niti aims to bring a paradigm shift in the choices available to the finance professionals through a deeper understanding of the CFO's role, and to draw inspiration from the life lessons of India's most accomplished CFOs. We believe there was a need for an in-depth book that can be a primer for finance professionals to design their careers and better understand the role of the CFO offices.

We are confident this book will bring a series of surprises on their roles and learnings that you can apply to elevate your performance and effectiveness. While the stories themselves are great fun to read for all, you should definitely pick this book if you are:

- A finance student looking to chart his/her path to the top of their field,
- A finance professional aspiring to be a CFO and wants to understand the role in greater detail and make choices to fast-track that aspiration,
- A CFO of a small/medium enterprise willing to understand how to grow in their careers, and
- Business leaders, vendors, or service providers who have CFOs as important stakeholders, and want to understand their operating model and key drivers. With ever-expanding roles, CFOs have become critical to multiple other functions, service providers and vendors alike. The understanding of their priorities can significantly elevate these interactions.

Whatever be your reason, you will find many opportunities to get inspired and learn from these leaders.

How it all came together

Like most great things in life, this book was more of a confluence of multiple happenstances than a planned exercise. At a chance discussion, both of us (Sandeep and

Pramod) debated on the importance and prominence of the CFO office. While we both agreed on its importance, we were not too certain of the prominence it has today within large organizations. Out of curiosity, we ran a search for the most important CFOs, and what we found was a bit surprising. About 90 per cent of the content was focused on the chief executive officers (CEOs) and their leadership styles. Another 9 per cent was on the chief marketing officers (CMOs), chief information officers (CIOs), chief technology officers (CTOs) and others. The CFOs were mentioned very few times, a lot less than the other CXO group. Next, we searched on Amazon for books on CFOs; the results were even more despairing. It was a bit strange that there was not enough content on this topic.

We thought this wouldn't do at all. Most large organizations, with strong finance functions, have a whole bunch of staff aspiring to be the CFO. All the newly minted Chartered Accountants and Masters in Business Administration (MBAs) in finance have the dream of making it to the vaunted CFO position one day. They could all do with some knowledge about the role and the people who occupy it. Why hasn't anyone bothered to put together some insights around how the CFO office functions, what makes a successful CFO, some inspirational stories etc.?

This small discussion led to an effort to find India's most important CFOs heading the largest, most profitable and impactful organizations, and chart out their life stories across multiple parameters. The aim was to not only figure out the secret sauce that went into the making of a successful CFO, but also understand their personal lives in detail; what values drive the CFOs, and what are the common factors that bring success in this role. The book would act as a guide to a student or a mid-career professional to understand what key elements they should inculcate in their careers and eventually target this coveted position.

This was in end 2018. What followed was a really exciting 24-month journey, where all our preconceived notions were proven wrong, and led to personally enriching series of discussions. This helped us attain the steepest learning curve we had ever witnessed in our careers.

We had several worries to begin with. Somehow, if we did manage to reach out to the CFOs, will they be convinced to open up about their lives and share it with us? Will the publishers be interested in bringing out this work to the readers? If everything did come together, will we able to take out time from our regular jobs and do justice to the content? The list went on. All the above were good reasons to pause, but we had a compelling urge to contribute and change. This set the ball rolling for us.

Taking a leap of faith, we started putting together the dream list of India's most accomplished CFOs whose life lessons could stand as a guiding light to comprehend the journey that took them there as well as their roles. We mailed them a detailed plan and requested their time—180+ minutes from their busy calendars (we ended up taking far more time), split into two face-to-face sessions of 90 minutes each—to contribute to this cause.

Let us confess. We didn't have much hope of getting a response. Nothing happened over the next 48 hours either. Then, the responses started trickling in—a few clarificatory questions, some polite declines and also a few requests for a meeting before taking a decision. After a few more calls, we cracked our first interview with Mr Ajay Seth, CFO of Maruti. His willingness to contribute and teach left a deep impact and motivated us to forge ahead. We started getting more responses over the next few weeks, and a few follow-ups later, we had set up interviews with six of India's biggest and most influential CFOs.

After the interviews were set up, we brainstormed on the overall questionnaire. We spent multiple days (and nights) to finalize a set of questions that would help the reader accomplish the objective—an in-depth perspective into the early life of the CFOs, the lessons that helped them prepare for their careers; the intricacies of the CFO office;

the manner in which the role has evolved; and finally, a little peep into their personal lives, such as work-life balance, hobbies, books, family, etc. The intent was to not only give the readers a view of what makes and sustains a successful CFO, but also the life lessons to guide them on their own journey.

Interview structure and questionnaire

Each of the interviews is divided into five distinct sections:

- Fireside Chat
- CFO Office Demystified
- Getting Personal
- Key Takeaways
- Extra Shots

The overall questionnaire was designed to make sure that we get to hear in detail about both the professional and personal lives of our CFOs, as well as learn from them about the intricacies of the CFO office, glean advice for finance professionals and their life mantra. Given below are a few of the important questions:

To start with, can you take us through your life journey?

We spent close to 40 per cent of our interviews discussing this. We expected the CFOs to give us some short narration of their life events. However, we were in for a pleasant surprise as they opened their heart and life, including very interesting anecdotes, initial successes and failures, and what they learned along the way. They wanted to make sure the readers understood their choices and the context behind them. They narrated it all as if the reader was sitting right next to them on a one-on-one mentor session. The reader will come across multiple interesting stories, including:

- A CFO who started his career as a cash counting resource in the Reserve Bank of India (RBI).
- Someone who almost made Molotov cocktails at the age of 18. We are not telling who!

  ...and many more such interesting stories.

Were you always clear that you wanted to head the finance function? If no, what did you aspire for early on in your life/career?

We included this question to understand when they realized their calling, and when they took on that path. Did they plan to be a CFO? Is there anything like a right time to start the journey? We got to know about:

- A CFO who wanted to be a fashion designer, and someone who aspired to be a doctor.
- A CFO who played cricket and was coaxed by the college to focus on cricket and not get distracted by studies.

  ....and many more discussions that we are sure will open a different perspective for you.

In your view, what are the top priorities for a CFO?

You would be surprised to read the list of priorities and the way it shapes the functioning of the CFOs today. One of the key surprise common elements was how important overall company strategy was to the CFO function, and the key role played by the CFOs.

We also spent considerable time on their office operations, personal schedules, future outlook and digital finance in the questions.

We have replicated the interviews as it is, if not verbatim. This was to make sure the intent of the CFOs to make the reader feel their presence as if on a one-on-one coaching was not fiddled with. We have included a few additional details and a separate section where we bring out patterns and commonalities when we stitched the stories together. You are likely to find these similarities yourself as you read through, and hopefully, you will gather your own insights around topics like:

- The nature of roles they were chosen/opted for. Can there be a set of roles one can pick up to fast-track one's career to be a CFO?
- Views on what their role entails. Is it just about creating true and fair financial statements, or does it go beyond that?
- The response mechanism when they encountered an uncertain role or situation.
- The principles of collaborations and interactions.
- The manner in which they stay up to date and relevant.

We started this book with an objective—to contribute to the larger community and act as a bridge between this untapped sea of knowledge and the beneficiaries. However, we ended up receiving a personal transformation as we heard these leaders detail out their life journeys, lessons and roles. While we have been closely interacting with global CFOs as part of our roles, these interactions opened our eyes to a completely different world of theirs. After many of these interviews, we would spend hours reflecting on deep life lessons we just witnessed. We were able to instantly achieve improved results in our own professional lives by applying some of these lessons. We firmly believe this book will have the same impact on the lives of its readers.

The reader can go through these interviews in any order. We recommend using the space at the end of each chapter to list out the learnings from the section, start noting down actions you can take, and the results you see as you progress. Our recommendation would be to put together an action plan for your own future as you flip through the learnings gained from the book.

We would no longer stand between you and the transformation you are about to witness.

Good luck!

Pramod and Sandeep

Ajay Seth

CHIEF FINANCIAL OFFICER
MARUTI SUZUKI INDIA LIMITED

Mr Ajay Seth is the Chief Financial Officer and Member of Executive Board of India's largest carmaker—Maruti Suzuki India Limited. Under Mr Seth's stewardship, Maruti Suzuki has witnessed a tremendous growth in revenue—from Rs 12,000 crore to Rs 80,000 crore at present—to become one of India's most profitable and professional companies. A seasoned chartered accountant (CA) with over 35 years of experience, he has occupied senior management roles at various other companies, such as Escorts, Joseph Cyril Bamford (JCB) and Eicher. He has been bestowed with multiple awards for his leadership skills, including the CA CFO 2020 Award (Large Cap Manufacturing & Infra) by the Institute of Chartered Accountants of India; Best CFO Award 2020 (Auto & Auto Parts) by Institutional Investor; Hall of Fame Award from the CFO India Forum (2019); Best CFO Award from Business World (2017); India's Greatest CFO from Asia One (2016–17); the Institute of Chartered Accountants of India (ICAI) award for Best CFO (manufacturing sector) in 2016 and (engineering and capital goods sector) in 2009; Best CFO in liquidity management from *Business Today* (2011) among several others. As a strategic driving force behind business, he lives by his mantra of *Take the initiative, look at the big picture and bring out-of-the-box ideas to grow the business.*

Fireside Chat

To start with, we would like to understand your life journey so far.

It has been a very interesting and rewarding journey so far, all thanks to the Almighty. I was born in February 1960 in Delhi in a middle-class family, where values, discipline and focus on studies were very important. My father was in government service and my mother a homemaker. I have a brother, born in 1963. We both studied at a government school, Kendriya Vidyalaya.

I was an extrovert and not too sharp in studies. During my initial schooling, I was more inclined towards sports and extracurricular activities, but my parents thought I must focus on something better, such as studies. Later, I was reasonably okay in academics and was keen to pursue science as a profession as I wanted to be a doctor. Though some of the science subjects were not my favourites, when my parents asked me if I would be interested in science, I responded in the affirmative. I still have a good connection with peers and friends whom I studied with; today, most of them are doctors, engineers and civil servants.

An academician in the family, who was the principal of a public school, recommended that I should explore the option of pursuing chartered accountancy. For me, it was more like Greek and Latin; I had no idea what this CA was all about! I was always very good with numbers and could do faster computations than most students, so he suggested that I should join the commerce stream. During the early

1970s, in Delhi, commerce as a subject was hardly available in schools, so I had no choice but to change my school to pursue it. I was reluctant to leave the school as I didn't want to come out of my comfort zone with my school friends, but in those days, career choices were primarily determined by parents. Hence, I ended up joining a public school and taking commerce. That was the beginning of a change in my life and career. The moment I took the subjects in the commerce stream, I started excelling—I even topped my class. The numbers, computations and accounting were all natural to me. The teachers were very fond of me and would tell the other students to connect with me and learn. It gave me tremendous confidence.

> *The learning in my career then was you must choose what you are good at, even if it demands getting out of your comfort zone. If you don't do that, you may forge ahead, but you will not be very successful in the long run.*

That was the time I decided to pursue CA. Not many people decide at that young age to pursue a profession. But when I was in the ninth standard, I was sure my next milestone was to be a CA.

Were you inspired by any CA you knew? Or did you believe CA to be the pinnacle of the commerce stream?

At that time, nobody in my family was a CA. Being the first one, I was an inspiration to my cousins who found the impetus to pursue CA. It was the ultimate proficiency for me in the field of the accounting profession, a belief that drove me to pursue this course. After completing my schooling in 1976, I joined Bhagat Singh College, Delhi University, to study for a BCom degree. I missed admission to the prestigious Shri Ram College of Commerce (SRCC) by a bit, as the cutoff percentage was very high, so the second-best option was this college. I graduated in 1979, and then started my CA articleship along with three and a half years of rigorous studies. My efforts paid off, and I became a CA in the first attempt at the 1983 exam. After all, a CA is a CA.

After finishing my CA, there were two options—either to start my own professional practice or do a job. Initially, fascinated by the idea of my own practice, I joined hands with a friend for a very short time only to realize that professional practice was not something meant for me. I then decided to switch over to working in an industry. That's when I began to look around for decent jobs.

I got offers from many companies. The choice was between Eicher and Hindustan Petroleum. At that time, it was believed the public sector companies were reliable, had long-term potential and were safe to work for. On the contrary, I was interested in working for private sector companies as I believed I could show my strong points and grow faster. I, therefore, joined Eicher and it has been one of the best decisions in my career. The human resources (HR) practices at Eicher Motors were par excellence. A great organization with tremendous discipline, teamwork, appraisal systems, key responsibility areas (KRAs), setting targets and goals, it was a good choice and I think I was fortunate to get my base right.

I joined as a junior executive on 1 August 1984. Subsequently, I was promoted as a senior officer. I worked with Eicher for about two and a half years, after which I decided to move out. You will not believe that even in 1986, Eicher had a system of an exit interview with any candidate who decided to leave. Anil Sachdev, the head of the HR department, conducted my exit interview and tried to convince me that I should not move out from the company. He is the one who does a lot of work for Maruti even now, so when he met me recently, I reminded him, 'You were the one who took my exit interview.'

I joined Birla Yamaha in 1986 after leaving Eicher. I was looking at the commercial aspects of the business such as setting up commercial channels, financing the point of dealerships, hire purchases, leasing and all kinds of other things. I stayed there for a year and decided to look around for a change as I wanted something more challenging. I got a very good break in JCB in September 1987.

JCB was a small company with a turnover of Rs 40–50 crore at that time, with opportunities of increasing scalability. I remember we had just launched the concept of an excavator loader, which was a very new concept in India. It was a joint venture (JV) between the Escorts group and the JCB UK group. There was a young CEO handling it, and I joined them as an assistant manager reporting to the head of finance. The concept of a CFO was not so relevant at that time because it was a small company. There was a head of finance with 20 people in the team. We started growing very rapidly. For me, working in that company was a great learning experience. I was given a free hand, and was looking at almost all aspects of finance independently. The job included multiple aspects of finance such as treasury, general accounts, automation and so on.

I got married in 1985. Soon after, my daughter was born in December 1986. I took up my job in JCB in September 1987. There were times when I would work continuously for three days, and not come home because of work pressure. Since the systems were manual, one had to do a lot of reconciliations. Ferguson's, our auditor, was pretty tough, which meant that pressure was high from the auditor. I was committed to complete my work and make sure the timelines were met. Those were the kinds of pressures and hardships I went through, but it was a great learning experience, especially automating the systems and ensuring the processes were streamlined.

Towards mid-1988, one year after joining the company, the person I was reporting to left. He decided to go to the Middle East because the salaries in India were very low those days. As the Middle East was offering good salaries, people went there to make some money and then return. Our CEO was a CA and MBA, a very competent person who continues to be my mentor till date. He called me and said, 'Sanjeev is leaving. Will you take up his role?' I replied, 'If you have confidence in me, why not? I will.' He said, 'We are doing this experiment with you. You are young, but we are going to give you this role as the head. We will see how you deliver.' That gave me tremendous confidence in terms of the trust the management had in me. That's how it all began. I got the position of a CFO at a very young age—at the time, I was a little over 28. I always tell my friends and colleagues that I have been a CFO from the age of 28.

JCB was growing at a pace of about 25–30 per cent every year. As we reached a size of about Rs 1,000 crore and started making huge profits, it was time to focus on automation heavily. We were also discussing multiple things, such as whether we needed to go in for enterprise resource planning (ERP) implementation, what is the best way of integrating systems and so on. I worked very closely with the consulting team from Xerox Solutions in business process re-engineering (BPR)—it led to significant changes in the way we ran our business processes. I thought that while finance was important to me, I should also look at other areas where I could add more value to the business. Soon I was working on different projects in several areas as a leader and I loved those challenges.

Certain things you need to establish wherever you are working are:

> *First, what is your ability to take the initiative?*
> *Second, are you capable of looking at the big picture?*
> *Also, can you do out-of-the-box thinking and add value to a business as a CFO or head of finance?*

After Rakesh, our CEO was Arvind Agarwal. He continued to entrust me with a lot of strategic work to handle. For instance, JCB requested us in 1995 to create a strategic business plan. I thought this would be an excellent area to work in as strategy was something I was always very passionate about. I was excited to be the project leader.

We worked with Dr Athreya for the plan and while on the job, I learned a great deal—about how to evolve goals and objectives, formulate them into strategy, and then eventually into action and timelines. We divided our teams into various groups to work in certain areas, interact with external people to understand the macro environment for the next 10–15 years in India. They would also assess what would work and not work, whether we should diversify or stay in the same business and so on.

This is very interesting because now people are saying CFOs should become strategic partners. But what you are saying is that right from the 1990s, you had a strategic bent of mind?

Absolutely.

> *One lesson that I tell everybody to keep in mind is that 'You need to look at the big picture.' If you look at the big picture, strategy becomes a part of it. Any CEO or any board will be happier with you if you work in that direction rather than just delivering numbers.*

So, we developed a strategic plan and after rounds of approvals, it was presented to the management and board. I still remember one compliment I got from the British team, which was that they could not have made such an effective strategic plan by themselves. It was a great job by our team and the credit went to us. So, that was my stint in JCB, a good 10 years I spent there with varied professional experiences. Unfortunately, it was not a listed company, so except for my interaction with bankers, there was nothing that entailed work with external parties.

> *One other learning you get when working with multinational companies is how you manage different cultures. You see Indians, you see Europeans and assess how to manage their DNA. How do you handhold them? How do you ensure*

there is a good rapport? How can you adopt best practices from them?

I had now reached a stage where I had gained experience in strategy, process improvement, automation and finance. It was a long journey, but I still thought there was more to do; there were more opportunities I wanted to look for because I had done my bit here.

In addition, I realized I was not financially very secure. I was very happy working, but the salaries in India were low at that time. It was for this reason that there was a craze to head to the Middle East to work and earn larger amounts. I decided to give it a try.

When you left the organization, what was the size of the finance department?

It consisted of about 45 people, with a turnover of Rs 2,000 crore.

Interestingly, you went from Rs 40 crore to Rs 2,000 crore and from 20 people to 45 people. So, just with the double number of people, you achieved 20 times the revenue.

It was mainly to do with automation and BPR. I benchmarked everything according to how JCB does it. I still remember a very interesting anecdote. Once when I was sitting with one of the business unit heads of the JCB excavators, I asked him, 'Jim, how do you manage the inventories?' Jim replied, 'Inventories? What do you mean?' I said, 'I was going through your shop floor and facility and could not see a place where you store your components.' He started laughing. When I asked, 'Did I say anything funny?', he said, 'No, no. You did not say anything funny, but we do not store anything.' This is 1992 I am talking about. We had not heard about just-in-time concept, Kanban and all that stuff till then, stuff that helps to track production and manufactured materials. I queried, 'How do you manage it then?' He answered, 'The logistics team brings the material directly to the shop floor. Trucks come every 30 minutes or one or two hours through the pull approach directly to the shop floor. It is picked up from there, and is replenished every few hours.' For me, his explanation was amazing! We had a store in JCB where we stocked all kinds of components, but once I got this information, we put into practice the concept of just-in-time, Kanban and logistics planning. All those were great learnings.

> *When you are working with the right organization, you should be willing to pick up best practices from there and adapt them. Sometimes, what happens is that people say, 'It works there, it cannot work here.' I think everything is workable. It is just the right mindset that is needed. You have to change your mindset.*

For me, my move from JCB to the Middle East was largely motivated by the lure of money. I thought I was going to experience tremendous exposure and learn a great deal working for the world's largest dealership of one of the largest car companies. After a lot of thinking, I decided to go to the Middle East with my family (my wife and two daughters). I reached there and got a very warm welcome from the HR representative, who is still a good friend. I was taken to my residence, which was a beautiful four-bedroom luxurious apartment, fully furnished with all the facilities down to the minutest necessities. We were wonderstruck at this different world.

But reality starts hitting you sooner than later. I started going to the office, and could not understand the culture there. I had gone there as a credit controller responsible for controlling the credit of all the group companies of the organization, institutional and retail. When I joined the company, I realized it was only working on its momentum. The culture didn't promote out-of-the-box thinking and lacked a challenging work environment.

I told myself that I had to take up more challenging responsibilities. I realized that while I may end up making a large amount of money in that organization, I would have a very unsatisfying professional life. Even my wife understood that I was not very happy with the job. She told me that I should not stay in the company for too long, but try to leave or change my job. I stayed there for a couple of years, then decided to go back to India. I had got an offer from Escorts, so I quit the Middle East job. This is how quickly the transition happened from there to here. I would have gone in for the change at less than half the salary I was getting in the Middle East. For me, my career was more valuable than money and to be professionally satisfied was more important.

Escorts was in a difficult situation when I joined the company in 1998. The tractor industry was going through a downturn and the inventories had piled up, leading to a working capital stretch. The challenges were manifold. I had to work on BPR, set the systems and processes right, and ensure the treasury was managed in a big way because we were short of funds. We were also high on costs, which meant that two jobs had to be done—one was to get more funds and the other was to reduce costs.

With this objective, we first took up ERP implementation. We did two projects with consulting firms—one on material cost reduction, where we did vendor rationalization, negotiations and aggregation. The second project was on process improvements, where we had set up a target of 5–10 per cent improvement over the costs of the existing processes. Still, the business was not doing well. When the business is not doing well, the pressure is on all the elements. You need to work on the costs and funds all the time.

My next job was the treasury, which is, again, a very significant part of a company. I think I learnt the most in Escorts when I had the mighty task of borrowing money in a distress situation. Being entrusted with responsibility is when one starts learning the best way to deal with structured transactions. We also started looking at the priority sector lending products because tractors were in the priority sector and realized we could do certain portions by factoring with various banks and getting cheaper rates. We did an exciting tie-up with an insurance company called Coface in Singapore, which had tied up with a local insurance firm in India to give guarantees to a third party who was lending us capital. We could get the loans at almost 200 basis points lower and could get the working capital cycle corrected over a period. I think those six challenging years in Escorts gave me significant satisfaction in terms of working in a situation of distress and not getting bogged down. You know it is very simple to say, 'It is too difficult for me to manage here. So, let me get out.' Instead, I took the situation as a challenge.

> *That's the learning young people should also get. If you are working on a challenge, it is the best time you can learn. Sitting in a cosy place passively is a very easy life—but sitting in a difficult position and turning it around is where your ability lies.*

One of the striking things is that you always got into a challenging situation rather than remaining in comfort. You have been very uncomfortable with comfort. Also, you have taken up challenges that you wouldn't have taken up before with ease, gone in and learnt to face and overcome them.

Absolutely, I think so. I am very restless when it comes to a complacent mode. If you can connect well with the business, the macro scenario, then it is easy for you to dive deep into these areas. In Escorts, I could connect well with what the tractor industry was all about—where we were vis-à-vis that, what our gaps were vis-à-vis the industry. If I can get the bigger picture clear, it's easier for me to focus on things and projects I work on. Many a time, I would make presentations to the management to say why we were different from Punjab Tractors Limited (PTL) because PTL was one of the benchmarks.

I was on daily speaking terms with Rajan Nanda, our chairman at that time. He would call me to ask how much production had taken place. What was the status of the funds? What happened to this and that? Even though I was not a professional with production competencies, I still made sure he got all the required information.

When I was leaving the company, he called me and said, 'Do whatever you want, whichever way you want to be happy.' I replied, 'I am very happy working here. There is nothing that's pushing me to go. But I want to take up a bigger challenge and I don't think I would get it here.' As Escorts was a Rs 5,000–6,000-crore company, I thought a more significant challenge would come from a company with a much bigger scale at about Rs 12,000 crore. Maruti was a significantly bigger company, and I wanted to showcase my ability to perform in a much larger set-up. That's how I changed from Escorts to Maruti. This was in April 2005. It has been over 13 years now.

Obviously, there is a size difference. Did you also see 10 years into the future and think that while Escorts would grow at x per cent, Maruti would be the behemoth it is today?

Escorts was a great place to work, and I have a very high regard for the group. I always believed in diversifying the business well, making it capable of earning a good return on investment (RoI), and improving the overall return on equity (RoE). Coming with the same thought process, you need to focus on your core in case you have a particular business dragging down the overall performance. You need to either turn around a business or get rid of it at the right time to prevent dragging the overall business prospects downwards. We should aim for rational thinking together with discussions and debates about what is right and wrong. These are some of the things that matter over the long run.

> *The key learning is that if you don't take the right decisions at the right time, you will end up in a place where you are either just surviving or struggling to survive. The scale is one part, but ultimately, it is essential to assess what the mission of the company is, how much it will grow, what its future is. Also, it is important to envisage what role you can play in shaping the future of that company.*

When I joined Maruti in April 2005, it had a different culture. The benefit was that I had worked in a variety of cultures and places and with many people by then. I could relate to people, and had led different teams. Almost all my teams were always motivated. At times, I had intense discussions with the team members, but all in the course of business. I have always made sure I take care of them in all possible ways, including their growth, enrichment and opportunities.

When I came here, the management was clear that somebody who could lead well and deliver more strategy and better inputs to the business was required to steer the company ahead. There was a different culture at that point of time. We had just transitioned from a public sector undertaking (PSU) to a multinational organization. Jagdish Khattar, the CEO, was a very fine man—whom I have a high regard for—and I give him a lot of credit for the success of Maruti. I started working there, and thought there were opportunities for system improvisation given the scale of business. We were onto some home-grown systems with legacy processes. There was a lot of scope for process improvisations, internal controls strengthening, possibility of synergies through migration and enterprise resource planning (ERP). ERP implementation had its own challenges. For me, it was an easy thing to do because I had experience in it. Within a year, we had the system in place. We implemented different modules in finance backed with good interfaces and legacy modules such as a vehicle tracking system, supply chain, marketing. All the systems started connecting to each other. We carried out a set of BPR initiatives as well.

We started growing in a very rapid manner. When I looked at what my priorities in Maruti should be, I focused on three things:

> *It is essential to track competition in a very significant manner because it is a highly competitive business, and everybody is eyeing our market share. How do you create entry barriers for competition, whether it is our pricing strategy or the cost competitiveness?*
>
> *How to continue to keep track of the costs and best practices? When you are growing, it is very easy to lose your sense of what the costs are and become complacent.*
>
> *How do you interface with the external world and ensure you are delivering according to their expectations? I am talking of the investor community because we have 44 per cent shareholding with outside stakeholders.*

Given you are flush with funds, do you think the company's relationship with banks is not as critical as Escorts is?

In the treasury, there are other challenges. One challenge is on the investment side—how do you get the best out of the money you have? How do you have the best system of no floats or no idle money lying anywhere, but within the policy framework of safety and liquidity? The other challenge is exchange risk management. It is a huge challenge here because we have reasonably large exposure, and the volatilities are ever increasing. Anything that goes wrong can have a significant impact on your bottom line. These two areas are always at the heart of a CFO.

As we scaled, we started working on backward and forward integration. On forward integration, we looked at setting up insurance business, True Value outlets, loyalty cards and finance facilitation for the customers. On backward integration, we set up engine plants, transmission plants and some key components such as plastic moulding, which we thought would make more sense if manufactured in-house.

Given the scale we were into, we spun out some companies as separate companies, and thought it would make more sense to merge a few of them to get more benefits in terms of scale. We did a couple of mergers over a period—although mergers are always a painful process. You have to go through checks and balances; pricing should be right, everything else should be correct and so on.

Then, there were a whole lot of things that happened during the last five to six years in terms of regulatory and compliance changes, ranging from corporate governance, international financial reporting standards (IFRS), demonetization, Goods and Services Tax (GST) and some tax reforms. For the scale and size of our company, we have to start preparation at least one or two years in advance for these aspects. Also, for us, we must meet all the timelines, cross all the dots; there is no scope for any delay in any of the implementations. We worked on a variety of factors over a period. For me, it was an important task to set up the teams and allocate areas of work, have a governing body to check the progress, identify the aspects that required to be seen by the supervisory board and so on.

In 2006, we introduced a system of internal financial controls called the Risk and Control Matrix. We use it till today, and is an excellent tool to ensure all the processes in the organization are running with adequate control; if they are not, then they are reported. If there are significant risks in some of the processes not being compliant, we have to report to the audit committee immediately, see why it happened and assess what remedial measures are required.

This gave much comfort to the CEO and me. When I need to certify books, I do not certify something with a blind eye. I look at that dashboard, see whether everything is working, and if the audit committee is comfortable with the status. I also spend a fair amount of time handling the investor relations, roadshows, talking to the external shareholders to ensure we understand their voice and tell them the direction of the company without disclosing confidential information. We also conduct the institutional investor survey that is initiated by a New York-based company. They rate the CEOs, CFOs and the investor relations' head every year. For many years, I have been bagging the first or second position in the CFO category.

My philosophy has been, very clearly, to be transparent with people, understand their issues and tell the management about it. There are issues raised on surplus cash, higher dividends, royalty and others. We listen to them, bring them back to the table, talk to the board about it and see what resolution we get.

My learning here has been:

When the scale goes up, you have to gear up to ensure you can cope with the scale in terms of your business processes.

At no stage should complacency set into the business because when the profits are going up every year, people think things will happen automatically—and that is the biggest worry. We always need to have a stretch for the next goal. Now, we are talking about five million targets in 2030 for Maruti, and we have touched 1.7–1.8 million. You can imagine we are talking of a size three times of where we are today. We are a Rs 80,000-crore company, planning to go up to something like a Rs 2.5 lakh-crore company over the next 12–13 years.

This is something that keeps me excited all the time because we have a goal, a target and a clear vision to be there.

The philosophy of simplicity helps you create wealth. If you were to look at the office here, for example, when you enter it seems like a very ordinary factory or an ordinary office. Inside the shop floors, you will find a high level of automation, but you will not find any luxury or signs of richness. At the sites, the people sit in the open, while I sit in an open office. There are no rooms for anybody. If you get into the habit of being extravagant, you will tend to spend more money on expensive things than preserving money for your business.

Even when I go to the Suzuki Motor Corporation factory in Japan, it is the same. In fact, we have a meeting hall here because of the old design of the factory, but in Japan, there is only an open meeting room with a table and chairs on the side to sit down and have a quiet discussion. I have travelled across the world, but one country that can give you significant learning is Japan.

From what we have heard, you are not only a CFO but also a change catalyst. The problem is that while change catalysts are some of the most dynamic people in an organization, they face the maximum resistance. How do you handle that?

A vital aspect of your success or failure is how you are being perceived by your peers and superiors. Because if you don't earn respect in their eyes, you will not succeed in any organization. It is for you to demonstrate your capabilities and articulate them in a manner that ensures they know you are working for their and of course, the organization's, benefit.

For me, it has also been essential to work on a collaborative approach. First, try and understand the context from which the other business unit head (or vertical head) is coming.

What is his problem? What are his issues? What are his concerns? Also, how can you facilitate bringing solutions to all the problems? It is also essential to connect with people—not only in a 'formal-formal' way, but also as 'informal-formal'. It is important to be at ease with them and they should be at ease with you. That is when you start to exchange positive vibes with each other; if you are capable, they will accept you as a change agent. They will have no problems at all. However, if they do not find capability in you or consider you too arrogant, you will not be accepted. Any relationship can only work for a short period because of fear, not for a longer period. Humility is very important.

For example, I know that in any situation I can call up any of my senior colleagues for help and be confident that they will listen to me carefully. Almost 90 per cent of the time, they will help me find the solution. Likewise, if they call me and discuss their problems, they know with a 90 per cent certainty that they would find a solution.

> *We do not look at our individual interests, but at the business' interest, at the big picture, as I keep telling them. Arrogance and ego at these levels become one of the major factors in taking wrong decisions. Therefore, the business and the organization suffer.*

How do you manage to keep that in check? We mean, very honestly, when you are one of the most senior people in Maruti.

You should also have a knack of doing it. Invariably, problems get sorted out with a team approach. Sometimes, it gets tougher because others are also in a difficult spot. You will have to see what intervention is required, whether you need to talk to the MD or the board or the chairman, and the manner in which you should do so. This has to be done without being too abrasive about it. I can only go to them once or twice in a 100 times, because if I go 10 or 20 times in a 100, they will not like it and it will defeat my purpose.

Who have been your mentors? How did they help shape your career?

I have had various mentors at different points in time. I still draw inspiration from my first boss, Jayaram Easwaran. He was my first boss, and I still relate to him as my first mentor. He is a great human being and an excellent leader. He is still in touch with me. He worked in a variety of corporates during his tenure, is a very successful person and now a well-regarded writer. He is my first mentor, and will always remain as one. I can talk to him on any subject where I feel I need advice.

I worked very closely with another CEO—Rakesh Chopra—when I was in JCB and Escorts after that. He is the one who helped shape my career. Even today, I seek his advice when I am confused or think I need guidance. He was the CEO of Escorts' tractor business, and before that, the CEO of JCB for many years. He is now retired. He is also a chairperson on the board of the Rajiv Gandhi Cancer Institute in Delhi.

Of course, I draw a lot of inspiration from R.C. Bhargava (Chairman of Maruti Suzuki), and can mention countless areas where he has helped me shape as a better professional.

Could you share a couple of examples of your mentoring someone through their career?

While there are many examples, but let me take a couple of recent ones.

A team of fresh CAs had to be recruited at Maruti Suzuki. I wanted an executive assistant, so we gave the recruits the option of working for different departments, including working directly with me. I promised that if the candidate did not meet my expectations, I would guide and mentor him/her to another role. If he was good at the job, I would offer him greater responsibilities. Lalit Khilani, a young CA, was part of that batch. He joined me in 2006, and started working with me directly. Imagine a bright and young CA at the CFO's office! I am a very demanding boss, though I never lose my temper and use body language to convey the necessary message. He was able to settle down fast and understood the requirements quickly. I was dealing with so many departments and divisions, and he, in turn, had to deal with several seniors. It was not easy for a fresher. I kept guiding him in the business and what his job was all about; his interactions with the various departments helped him gain knowledge and experience. He had a 360-degree view of the business and everyone gave a positive feedback about him. Eventually, we moved him to a treasury job where he again outperformed, doing very well in that job because he had acquired the basic skills. The result is that now he is heading the treasury for a reputed company like ours. That is one good example of mentoring.

The second example is that of Rishabh (another direct reportee), who joined after Lalit left. Initially, the pressure on him was intense but slowly, he aligned himself. The point is to understand the qualities of a person and use them effectively for mutual betterment of the individual and the organization. Monitoring his work, we knew he was very good at accounting—as his specialization was in numbers, I used him effectively in that area. We also groomed him for his soft skills, presentation skills and so on. Now, he is heading the corporate accounts for us. With proper mentoring and appropriate guidance from time to time, within a period of 8 to 10 years, potential candidates are capable of becoming departmental heads in an organization of a large scale, like ours.

What advice do you give to someone who leaves the organization?

If a person is leaving because he/she is dissatisfied with the job profile or career growth, I do some introspection and offer a job rotation. However, if the reason is purely dissatisfaction with the salary, there is very little one can do. My advice to a person leaving for this reason is very simple. I say that eventually, you will get what you want. Depending on your competency, if you are leaving a good organization for a more suitable job profile, it is fine. However, shifting only on the basis of salary, and then not being comfortable in the new organization, is not a wise decision. Today's generation is very restless and wants quick money, promotions and higher designations, but I have seen that some younger people realize after a couple of years that they have made a wrong decision and try to come back. It is against our policy to hire them again. The opportunity, once lost, is lost, but we try to help if possible. For example, a person was very confused about his present career. We gave him a chance by rotating his job from direct tax to control assurance, and he is happy now. Then there was this girl who was doing very well in her tax job, but she resigned because her promotion got delayed by a year. The feedback I gave to her reporting head was that if she was not given a promotion, she should be informed of the reason for the delay and the time she would likely be assessed next. It is important not to let people in the organization get into such frustrations as one could lose a good resource. This is how we deal with different people and situations.

CFO Office Demystified

The CFO's office has transformed drastically over the past 10 years from controllership to conceptualizing strategy. How do you see it changing over the next 5 to 10 years?

The CFO's function is now hand-in-glove with a CEO. As a CFO, one should be aware of the business progress, risks involved, changes in the market. All this is possible in a large organization like ours only through data analytics. It is very important to use new-age technologies such as automation, analytics and artificial intelligence. The CFO's office, consisting of key managerial personnel, is an army in itself equipped with strategic path-breaking insights. The CFO is expected to steer the organization through cyclical peaks and troughs. The organization and the CFO have to now think through every situation very differently.

When I do my review meetings with my team members and different departments, the questions are:

- What is the value in what we are doing?
- What are the insights derived from what we have been doing?
- Are there any red flags or concerns emerging from the data? Most people are keen to give only good news, but I prefer the givers of bad news because they have identified the concerns. Once a problem is identified, it is easy to rectify it.

We gear up during our internal audits with many data analytics tools for reports, exceptions in business, external environment, overall operations and so on. It gives us an overview of what is right or wrong; this provides enough input for my meetings with the CEO and MD. For instance:

- If we find there are concerns of sourcing in the supply chain, or our localization levels are very low compared with what they should be, we raise a trigger;
- If we find there is an abnormal pattern of purchasing, we will raise a red flag;
- If we find something on the macro front, whether with oil prices, the interest rates or anything else, we will raise a red flag. This might impact the sales moving forward, or become a concern. How do we fix it proactively?

As you can see, there are variety of things we do now. But this is just a beginning.

There is much more to do since the business is going through a lot of transformation. What is relevant today may not be so the next day. So, one thing I have been saying to my team members is to have fun, learn along the way and not repeat mistakes. The past is only a reference. Hence, it is important to learn and relearn. For instance, in the next few years, the automobile industry will go through transformations, such as going in for electric vehicles, hybrids and so on. A variety of things are going to happen, and it is going to change the DNA of a lot of companies. Some companies will try to take advantage of the situation, while many may not be able to cope with these challenges. So how do we deal with it? What is the right strategy for it? That is where I think the role of a CFO becomes the key – to articulate facts about the situation, present the risks the company is exposed to, and suggest measures to mitigate them.

When I joined Maruti Suzuki, the competitive intensity in this industry started peaking with most of the global automobile brands eyeing the Indian market with bigger ambitions. In such a set-up, the CFO's role becomes much more demanding. When it comes to margins, from top management to minority shareholders, all eyes look towards the CFO to deliver best-in-industry results. You have to strategically and tactically ensure that the virtuous cycle of ever-reducing costs and increasing volumes doesn't break and you continue to maintain your competitive advantage. A strategic bent of mind helps you ensure that areas which need more nurturing get adequate funds and the areas that have flab experience stricter cost control. You need to act as a catalyst to initiate various projects like aggressive localization of imported components. A very reliable information system about finer aspects of cost and its inter-linkages with operations comes in handy to the CFO. A system of activity-based costing for in-house value addition and standard costing for an outsourced components set-up in earlier days proved to be very effective in improving cost structure. The design to cost concept also helps in ensuring that cost is controlled at the design stage itself. Extensive use of component design benchmarking, a very effective tool for cost control, helps in identifying various value engineering ideas and reducing costs.

Apart from strategy making, today's CFO must also have a bent towards investor relations, that is, as a spokesperson for the company. Meeting the expectations of its shareholders, handling investor queries, maintaining transparency of information and vision, clarifying investor doubts and taking back their inputs to the management is equally important in the role of a CFO. I keep attending conference calls and have one-on-one discussions with the investor community. I listen to them, give them clarity on the company thought process, understand their inputs, discuss these inputs with the management and then work around it. This entire process ensures principal trust in the eyes of the shareholders. With regulatory bodies making regulations stricter, the challenge is going to increase manifold in future.

Investors are key sources of capital; and in many ways their investment criteria have evolved over time. From looking at financial returns earlier to triple bottom line performance now, their approach is around sustainable long-term returns. A company delivering consistently good returns by taking care of the environment and managing the expectations of its stakeholders will be rewarded while a company delivering high returns by exploiting resources can face trouble and erode the wealth of investors.

The starting point in sustainable growth approach is to have greater degree of engagement with its stakeholders to understand their expectations. Besides, the company should also assess impact of its actions on environment and society. These two exercises bring out critical issues which can present risk and opportunity for an organization. These issues then have to be addressed through risk management and strategy formulation process, respectively.

A CFO should often engage himself in such an exercise for strategic allocation of financial resources. Being a leading member of Corporate Social Responsibility and Risk Management Committees, I had that opportunity to deeply understand the critical issues of the company and accordingly allocate resources for sustainable returns.

I am also a part of investor relations programme of MSIL and well aware about investors' requirements. Investors are increasingly demanding companies to articulate their sustainability approach in their annual report. And presently, integrated reporting framework is being recognized as the most accepted framework in investor community. SEBI has recommended to adopt this on a voluntary basis. But as a proactive company and for larger benefit of the investors, we adopted the Integrated Reporting Framework since FY 2018-19.

You mentioned robotic process automation (RPA), data analytics and artificial intelligence. Are you hiring or looking to hire specific talent? Or are you retraining your existing employees to use these processes? How are you approaching this?

We adopt different strategies for different processes. We outsourced the RPA process, and had a workforce that understood it. We started with RPA in treasury and operations, which reduced the time taken to four hours from four days. Reduced time increased productivity, and errors became almost zero. Initially, we start with external help; over a period, we provide the necessary training to our staff. Now we have RPA running in the areas of treasury and operations as well as GST reconciliation and capitalization areas. We have been working on data analytics for over two years now. We are poised to move to the next level, involving machine learning, artificial intelligence and so on. However, where artificial intelligence is concerned, I feel there's a long way to go.

The auto industry is expected to transform radically over the next few years. Going beyond RPA and artificial intelligence, you will have processes such as battery technology, for example, which is relevant just to your industry. How are you planning to tackle some of those?

The auto industry is going through landslide changes in terms of government regulations and customer demand. In this ever-changing dynamic environment, it is difficult to predict anything with surety. The government has been talking and pushing the future use of electric vehicles (EVs), amongst other things. But the penetration, timeline and issues related with this technology are still unclear. We are thinking on all these issues and planning accordingly. For example, we are working on a JV between Suzuki, Toshiba and Denso to produce batteries. We already have a plant in Gujarat for this. Another issue which comes to my mind is again related to the disposal of batteries. There must be a proper disposal mechanism for used batteries and all of the planning is happening now.

You would have heard about the corporate average fuel efficiency (CAFÉ) norms, which in itself is a huge step. So, when we do CAFÉ in 2022, and again in 2027, it might change the mix altogether. We might need to have more alternate fuel vehicles. Now, what will be the price point for these vehicles where the customer can buy? And what will be the cost structure and profitability? These are various questions to be answered.

The point that I am making is that it will be a massive transformation and the steps we need to take must be planned. While some of them will be immediate and others at a later stage, some will be very difficult to decide about now because we do not know whether there will be volumes to support those decisions or not. We are creating business plans, running sensitivity analysis, risk assessment and so on to make the right decisions.

How do you stay updated with current events since there is an information overload today?

A significant source of information is the review meetings, where my peers share much relevant information on the relevant departments. We have a system of mailers from a defined team that collates and circulates information on the happenings in the trade bodies. So, it needs a bit of intense reading; additionally, intense listening in the meetings is vital to understand the key issues in the industry. We all take notes, so we are updated in every weekly meeting on what is exactly happening.

Also, I religiously read the few specific mailers that give me a gist of the notifications, tribunal orders, high court orders and so on. It is just a small summary in one paragraph, and very easy and seamless to read. After reading the summary, if you want more information, you will have to dig deep. That is how it should be done. These are the kinds of mails I read, not the very detailed ones in high-flown language. I honestly do not have the time to go through them.

How do you also keep in touch with other CFOs?

I stay connected through various forums. For instance, I am a member of the Institute of Management Accountants

(IMA) forum and CFO 100. Also, many events happen at the Institute of Chartered Accountants of India. Further, there are occasions where we invite people to give a talk at our office or I am invited to talk at other organizations.

We stay connected via e-mails and WhatsApp groups. I am in at least three such groups—a CFO group, a CEO and CFO group and a CFO treasury group. I find a lot of quality information is shared on these groups. Some of them are very helpful. The discussion is only on business; the groups are not bursting with images of routine greetings and I have just complimented one of these groups on doing a good job. We stay updated on what is happening in the market—the global and domestic scenario—what the banks and foreign institutional investors (FIIs) are doing and so on. There is enough technology to stay connected with your counterparts.

If a young CA wants to join your organization, what would you be looking for before deciding to take them in?

First, I want somebody who is not superficial, has some depth in what they are saying as that is very important for me.

Second, I want to see how steady they are. I want longevity in the job and do not want people coming here and seeing the organization as a training ground to work in for one or two years and then join another place. So, I want to see whether they are likely to stay here for a longer period.

Third, I look at their flexibility in the roles that would be assigned to them. For example, I do not want people with a fixation to work only in tax or accounts. During the initial years, they should be flexible enough to work in all areas; that is how we groom people to eventually take higher responsibilities.

We think the related part is what would you advise a young finance professional trying to begin a career in finance?

The children of today are very different from what we were. They are very clear in their minds regarding what they would like to do. Assuming one wants to pursue a career in finance, there are various options available. What is important is one should be clear about what one eventually wants to be in the future—whether one would like to be an investment banker, or work in a corporate, eventually taking on a CFO role, or be a consultant looking at a specific area of consulting and so on. It is a question of what one's ultimate ambition is—only then can one decide on what is the right path to be taken.

There are a variety of courses available. CA is only one part of it; you have economics and many more choices in India and abroad. So, depending on what is the right mix of the course you need to adopt for your chosen career, work on that and fulfil your dreams. For instance, my daughter was never interested in finance; she did her MBA from the Indian School of Business (ISB) after earning her Economics (Honours) degree from Lady Shri Ram College, New Delhi. She did her MBA with specialization in strategy and marketing. Certain that she would not work in finance, she took up a career in sustainability practice, working for about seven years, initially with KPMG and then with PwC; after that, for two years, she worked with an organization called Dharma Life. She used to go to the villages to do qualitative research. She was very clear about what she wanted to do and followed her path decisively.

My younger daughter is a lawyer. She declared she wanted to study law as soon as she passed out of school, and I supported her. She has been practising corporate law for the past three to four years. I would advise parents to never pressurize their children, but to go with the flow. All we have to do is to guide them in the right direction.

Getting Personal

Moving to the personal side, work–life balance itself has different meanings for different people. What does it mean to you? How do you achieve that balance?

If one is organized, process-oriented, effective in the delegation of jobs and keeps the team accountable, one can ensure that one has a stress-free weekend with the family, if not the whole week. Of course, there may be some situations otherwise, which is very rare. We also have two shutdowns every year in June and December. That is when I plan my long holidays. So, there is a good work–life balance.

What does your normal day look like?

I wake up at 5 a.m. and work out for an hour every day. It can be either walking, cycling or even using the treadmill at home. By 7.30 a.m., I get ready and leave for office. I am at the office from 9 a.m. to 7 p.m., and back home by 8.30 p.m.

In the office on a normal day, I would spend the first 10–15 minutes looking at my priorities for the day. I spend the next 30–45 minutes with my direct reports to discuss the priorities for the day as well as the week. I also ask about any feedback my team wants to give on anything that is concerning or needs attention, and we accordingly divide our work. After this, I spend some time on my routines because there are approvals and other stuff to do. There are several meetings listed in the diary, so I tend to attend at least two to three meetings in a day, if not more. They are at different locations, so one has to travel to the head office and other offices. Some of these meetings are to do with business, some with the operations and some with strategy. There are weekly one-on-one meetings with the MD where we discuss the overall issues concerning finance and business, and any directions we need from the MD. We also have a weekly management meeting where all the peers discuss the operations and the future directions. Then, we have a monthly management meeting where we typically have comprehensive business analysis, also attended by the MD and chairman. In this meeting, we also talk about our areas, concerns, issues, scan of the market, environment and so on and the steps required to be taken.

Does work extend beyond office to home once you get back?

Unless there is an emergency, I generally avoid working from home. The whole purpose is to delegate work effectively. If you have enabled your team—competent enough to do what is required—to take decisions, you can be sure you will get the right outcome. They rarely need directions because they are well-guided from the beginning. It is also essential to have the right quality team to deliver. If you have that, then I think it is much easier for you. Some leaders may prefer to be self-styled kings—as they never delegate, they are very dangerous as leaders. It is very important that you have an enabled, dedicated and competent team. You should also create space for them, and ensure that they are ready to step into your shoes at any point in time. We have done that over a period, and I think it is working well.

What do you generally do on your weekends? Is it a five-day week or a six-day one?

After a long time, we now have a five-day work week. I prefer to spend the weekends with my family and do the things I love. I am a music lover and recently bought an old record player, a gramophone. Those records are pretty expensive, but make me feel pretty nostalgic since they remind me of my school and college days. I prefer old songs and traditional music. Apart from that, I speak to my kids, one of whom is married, while the other stays in Delhi and is currently working. I spend time with my wife and have get-togethers with my family and friends almost every weekend. My wife is an avid reader and loves reading spiritual books. I also read the books in her collection.

Are there any books that have shaped your thinking as well? What are the top five books you think influenced you through this entire journey?

I have read many books. My favourite ones are:

1) *Chandrakanta* by Devkinandan Khatri. What he perceived 50–60 years ago is a reflection of what is happening in technology today. I like the entire series by the author.
2) *Autobiography of a Yogi* by Paramahansa Yogananda.
3) *Art of Happiness* by Dalai Lama.
4) *Good to Great* by Jim Collins, where I can relate to the journey we are taking at Maruti.
5) *The Maruti Story* by R.C. Bhargava.

These books are very easy to read and understand, with not too much jargon. Some give you inner happiness, let you meditate and think positively, while others provide you with the insight to understand management styles, how to improvise and achieve more.

Very interesting. Do you get inspiration from anything else as well, such as movies, plays, paintings, travel, some experience, etc.?

I like movies and plays. I go to the Kamani Auditorium often. A play I recently saw was *Aladdin*, a Broadway show.

I have seen *The Lion King*, another Broadway show. I like plays which reflect history and culture. I saw *Ravana* for example, a tremendous play done by Vishal Bhardwaj, the well-known film director.

Generally, I like to watch thriller and comedy movies for relaxation. There are many movies I have seen that have given me lessons. For instance, I have seen the old war movie *Escape to Victory*, a great movie conveying many lessons on how you convert a failure into success and so forth. The movie called *The Mountain Man* shows how determination brings a person towards an unrealistic goal achieved by breaking a mountain. Amazing! There is a very old movie—if you are a movie fan, you would have seen it—called *Do Aankhen Barah Haath*. It is a movie about transformation, how one can transform someone's hardened attitude into something which works well and is productive. I still remember a dialogue in, I think, *Matrix*. The guy wants to jump from one building to another, and is scared. He thinks he cannot do it, and then his inner voice tells him that he must walk his path—and that's how he strengthens his determination and does it, achieving his goal. In your real life, you come across many situations and hurdles where you think you cannot handle them. However, that voice tells you, 'You must walk your path and find your solutions'.

Do you have any other specific hobbies apart from the things you mentioned above? Any hobby you have pursued over the years?

Both my wife and I love travelling. So, whenever we get an opportunity, we travel. We try to explore places in India and overseas. Our kids also travel quite a bit and act as our inspiration. They have experienced the toughest journey to Manasarovar, which took 21 days or so. You have to apply at the correct time and then permission is granted if you are medically fit. It is a question of exploring different places. You cannot claim you have seen India if you have visited only metros like Kolkata, Mumbai, Chennai and Bengaluru. Therefore, we are trying to explore more places, except the ones which are difficult to access at this age. I love seeing different cultures and countries. I have been to many countries and we have realized that if we want to learn about a country and its culture, we need to spend more time there. This is what we are planning to do now. For instance, we went to Myanmar this year and spent an interesting week seeing all the different places around the cities. We went on a similar trip to Japan this year.

Which is your most memorable journey? The journey you would say, 'Okay this is one visit I can't forget'?

I fell in love with Scotland. We visited the countryside, wineries, churches and historical buildings. The scenic beauty is awesome, and the Scots are very friendly people. We enjoyed every moment there, and would love to go back.

Is there any specific life-changing experience you would like to talk about?

I did have an experience that went a long way in impelling my reflections and growing professionally. In one of my roles, the company was going through difficult times; we were making many efforts to optimize the costs. We tried ERP implementation and many other ways to rectify the situation; yet, there were lots of issues and concerns. Even with the many steps taken, the business was dipping. Liquidity was a concern, and we were making an effort to solve it by speaking to various banks. Then my boss passed a comment, saying that I was capable of running only a small business, which is why I was unable to do well in a big company. This affected me very much, but I took it positively and spent time with him to understand where I was going wrong. This was a lesson that made me realize what my priorities should be and how to handle such situations. The priorities should be to look more at the business. For example, the priority is in terms of restructuring, depending on what the need of that business is in terms of cost optimization, an enabler to other verticals. Some of the other routine and operational details needed to be delegated to other people. One had to let them do it—that is how it should be managed. Over a period, such feedbacks and many others have helped in shaping my career.

Six months ago, I sent him (my ex-boss) a message on WhatsApp: 'Dear Sir, Happy to share my recognition as the CFO champion by *Business World* and Yes Bank in an award function yesterday. I owe my success largely to you and your mentoring. I remember you did mention that you would like to see me among the top CFOs in a large MNC. Thank you Sir, for all your guidance and support, without which this would not have been possible.'

He responded, 'That is not true. You have reached where you have due to your nature, hard work and capability. I am delighted to see your success. One piece of advice, however, from an elder brother, is you should not make his mistake. Work is very important, but so are a lot of other things. I wish you a full life. Warm regards, best wishes and God bless you.'

Thanks a lot, Mr Seth. This has been inspirational!

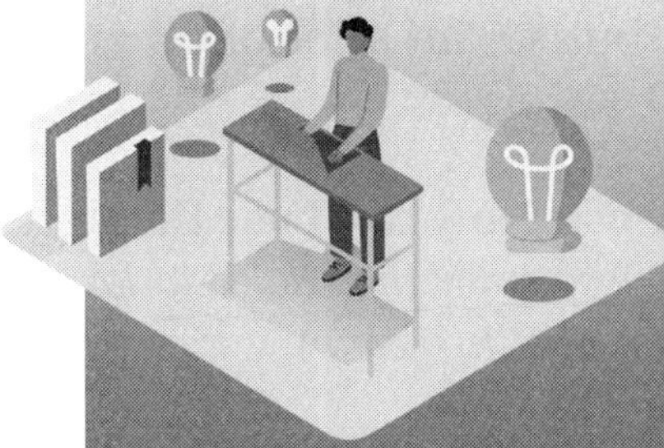

Key Takeaways

AJAY SETH

Take 1: Choose what you are good at, even if it demands getting out of your comfort zone.

Take 2: You need to look at the big picture. Strategy then becomes a part of it.

Take 3: When you are working with the right organization, you should be willing to pick up the best practices from there and adapt. It is all about mindset.

Take 4: If you are working on a challenge, that is the best time you can learn. Sitting in a difficult position and turning it around is where your ability lies.

Take 5: Take the right decisions at the right time, otherwise you will end up at in a place where you are either just surviving or struggling to survive.

Take 6: At no stage should complacency set into the business. We always need to stretch ourselves for the next goal.

Take 7: The philosophy of simplicity helps you to create wealth.

Take 8: A vital aspect of your success or failure is how you are perceived by your peers and superiors.

Take 9: You must walk your path and find your own solutions.

Take 10: Work is very important, but so are a lot of other things. Have a full life.

Key takeaways that inspired me most. How can I use them to change my perspective? (*This space is for the reader to jot down the lessons that they learned from this interview*)

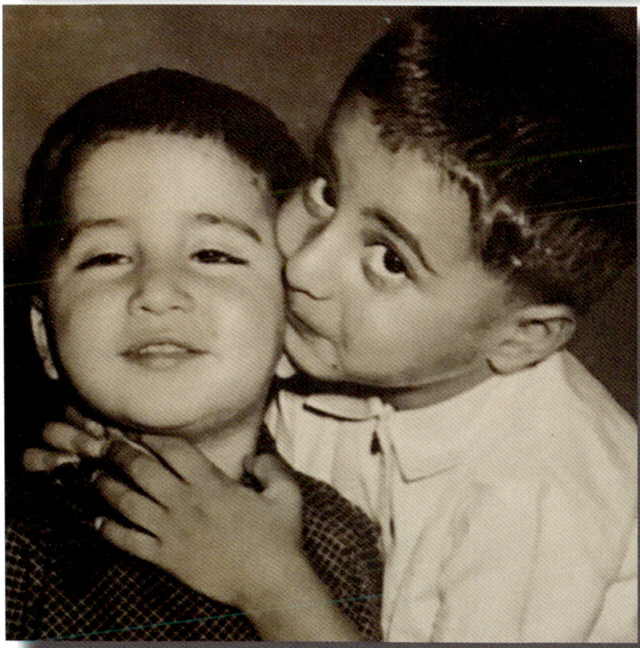

With parents (above) and brother Anil

(Top and bottom) ***Integrating Business with Finance:***
During the Eicher stint in 1985

(Top and bottom) On Escorts JCB ride, moving swiftly ahead

Felicitation by Mr Rakesh Chopra, CEO, Escorts Limited

Felicitation by Mr Kenichi Ayukawa, Managing Director and CEO of Maruti Suzuki India Ltd, in New Delhi

Receiving the 'Business Today Best CFO Award' from Finance Minister Shri Pranab Mukherjee, in New Delhi in 2011

Out Bound Training in May 2018

With mother, brother and entire family

Speaking at the CFO Asia Conclave

With Mr R.C. Bhargava, Maruti Suzuki Chairman, during an investor roadshow

Receiving the CA CFO - Large Corporate (Manufacturing & Infrastructure) Award from Shri Nitin Gadkari, Union Minister for Road Transport & Highways and MSME, at the 14th ICAI Awards 2020 in New Delhi on 20 January 2021

Driving Growth in Maruti's Car

Extra Shots

Ajay Seth

Do what you are good at and live a full life…

The meeting with Mr Seth was special because it was also our first meeting for the book. We visited the Maruti plant at Gurgaon (Gurugram). It is a huge set-up with multiple entry points, always teeming with incoming traffic. We were a little anxious, expecting to be turned away at the factory door by the guards who didn't know who we were. We had taken printouts of all emails from Mr Seth, just in case. What happened took us by surprise. Our badges (VIP passes) were ready and kept at the guards' door. The security incharge knew we were coming, and a car was waiting at the main gate to take us to the administrative building. A small thing, but a great lesson on 'detailing' and 'treating people well'.

We were asked to wait in a conference room—comfortable in a practical way, but nothing fancy. All the offices in Maruti are built around the assembly line. We waited to be taken to a larger cabin to interview Mr Seth, but to our surprise, he was sitting right there in the open area with his team. The CFO of India's largest auto company was right there in front of our eyes, acting no different than other employees, with no airs, expecting no special treatment. It was only later when Mr Seth explained the *philosophy of simplicity to create wealth,* that we could truly appreciate the Maruti culture and how it was ingrained in each employee.

Learnings in Action

The journey for this book lasted close to 24 months. It was the steepest learning curve but at the same time, not all moments were comfortable. We were working through multiple things—making schedules work for the CFOs and us (we were in full-time jobs), travelling to different cities to record the interviews, making transcriptions and doing multiple levels of edits, and finally, the actual publishing process. All of this was not particularly fast.

Rightly, we got a stinker from a CFO when he didn't see progress, letting us know his view which in summary gave us the message that we were not serious about doing this and he no longer wanted to invest time with us. The fact was, we were giving our best but it was still not enough. There was a moment when both of us thought, 'Can we do this, or should we quit?'

All of us have been through tough projects. We give our best, and still, there are moments when nothing seems to work. And the instant reaction is 'Give up'.

That is where one of the learnings from this discussion becomes pivotal. *'Sitting in a difficult position and turning it around is where your ability lies.'* As you read this book, you will get the same message over and over again from our leaders. Giving up is not an option, and every crisis is an opportunity. We brought in extra outside help for transcription, had more frequent interactions with the CFOs, and organized our time better. The fact that you are holding this book in your hands confirms that it worked. Do take a few moments before you move to the next interview to think about whether you are doing enough before you give up on a task, and what would you do if the option of giving up was taken off the table.

Koushik Chatterjee

CHIEF FINANCIAL OFFICER & EXECUTIVE DIRECTOR TATA STEEL

Mr Koushik Chatterjee, CFO and Executive Director, Tata Steel, joined the company in 1995. Mr Chatterjee is a Fellow Member of the Institute of Chartered Accountants of India and is on the board of several Tata Steel Group companies. Mr. Chatterjee has many laurels in his hat for his outstanding contribution as CFO—he was declared one of India's best CFOs by *Business Today* Magazine in 2005 and 2006 and by *CNBC* in 2007; he was awarded the 'Best Performing CFO in the Metals Sector' by *CNBC TV18* in March 2012; he was declared India's 'Best Executive' for the year 2009 by *Asia Money* Magazine; and he was honoured with the Lifetime Achievement award by the *Financial Express* at the FE CFO Awards 2019 that recognizes veteran finance professionals who have made an exemplary contribution to the industry.

Mr Chatterjee is an active speaker and has been a speaker in various conferences in India and abroad, including the McKinsey Global CFO Forum 2008, conferences organized by the *Economist* and *Financial Times*, London, the IIRC and the Confederation of Indian Industry (CII) conferences, the Challenge of Government Conference 2018 at the University of Oxford, guest lectures in the past at London Business School, Indian

Business School, Hyderabad, and other institutions. He is a member of multiple global bodies, including the Task Force on Climate-related Financial Disclosures (TCFD), set up by the Financial Stability Board, Basel, the Institute of International Finance (IIF), Washington-sponsored Task Force on Scaling Voluntary Carbon Markets, and a council member of the International Integrated Reporting Council, London. He is currently a member of the CII National Council and several sub-committees.

Receiving the Lifetime Achievement Award at the *FE* CFO Awards, he said 'You do not need rocket science..., just stick to the basics, put in a lot of hard work with integrity and fairness and enjoy the experience of your professional life. There will be ups and downs but if you stick to straight, simple and narrow and look at the best interests of the organization, you will find the journey interesting.' His life journey stands as a bright epitome of these principles. Faced with many unexpected twists and turns, his ability to simplify an otherwise complicated situation, pick learnings from any position, hard work, embracing the unknown, and his steadfast integrity stand out. Apart from his work, he is an avid reader of anthropology, a public speaker, a teacher, and above all, a family man.

Fireside Chat

Can you please take us through your journey, especially your growing-up years?

I was born in September 1968 and had a straightforward, uncomplicated township life during my growing up years. My father, an electrical engineer from Banaras Hindu University (BHU), used to work for the Steel Authority of India Limited (SAIL). His first job was at the Indian Iron and Steel Company (IISCO) as he was recruited directly from the campus, and was a career steel man throughout. IISCO along with Tata Steel are considered as the founders of the Indian Steel industry. IISCO was owned and managed by the Martin Burn group in those days till it was nationalized in early 1970s. Burnpur, which is about 200 km from Kolkata, was a world by itself for most of us during our growing up years.

We lived in fairly spacious and well-organized bungalows in a planned township very close to nature. My extended family was also from that area as my paternal grandfather was employed with the Equitable Coal Company (later nationalized as Coal India) and my maternal grandfather was an ex-army doctor who practiced in Asansol after leaving the army post World War II. My paternal grandmother, my maternal grandparents and other extended family used to stay close by. Burnpur was a cosmopolitan steel township and I had the pleasure of mingling with people from all over the country and hence was exposed to a variety of cultures and traditions since childhood. This multicultural exposure helped me a great deal later in life.

I believe we imbibe most of our value systems in the early years from home and school and they prove pivotal later in life.

I did my schooling in a century-old Irish missionary school, St. Patrick's, in Asansol. The school was built in 1891 initially as a Scholasticate for Belgian Jesuits but subsequently converted to a school run by the Congregation of Christian Brothers, a Catholic religious institute in Ireland.

The motto of our school was 'Sola Nobilitas Virtus' or 'Nobility is the sole virtue of life'. After so many years of leaving school, those words of wisdom and values have stayed ingrained in my mind.

The Brothers of the order ensured strict discipline and we had many extracurricular activities to help us grow up as more rounded personalities. I was moderately good in studies but was more distracted by sports and extracurricular activities like theatre—both in school and in the township. We spent most evenings on the playgrounds after school hours. In summer, we played football and I used to be a goalkeeper. During winter, we played cricket where I was a wicketkeeper-batsman and also bowled handy off-spinners. I also played badminton, basketball and table tennis, mostly in school. My mother used to play sitar in her younger days and even though I didn't learn to play any instruments, over the years I developed a keen sense of classical music which remains a de-stressor for me even today. This is how I largely spent my childhood—a middle-class upbringing with friends and family nearby and lots of outdoor and indoor engagements. Essentially, I had a stable, grounded, relatively uneventful, and straightforward formative years.

Were you always clear you wanted to join the finance function? If not, what did you aspire for early on in your life/career?

Far from it! I was in the science stream till Class 12. I was keen to follow in my maternal grandfather's footsteps and become a doctor, but that did not fructify. Maybe I was not serious enough at that age. That was an early failure in life and compelled me to reflect deeply on the way forward.

I ultimately followed the advice of a close family friend who was a chartered accountant and decided to pursue a degree in commerce, followed up with the chartered accountant qualification. It was during college that I started getting interested in finance. The real trigger to dive deep into the subject happened much later when I taught at the Xavier School of Management (XLRI), Jamshedpur, as a visiting faculty member. In some ways, that teaching stint was a great learning period and led me to focus on specialized areas of finance and new-age finance subjects.

Interesting. Can you take us through your formative school and graduation years?

I finished Class 12 in the science stream. Post some introspection, I ended up choosing commerce for college. I joined the University of Calcutta to pursue an undergraduate degree and thereafter also decided to pursue a degree in chartered accountancy. I come from a family of engineers and doctors—nobody in the family was from a commerce or finance background. I was inspired by a family friend who was a few years elder and had just qualified as a chartered accountant. He motivated me to pursue the course. I joined the Goenka College of Commerce and Business Administration, University of Calcutta, in 1986.

I had a few relatives in Calcutta and the city was familiar to me as we used to visit it during winter vacations. But my father insisted that I stay in a hostel and get the feel of the real world outside the safety and comfort of home. As I couldn't get accommodation in the college hostel, I got a place in the Salvation Army Hostel located opposite Mother Teresa's Home on Lower Circular Road with the help of a close family friend. The Salvation Army Hostel in Calcutta was a part of a chain of hostels with headquarters in the UK, but mostly known for hosting the homeless. The student hostel in Calcutta was fairly well maintained. It was not a college hostel, so there were all sorts of people as residents. Some boys were from prosperous families, some came from humble backgrounds, and some were even working professionals. A few were wasting their lives on drugs and other distractions while most were engaged in studies or jobs.

I was 18 years old and my roommate was a 45-year-old Bengali gentleman born and raised in Tanzania. He returned to India with his parents when Tanzania got freedom and settled in the erstwhile French colony of Chandannagar near Calcutta. From lording over my own room in a rather spacious bungalow in Burnpur to sharing a room with somebody unknown and much elder to me was a challenge in itself to start with. As time passed, I realized he was a congenial non-interfering soul and quite accommodating in nature. He had been impacted by polio in his childhood. He worked in the State Bank of India in the foreign department, was married, and had a daughter. He used to come from Chandannagar on Monday morning, attend office through the week while staying in the hostel, and return home on Friday evening by train. He had a very regimented schedule and routine lifestyle. On Fridays, I would feel liberated as I was the sole occupant for the weekend and it gave me space to follow my own routine. That was the regime for almost eight years when I was in the hostel.

The other hostel mates were from different backgrounds—some studying for postgraduate courses, others whiling away the time drinking and doing drugs, some working, and some even retired and old. It was a world in itself—noisy, distracting, and very easy to lose one's way. I juggled my hostel life and studies and before I realized it, I had completed my graduation. For a small-town boy, I think my mental battle every day was to keep myself focused and ensure I achieved the purpose for which I had come to Calcutta. At first, I felt very uncomfortable and awkward about the environment in the hostel and wished I had a better place to stay. But I forced my mind to accept and adapt to the environs and steel my mind to reality. Over time, my mind became numb to any distractions. I had a few other friends in the hostel who were equally focused and it was they who gave me company on this journey.

I did my articleship in Calcutta and a lot of time was spent doing audits. Unless one is disciplined, there is always a risk of losing study time. I used to avoid audits that required travelling as I did not want to divert my focus from studies. Audits can be exciting with clients—the excitement of accounts closing and being part of senior client meetings, and so on. However, I used to avoid all the glitz whenever possible and rush back to my hostel to study for the examinations. I had many distractions in my hostel life anyway to deal with!

After I completed my intermediate examinations in chartered accountancy, I wanted to get an early exposure to the industry. There was an opportunity to be an Industrial Trainee in Britannia Industries in their Calcutta factory and regional office in 1991. I considered it a good break because I knew I would get to learn something different. I worked on the management information system (MIS), performance assessment and management reporting, as Calcutta was a hub for external processing franchises. It was a fascinating role with very helpful people around and a positive environment. As a collateral benefit, I got a princely stipend and my standard of life improved! While I continued at the Salvation Army Hostel, I could go out for a good meal or travel in a taxi and recalibrate my budget beyond what my father sent me for monthly sustenance. Britannia had an excellent canteen, where good quality food was available at all times at a nominal price.

I was fortunate to have the company of outstanding senior colleagues. Britannia Industries was a very professional and well-run organization and I learned a lot during my training period. I had two amazing superiors—Mr J. Rajagopalan and Mr R. Eswar. They were very supportive of me and helped me in every way during my stint in the company. Towards the end of the one-year training, the Babri Masjid demolition happened in December 1992, which resulted in unfortunate events in Calcutta, including communal riots. These incidents had a deep impact on me and I decided that I would leave the city if I got a better opportunity. Mr Eswar asked me to meet Mr P. R. Ramesh who was then the Regional Partner at S. B. Billimoria & Co (SBB), now part of Deloitte, in Calcutta. I went to meet Mr Ramesh in his Circus Row Calcutta office and he was surprised when I told him that I wanted an opportunity to work outside of Calcutta as most people do not want to leave the city. He said there could be a vacancy in the Jamshedpur office and asked me if I was willing to relocate there. I told him I was ready to go. I had never been to Jamshedpur, but it is a steel town after all and I have grown up in such a town.

He still insisted that I go to Jamshedpur for a day at the firm's expense and see the place before I took a decision. So I went to Jamshedpur for a day and met my future colleagues, including Mr N. Venkatram who was then heading the Jamshedpur office of SBB. I came back and told Mr Ramesh that I was ready to join the firm in Jamshedpur. I felt it was the right decision to take at that time. I was looking forward to another phase of learning and experiences compared to the last eight years spent in Calcutta.

So your Jamshedpur story started in 1993. How was life in Jamshedpur and how many years were you there?

Jamshedpur was a breath of fresh air. Life in Jamshedpur was much more organized and calm compared to Calcutta and I felt at home. During my tenure in the firm in Jamshedpur, I got involved in many audits for Tata Group companies, including Tata Steel and Tata Motors. It was quite a fascinating experience to work with a wonderful set of people like Venkat and Ramesh, and undertake audits of large companies. The couple of years that I spent at SBB were very interesting and I enjoyed every bit of it. I shared a chummery with two other colleagues—one was an intelligent Malayali boy born and bred in Jamshedpur who was an article in the firm, and the other was a bright conservative Tamilian from Cuddalore. It was quite an interesting experience, often bordering on being hilarious, as we had a tribal boy from Jharkhand named Chitto as our Man Friday, who was very patient with us, but used to get completely lost and at his wits' end trying to make food commonly liked by all of us! The good thing was everyone was sporting, not fussy about such matters and our camaraderie was very strong. Ramesh was a very serious, sincere cricketer and used to come down from Calcutta to play interoffice cricket over the weekends in Jamshedpur. We used to play against all the Tata companies on different grounds, including in the Keenan Stadium. Come winter season, cricket used to be a major weekend engagement and everyone would look forward to it. Weekend winter trips to the highway *dhabhas* from Jamshedpur to Ranchi were very common and these outings provided opportunities to bond and have fun with the team. After a couple of years in SBB, I got an offer to join Tata Steel. It was a genuinely hard call to leave the SBB as I was enjoying every bit of the experience amidst some wonderful colleagues and the leadership of Venkat, who used to keep us all together as a family. From a long-term career point of view, Tata Steel appealed to me as I wanted to broaden my repertoire beyond audit. Coming from a family with strong links to the steel industry, I decided to take the offer. I went to Venkat and explained my decision. While he was initially disappointed and reluctant to let me go, he understood my career aspiration and we share a very good relationship with mutual respect. I learned a lot from him and Ramesh both professionally and also from their leadership styles.

I joined Tata Steel in November 1995 in the Synergy Group which was part of the Managing Director's office. It was the corporate centre for Tata Steel's investments in subsidiaries and joint ventures, evaluating new ventures, and undertaking capital planning for the company. It was a multidisciplinary group of about 10-15 people with a dual reporting system, and we reported to both Managing Director Dr J.J. Irani and Finance Director Mr Ishaat Hussain. As I settled into the new job, I realized that the Synergy Group was a flat organization within an otherwise hierarchical company that had multiple levels. Any assignment could go to anyone depending on the skill sets required or the kind of assignment. There were different types of projects available at any point of time apart from the performance monitoring of the portfolio—evaluating and developing a business case for new joint ventures or a new business, evaluating large capital projects, taking direct oversights on special situations in any of the subsidiary companies, developing turnaround plans, and so on. I had a wonderful set of senior colleagues especially my immediate senior and friend Harinarayan Sharma who was my guide during the initial years. This was a great learning phase for me as I was involved in many interesting projects which shaped my thinking—a skill that I have used throughout my career.

Life in Jamshedpur was almost too perfect and organized, thanks to Tata Steel's deep commitment in enhancing the quality of life for the citizens of the city. There is a lot of time available for the citizens to pursue interests, especially in extracurricular activities. For the more seriously inclined, one of the opportunities that many young professionals pursue in Jamshedpur is to undertake an MBA course in XLRI. I too was interested in undertaking the course but instead I landed up teaching at the institute. I started by teaching the evening programme and from the second semester onwards I was asked by the institute to teach in the regular business management day programme on corporate finance courses, including electives. This phase of my life was one of the most fulfilling periods of my learning contribution cycle. The students, largely in my age group, were very intelligent and came from very good undergraduate institutes. So handling a class of 70 bright students was both challenging and interesting. In Jamshedpur, there is hardly any distance to travel as the campus was only about five minutes away from my apartment. So I used to spend a lot of time late in the evening on the campus, especially in the library to read and prepare for the classes. The four years that I taught in XLRI were a very fulfilling experience in more ways than one. Many of my students became my friends and continue to be in touch—they have done well in life which is so good to see. The experience also helped me to broaden my vision and knowledge about many varied issues and subjects that came to good use later in my career. My passion for teaching started from my XLRI experience and I am immensely thankful to XLRI and senior professors like Dr H. K. Pradhan for all the support.

Dr Irani was the Managing Director of Tata Steel based in Jamshedpur while Mr Ishaat Hussain, the Finance Director of Tata Steel, was based out of Bombay (now Mumbai). The mid-nineties was also a period when Tata Steel was going through one of its deepest restructuring and renewal phases in its history with multiple multiyear initiatives to make the company stronger and robust following the liberalization move by the Government in 1991 to open up the economy. Dr Irani aligned the entire company to focus on some very hard decisions including organizational right-sizing, investing in new technology, developing an integrated supply chain capability, focusing on being a cost leader in the global industry, bringing in new products, and rewiring the commercial functions to best adapt to market realities. This phase of five to six years was at one level tough for the company, its leadership, and the employees but will also go down in history as the period when the foundations were laid to make Tata Steel future ready and globally competitive for decades to come. Dr Irani was a firm leader with a deep understanding of the industry and focused on outcomes but was also very compassionate. The package that was designed for separating employees was a case in point. In a country that has no social security plan and very few livelihood opportunities around Jamshedpur, the early separation package was designed uniquely to help the separating employees maintain a steady stream of earnings equivalent to their basic salary till they would have normally retired. The separation was also done humanely with soft loans to build houses and medical benefits. Every month, there used to be celebratory events to recognize the employees' contribution to the company where the retiring employee and his family would come and meet Dr Irani, the leadership team and the unions—all of whom would be present to bid the employee farewell. What could have been a painful experience for the employees was converted into a celebratory and participative process that was inclusive in spirit. As a youngster and an observer, this style of management left an indelible mark in my mind. Dr Irani was a standout leader who could take hard calls and implement them most appropriately. He is someone who would be logical even when speaking the unpleasant truth to the senior leadership. The actions taken in those years became the foundation stone upon which the successive leadership in the company build upon. He walked the talk and always put institutional interest ahead of everything else. Dr Irani and Mr Hussain were close partners in this journey along with other senior leaders of the company.

Mr Hussain used to visit Jamshedpur once a month for a couple of days for work. During one such visit, I was asked by my reporting superior, Mr Sharad Kale, to go and visit him with the analysis of a proposal on the acquisition of a downstream tube business in Pune. It was a Saturday afternoon and I was to meet him at the Director's Bungalow (DB) in Jamshedpur. For people who have been to Jamshedpur, the Director's Bungalow constructed in 1918 is still a famous landmark in the city. It has seen a lot of history and has played host to great personalities over the decades. For a youngster like me, to go to DB, as it is popularly called, was an event in itself. I went to meet Mr Hussain armed with sheets of analysis (laptops were not in vogue those days).

I introduced myself to Mr Hussain. He somehow sensed that I was nervous and started with a casual conversation to make me comfortable. Known for his relaxed informality, he could adjust his conversation depending on whom he is speaking to. He asked me about my interests other than work, and we discussed a lot of other subjects including sports and life in general. He is a very down–to-earth person who has no airs about his position, and I felt at ease instantly. Our meeting lasted for an hour over some tea and the famous Fakira's *Farsan* of Jamshedpur which he liked a lot. I presented the business proposal and discussed its merits after which left the meeting relieved and happy.

After a couple of months, on another visit to Jamshedpur, Mr Hussain asked me to come to Mumbai for a stint of three to four months in the Head Office (Bombay House) to get exposure to corporate finance and treasury activities. This was in the summer of 1998 and I came to Mumbai in September 1998 for a few months. As it happens, I eventually stayed back and the city has been my home for the last 22 years!

Around the same time I came to Mumbai, Mr Hussain was appointed as the Executive Director of Tata Sons and I started getting further exposure to new subjects on corporate strategy, corporate governance, new investments including mergers and acquisitions (M&A), financing, and restructuring. Mr Hussain eventually moved from the role of Finance Director, Tata Steel to Executive Director with Tata Sons and Mr R.C Nandrajog took over the CFO role as Vice President (Finance) in July 1999. From 1999 to 2004, I worked with Mr Hussain and got the opportunity to work on some very interesting assignments including privatization bids for some of the public sector undertakings (PSUs), joint ventures like Tata Sky, Tata AIG, divestments like Tata Infomedia, preparation for the Tata Consultancy Services initial public offering (TCS IPO), implementation of economic value added (EVA) methodology in group companies and several other strategic initiatives.

Every day in Tata Sons was a learning process and it increased my understanding on a very wide range of subjects. The breadth of varied industry exposure and the opportunity to engage deeply in multiple projects at the same time was a great experience. There were several governance and policy framework initiatives that were developed by the Group Executive Office in Tata Sons during that time and I loved working on them. It provided me the opportunity to learn and research governance as a subject of interest. The other great self-learning experience was to observe the leadership styles and situational application of the top leadership of the Group during work. This was an invaluable experience because I had the opportunity to observe how situations are assessed, policies are formulated, strategies are developed and decisions are taken. I don't think any B-School curriculum could match that experience.

I believe when we have an opportunity to learn, we should make the best use of it. I used to put myself in the position and situation of leaders and enact the same in my mind to test whether I would have done anything differently and also learn from the decision-making process. I would always have my hand up and was open to any assignment that came my way.

Mr Hussain was ever willing to give me opportunities so long as I was able to deliver the outcomes. We were a very small team and Mr Hussain's leadership style was anchored on empowerment with accountability. The exposure and experience in Tata Sons helped me to grow intellectually, and enhanced my multitasking abilities and maturity to look at high-stakes subjects objectively for decision-making. The working ambience was perfect for a youngster like me to stretch myself, learn, and contribute without any fear or stress.

So how did you come back to Tata Steel?

That's an interesting story. In late 2002, Tata Steel was evaluating the acquisition of a distressed steel company in India. I was not connected with Tata Steel at that time. I had a few colleagues from my earlier stint in Jamshedpur who used to seek my help in evaluation and financial modelling. I participated in the review of this evaluation as well, which was chaired by B. Muthuraman who was then the Managing Director of Tata Steel. One day in early 2003, Mr Hussain's secretary informed me that Mr Hussain had received a fax about me from Mr Muthuraman. I was a bit surprised as I had nothing to do with Tata Steel at that time and was busy with the TCS IPO project. Mr Hussain didn't mention anything to me the whole day about the fax. The next day I got a call from the Tata Steel Managing Director's office that Mr Muthuraman wanted to see me. I went to meet him and after pleasantries, he talked in detail about his vision for Tata Steel in the next decade. He then mentioned that to help him implement the strategic path he would like to have a strategically-oriented finance leadership. It seems he had done his research and run references on me. He asked me to return to Tata Steel and go to Jamshedpur as the understudy to the Chief Financial Controller for a while as he was retiring in a year. The CFO of the company was also due to retire in about 18 months. He mentioned that if I did well and demonstrated the leadership that Tata Steel needs and understood the complexity of Tata Steel, I stood a chance to be the CFO in about 18-24 months. This conversation was a big surprise to me. The thought of becoming the CFO of a large company like Tata Steel at the age of 34-35 was beyond my aspirations.

At that point, I was handling the formation of the Tata Sky joint venture and was also involved from the Tata Sons side on the TCS IPO initial public offering, India's largest IPO at that time. It was a fascinating work for me. We were a young family and my son was an infant, so to take such a big call needed some reflection and introspection. I sought some time from Mr Muthuraman to think through my decision. Over the next few weeks, I had several conversations with Mr Muthuraman to understand the company strategy, his expectations, and why he was looking at me given that I had not gone through the grind of a typical finance career. He was quite insistent and clear in his mind that I could meet his expectations. I finally relented. On one of his visits to Mumbai, he called me and mentioned that he would make the announcement in the next town hall in Jamshedpur scheduled the same week. And he did. Mr Hussain, Mr Muthuraman and I worked out a transition plan from Tata Sons to Tata Steel, as we were in the final stages of closing the Tata Sky joint venture and TCS IPO preparations were peaking.

As I started getting my feet wet in Jamshedpur, the controller function in Tata Steel looked more engaging than I had assumed, and I started getting really hands-on as I did not want to waste an opportunity to learn. Around the same time in November 2003, Tata Steel started looking out at opportunities for inorganic growth and I became involved in the process. One such opportunity was in Singapore that culminated in the acquisition of NatSteel in August 2004. I spent the 12 months between June 2003 to August 2004 in heightened multitasking between Tata Sons and Tata Steel and between Mumbai, Jamshedpur and Singapore. With a full plate at work, I became like a visiting guest at home. I can say that my wife and infant son hardly saw me during that period.

And then you were appointed as the CFO of Tata Steel in 2004. How prepared were you?

In August 2004, I was appointed as the CFO of the company at the age of 35. The position then was called Vice President (Finance). If you ask me whether I was formally trained to be the CFO at that age, no, I wasn't. But did I have the courage and conviction to take the responsibility? Clearly, yes. In my mind, once the commitment is made, I become duty-bound to make it work. By this time in my life, I had got used to being out of the comfort zone and I could mentally adapt to the new situation and playground.

> *I feel it is important for any professional to have the ability to step up the game when the need arises and to a large extent it is the mental agility and clarity of mind that are enablers for human beings to go outside the comfort zone and take on bigger challenges.*

Mr Ratan Tata, the Chairman of the Board, Mr Muthuraman, Managing Director of the company, and the Board of Directors had placed their faith and trust in me to take the responsibility. It was, therefore, my duty to ensure I provided effective leadership to the functioning of the company and deliver on the same.

There were a couple of other reasons why I felt comfortable in the role:

Firstly, because it was Tata Steel—this is a unique institution where people are very passionate about what they do and are aligned with what is best for the company. If you are in Jamshedpur or any of the operating locations be it in the mines, collieries, marketing network, etc., you can feel the culture of the company through the passion of the people and the communities around them. When you walk back into such an institution you know the only thing that matters is to focus on what is good for the company. This has been a multi-generational attribute of Tata Steel and that's how the organization's DNA has developed over decades.

Secondly, I was going back to a company and industry that I was most familiar with and hence it was a homecoming even though a lot had changed within the company.

The one year of transition into Tata Steel helped me get a better understanding of the role, the people, and their expectations. The senior leadership of the company were much older and experienced than me but were also very supportive and I quickly settled down in my new role. We were amid the first overseas acquisition in South East Asia, so it was like jumping in at the deep end from day one. For a professional, it couldn't have been more exciting.

So how was it going back to Tata Steel? Did you have any awkward moments?

Before I was transferred to Tata Sons, I was very junior in Tata Steel and as is customary, I used to call the seniors 'Sir'. When I returned to Tata Steel at end of 2003, they were still there and were aspirants for the position of Chief Financial Controller which I was appointed to. Naturally, in the initial days, there was some awkwardness because they were my seniors and now they were reporting to me. They were understandably unhappy with this development and the same was reflected in the initial conversations when I became the joint chief financial controller. To me, such situations are a test of the strength of your character and emotional intelligence. You cannot use your positional hierarchy to manage such situations. I felt deeply for them and said to myself that it is as much my responsibility to not only make them comfortable but also help them continue to aspire for professional success. I was a stakeholder in their career and I wanted everyone to be happy and motivated. I spent a lot of time with them, gave them space, respected them, valued their advice and never made them feel that I was higher in the hierarchy. Eventually, I tried to provide exposure and opportunities to most of the senior leadership in the finance function based on what I felt best suited their experience, skills, and capabilities.

> *Dealing with people's emotions is an integral part of leadership qualities which I learned from the leaders that I worked for. For me, patience and calmness are critical attributes. Leadership styles that are temperamental and create an environment just to drive outcomes without looking at the long-term institutional and people impact can hurt the institution.*

My priority as the CFO of Tata Steel was to realign and refresh the finance team to the new corporate strategy of Tata Steel, especially around growth. Tata Steel as a company always had very strong systems, controls and processes. The company had very efficient processes in financial accounting, transaction processing, financial reporting, and many such positive attributes. In the first few months, I assessed the finance talent capability that would be important for the future, the leadership attributes, and the self-driven mindset that I was looking for in the team members to align with the company's strategies. I was not looking for an extensive external recruitment or to build a larger team beyond what was already there. As a company, Tata Steel had just come out of a huge organizational restructuring a few years back, and hence the company was very sensitive to any increase in the numbers. What I was looking at was critical capabilities and how to give exposure to the bright professionals in the company to newer areas of finance like M&A, treasury, risk management, investor relations, financial planning and analytics, etc. It was not an overnight transition but a structured programme over two years without making it apparent to everyone that we were doing something big bang. I prepared a very detailed road map outlining my vision for building capacity and capability and discussed it with Mr Muthuraman, who was extremely supportive. That 15-page document became the anchor for talent management for finance over the next few years.

Over the next few years, Tata Steel ventured into overseas acquisitions in South East Asia and then in Europe. As a team, we learned the process fast, both in terms of planning and execution of the transactions efficiently, including financing. What was also important was to do a risk assessment of such growth so that everyone was aware of the decisions. Raising $10 billion in the international markets was both a challenge and an opportunity—our focus was to get the best transaction for Tata Steel under all circumstances. Today I can proudly say that we have one of the best finance teams in the country, and that is our major strength. Over the years, the finance team of Tata Steel has raised roughly about $60 billion capital (gross), including refinancing and new capital. That is not a small number by any team and if you were to benchmark the terms, the pricing and the timing of these financing, you would find that we would be right ahead of any peer.

The team members have consistently showcased their ability to be innovative, embody a bold spirit, and to do the right thing by respecting the boundaries, both in letter and spirit. The team has gained credibility and earned praise from stakeholders by taking on stretch targets.

> *The tasks were difficult and we faced many hurdles and uncertainty, but when one's intent is right, one's sincerity is high, and when the objective is clear, things do fall into place—even if one trips once in a while during the journey.*

These are the attributes that helped me and my team surpass all the adversities, including handling the financial stewardship during the global financial crisis, the 2015 commodity downturn, and the recent Covid crisis. We must continue to build on the legacy that will help the next generation of leaders to learn from and take the institution further.

How do you cope when things don't go as planned or take longer than what you expected? What would you advise others to do when faced with such situations?

Many things didn't go as expected. My life story has numerous falls right from my early adult life. As a young boy from a small steel town with middle-class value systems, merit is the only capital one has. The hunger to do well was always there and the more adversity around, the more determined I became.

> *While it is normal to get disappointed, I have learned over the years to be calm and resilient in the face of adversity. My father, who studied in Ramakrishna Mission—Belur Math, had gifted me a small plaque when I was perhaps in Class 12. The plaque had a quote from Swami Vivekananda saying 'No good thing can be done without obstruction. It is only those who persevere to the end succeed'.*

The plaque has been with me for the last 34 years and in some way has helped me in developing my mental strength to pick myself up every time I trip or face adversity.

> *A sense of equanimity is very essential to live in today's uncertain world. Especially in leadership roles, it is very important to remain calm, get deep into the issues at hand, and provide space and confidence to the team to meet organizational goals with patience, focus, and objectivity.*

While there are numerous instances, I will give you one example. When we were restructuring the £15-billion UK pension scheme exposure from 2015 to 2017, we went through a lot of complexities and negotiations with multiple stakeholders to find a fair solution for the scheme, pensioners, and the company. It was a fine balancing act. It took us 18 months to go through the multi-stakeholder negotiation process with lots of twists and turns. It was also not a slam dunk restructuring—it was customized and rare in the UK pension history. But we stuck our necks out and persevered till we could get the outcome that reduced the risk to the company and yet was fair under the circumstances to the pensioners. It was not a financial de-risking we had in mind. We were also looking at the societal equation with 130,000 pensioners whose pensions were at stake and hence a sense of fairness was very important. This process required very careful navigation and I was blessed to have colleagues in the company both in India and the UK who were completely aligned. In the end, we were able to achieve an outcome acceptable to everyone.

> *In summary, I believe that setbacks and adversity are part of the journey. The most important part is how one faces adversity, how one can train oneself to hold their nerves, maintain calm, remain patient and focus on the path rather than get distracted from the core purpose of life. From all the setbacks that I have been through, there have been learnings that I reflect on often and they have helped me plan better for the future, understand people and circumstances better, and make me more realistic as a person. To quote Leon Brown, the famous baseball player, 'Nothing goes to waste in the journey of life, both good and bad experiences shape your mind and heart for what is to come'.*
>
> *If you are passionate, then you will always want to succeed and not succumb to adversity. Our intuitive powers and judgement capability gets far sharper as we go through complex situations.*

Today, our core team is capable of doing the same. Even a person, who was a newcomer in 2005, has had a similar experience like mine at some level after 12 years.

What has been the role of mentors in your career? Can you share a few of the life lessons instilled in you by your mentors?

I feel that as we grow up, elders and peers have a strong influence on our lives. Some are explicit guardians, while we follow others implicitly or even seek advice from. I have been fortunate to come across many such personalities in my life and have taken advice and inspiration to shape my thinking and personality.

My father was my life coach in my formative years and his influence helped me define my character and personality. His value systems, straight thinking and mental strength to face adversities drew me to him. He never scolded me but inculcated in me a sense of responsibility, integrity and fairness to all. He also encouraged me to reflect and introspect on small and big moments in my life to learn from experiences and put them to practice later in life.

Later on, when I worked closely with Mr Hussain, I looked up to him as my mentor and I learned a lot from his way of dealing with situations. He was not a person who would 'advise' you on anything but I learned a lot by observation. He gave me a lot of space to develop myself. He was like a lifeguard at the deep end. If you required his advice, he was just a shout away but otherwise, he would not intervene at all. That approach helped me become mature and get comfortable taking more responsibility. To both my father and Mr Hussain, it was very important to be a good human being and to be fair first before looking at outcomes. In many ways, my world view has been significantly influenced by both of them. Interestingly, none of them ever explicitly advised or mentored me consciously.

CFO Office Demystified

In your view, what are the top priorities for the CFO?

I have had the privilege to work with three CEOs and three Chairmen in Tata Steel and I feel CFO is the co-pilot to the CEO and the Board. As a CFO, I have worked with all CEOs very closely and in the recent years, Naren (T.V. Narendran) and I have being working very closely and collaboratively in the long-term interest of the company under the guidance of our Chairman, Mr Chandrasekharan.

The CFO is also the true trustee of all stakeholders and hence in a position of not only responsibility but also trust. The CFO, along with the CEO, has a bird's eye view of the organization, and the internal and external environment. Hence, the CFO must develop a higher degree of sensory capabilities, faster and better than anyone in the organization. This helps the CFO to be pro-active and develop better instincts for potential strategic risks and opportunities to the organization. With the advent of data and analytics in the modern world, it becomes even more critical for the CFO to play the strategic partner role with the CEO and help the discussions at Board meetings.

In my view, the CFO has to balance the immediate-term sustenance and the long-term value creation of the company. The daily focus undoubtedly will be on driving performance, cashflows and managing risks, along with focusing on the financial stability of the company. including balance sheet management and financing. This is a classical daily management focus in top quality management (TQM) philosophy without which the financial fabric of the company will be at risk. At a time when the external environment has a significant impact on the company, such as the outbreak of the Covid-19 pandemic or earlier due to the global financial crisis, the role of the CFO doubles up many notches as the crisis manager for the company. As the company pivots all business decisions on cashflows and drives cost takeout programmes, it becomes imperative for the CFO to anchor some of these initiatives and work with business colleagues to create a cohesive cross-functional strategy to drive the outcomes. To do so, I would again emphasize that the CFO must keep his equanimity and not get flustered because the worst thing that can happen to an organization in a crisis management mode is to have senior leadership that do not have the patience and calm to handle a crisis. Yes, we need to drive outcomes but not by being rash and abrasive. It can be achieved by motivating the team to look at ways to think through options and take conscious calls that will not only meet the objective but also protect the long-term interests of the institution.

In the long term, strategic priorities of the CFO revolve around anchoring the strategic agenda, including deployment of long-term capital for value creation, strategic risks and opportunities, and scenario-driven stress test to ensure that the company's strategy remains alive to the long-term objectives at all times. There is a need to focus very critically on talent management and creating long-term bench strength. As the world is rapidly adapting to technology and digital enablers to become more efficient and effective, it is important to look at talent differently. The CFO has to look at the skill sets of the finance team very carefully and assess and map the skills of the future which will undoubtedly be very different.

What were some of the important attributes and choices you made that shaped your role as a CFO?

As I mentioned earlier, I was not trained to be a CFO at the age when I was given that responsibility. I took it and worked hard to ensure that the people who decided to trust me stood vindicated by their decision later. A few factors did help me to take on the role with confidence.

- First, my experience of working on a wider canvas in Tata Sons ensured that I was not overawed by the situation.
- Second, I had the experience of surviving and sustaining myself outside my comfort zone and in unfamiliar situations. Be it my life and times in the Salvation Army, the stint in XLRI or the subsequent experience in Tata Sons on many projects and assignments, unfamiliarity to me was quite familiar! My mind is fairly adaptable to any situation. That helps when you are thrown in at the deep end of the pool!
- Third, I am happy to be a learner and have no issues in saying 'I don't know'. People who know me will tell you that I have an inconsequential ego and that lack of ego helped me to apply myself without any hang-ups and I got a hands-on view of the issues. I must also thank my colleagues in Tata Steel who were always helpful, cooperative and constructive in their approach, including my seniors—Mr Muthuraman, the Managing Director, Dr T. Mukherjee and Mr A. N. Singh, the two Deputy Managing Directors, as well as other senior colleagues over the years.

> *To me, good leadership requires the ability to deep dive into issues, declutter one's mind, and look at the bigger strategic picture. This is important for high-quality judgment and decision-making in any given situation.*

This is a continuous process and my fundamental approach has remained the same. I feel that as a professional, once you get into leadership positions, it is the institution and not you that matters. That is why senior leaders across the world work so hard sacrificing their personal lives to make their institutions stronger and better.

What are the top qualities you recommend for young people who aspire to have a successful finance career?

I believe very strongly that one needs to develop a strong work ethic as a professional, without which no matter how bright and talented a person is, it would be difficult to sustain and succeed in the long run.

The second quality is a learning mindset. The world is moving very fast and while professional degrees will give you the passport to start a career, the actual learning starts only when you start working.

> *Beyond the professional craft that one acquires with a degree, your career needs to be seen as a lifelong journey of learning, finding the opportunities to apply the learnings with allowances for failing sometimes (and failing badly), the ability to pick oneself up from failures quickly, stand back from disappointments and reassess the situation, be calm and sporting even when you are judged unfairly, build an enormous amount of mental strength, look at success only as a milestone and not as an outcome in itself, respect everyone for whatever they contribute, judge people fairly without a bias, and try to be happy and content after you have given your best.*

Not all of these qualities come to everyone in the same measure at the same time because we are all very different human beings and not clones of each other. But it is important to recognize that these are important virtues to learn and imbibe to be happy in our professional and personal lives.

How do you see the finance function evolve in the future?

The world of finance function has been rapidly changing in the last decade, with the CFO and the finance function moving away from the primary focus on financial operations and controllership to a larger role in strategy and stewardship. With the acceleration of technology in recent years, the world of finance is now focused on, in my view, the 3Ds—Digitalization, Data and Deep Learning. Digital tools are providing new capabilities to finance teams and many of the core processes in the finance function are adopting robotics process automation, visualization tools, cognitive computing, advanced analytics, and blockchain. Robots or bots are automating recurring routine tasks and processes; visualization tools are making decision-making easier by 'seeing' the analysis; cognitive computing is using natural language sciences based speech recognition; machine learning is making data and analysis available almost instantly and in real time; and advanced analytics is providing deeper insights and better predictions of future scenarios. As these digital tools and technology become more accessible and affordable, it is clear that the finance of the future across all areas will become more and more aligned to technology and adaptable to disruptions.

You may be wondering what will happen to the people and what the future of the finance professionals will be. In my view, people will remain at the core of the transformation. It is the professionals in the finance function who would be the users of these digital enablers to become more efficient. The one attribute that will be required is to be quick learners and adapters. Other emerging areas are also becoming important skill sets for finance professionals, for example, climate change and sustainability, risk management and stewardship skills.

The skill sets of the finance team will have to be different and traditional functional skills will be a very small part of the overall capability set. Young professionals or aspiring professionals will have to get trained in technology and data science to be successful in future. Future finance professionals will have a wider repertoire of skills beyond traditional finance skills. As the world comes out of the current pandemic, the next challenge which is already here is climate change and carbon economics, and they will play a significant role in the global standards of banking, capital allocation, project financing, insurance, risk management, and many others. These are areas apart from digital technology and data science that finance professionals will have to be trained in and will have to engage deeply in the future. In my view, climate change will significantly reshape the debate on corporate and portfolio strategy, capital allocation and risk management standards of corporations around the world in the next decade. The purpose of a corporation will be redefined around sustainability and climate change in particular. The boardrooms are still getting a feel of the issue but very soon it will be the front and centre of the boards around the world. It's started to happen in many geographies, and the way I see it, the financial markets are very reactionary. So when the trigger will seem real, the financial markets will react suddenly and corporates who are not prepared will face significant challenges. And on this path, the CFO and the senior finance leadership of companies need to have the knowledge and understanding to be able to collaborate with the rest of the organization and shape the agenda within the organization to mitigate the impact of climate change. There are many global initiatives starting from disclosure standards like the Task Force on Climate-related Financial Disclosures (TCFD) to developing markets for carbon offsets, which are all aimed at mitigating climate risk. It's a topic where the finance function cannot afford to be behind the curve.

As a CFO, how much do you interact with other functions and with your customers? How often? How has it evolved?

To be effective in the role, one has to understand the business very well. Having spent 25 years in the company, it comes with experience. But business dynamics change all the time and hence the continuous conversations and insights with colleagues in the business and other functions are vitally important. And it's just not me but the entire senior leadership in my team who work very closely with the business leadership daily to ensure that we are keeping our eyes open and ears close to the ground, and also to support and facilitate business decision-making continuously. Working collaboratively with my colleagues in the business domain is essential to ensure that we all are aligned on major issues of the company and we are on the same bus journey to drive organizational objectives. For an effective finance function, understanding the business and the issues facing the business are very crucial. We have an open organization and I encourage all my colleagues to be in close connection with their counterparts in the business and be part of the problem-solving process. That helps their learning of the business and also appreciation of the business issues and complexities that we need to resolve together. So the finance team right from business analysis, financial operations, financial reporting, tax and corporate finance, treasury to investor relations and risk is deeply involved in the business to provide a high standard of financial stewardship to the organization.

What is your advice to a new CFO?

For a professional, it is important to develop self-leadership skills and leverage them to fuel organizational leadership success. There is no finite prescription in life's journey except for some simple principles of leading oneself in a straight and uncomplicated manner.

> *Professional life is a journey of experiences and one can never be trained for all situations, hence it is important to ensure that we approach all experiences to the best of our abilities, be honest to the cause, and exercise our judgement in the best interest of the situation.*

My first advice to a new CFO will be to feel secure and confident in their abilities because that is what has brought them to the position. It is not good for an organization to have an insecure or temperamental leader or someone who clamours for credit for every accomplishment of the organization. We are living in a world of continuous disruptions and hence it is important to develop a mental framework to maintain equanimity across varied situations.

Second, the CFO needs to build a core team from people in the organization and if required, hire selectively from outside. While building a team, it is also important to acknowledge that all team members will not be the same in behaviour, attitude, capability, etc. They need to be committed to the common cause of the company. It is important that the CFO gives space to the team and allows the team members to give their best. It is essential to keep an open office culture where members of the team should be free to air their views and not to hold it against them if they don't agree with you (the CFO). That's very healthy for the organization, as long as the discussions and debates are constructive and the spirit is to address organizational priorities. I have never sought to have people who want to be personally loyal to me—it makes me uncomfortable. I have grown up to be personally loyal to the organization and be true to my craft, taking everyone along in my journey. I have not regretted it even if circumstances have not been always smooth or people have developed misperception because of the way they saw things. It is fine with me because in both professional and personal lives we have to build mental resilience to face the world and external exigencies.

Finally, the journey of a CFO can be challenging and stressful; hence it is important to keep a calm head that can multitask around the priorities of the organization. I feel that to be effective, a leader also needs to be kind and large-hearted. In today's world of collaboration and team effectiveness, the performance of teams is much higher if the members are dealt with respect than the archaic taskmaster approach of yesteryears. When I became the CFO of Tata Steel, I was 35 years old and I was given the opportunity and a big responsibility to lead the finance function. I took it upon myself to be a quick learner and focus to raise my capability bar to fulfil the requirements of the role. When the time comes, one has to stand up and be counted. While on that path, it was important for me to build a core team from the professionals working in the company and excite them about the future challenges so that they could collaborate and give outcomes that the company needs and values.

For a newly appointed CFO, it is important to meet as many people as possible and have a very deep understanding of the business, the strategic risks and opportunities of the company and the industry, an in-depth understanding of the people and talent issues, and to keep an open mind and learn from colleagues about the business. Keep the learning-contributing cycle going as that's the best way to renew knowledge and deliver in accordance with the organization's requirements.

Getting Personal

There seem to be so many activities at work and you also are a man of many interests. What does your normal week look like?

Pre-Covid, for the last 15 years, I travelled both within and outside India, something that had become a part of the routine. I assumed a lot of professional responsibility early in my career at a fairly young age when I also had a young family. I agreed with my wife that wherever I am during the working week, I will be back home over the weekend and be with my family even if it required to work from home. I read late into the night as it helps me concentrate and reflect on the day gone by and the priorities for the future. When in town, I do yoga and stretching in the morning before I go to the office. I generally leave the office by 8 p.m. to get back home and spend the evening with my family. Weekends are mostly spent working and reading at home, engaging with the family, listening to music or watching a game or movies.

During the last 10 months, with the outbreak of the pandemic, it has been a new way of looking at life and work. First of all, my wife tells me that it feels odd to see me all day at home as that is an unfamiliar sight for the family—no travel, no late working in office which is what I have been associated with for all these years! On the positive side, I have been helping out at home with some apparently simple but very critical chores that one normally passes over and takes for granted. The other interest which I have taken to is helping my 'plant mom' wife in gardening.

It gives real positive energy to be with plants, taking care of them and see them bloom. We also participated in the Shrewsbury Online Flower Show in the UK which was a great experience. Work from home can get monotonous but if it is interlaced with some completely unrelated and interesting activities it can be fun and keep you energized. I feel that the world is at an inflection point and we are now in the process of reassessment of how the definition and scope of work will evolve, how the workplace will perhaps become agnostic where location is concerned, and the skills required for the future will have to be more relevant to the emerging needs of the business.

How do you define work-life balance? With so much going on, how do you find that balance as a CFO? What are your passions outside work?

Well! Maintaining a healthy work-life balance is of great importance to everyone to make life more wholesome. A large part of our existence is beyond work and we need to nurture that, or else we can rust as a personality. Personal life does get affected when you are in a position of responsibility early in your professional life. And unless the entire home ecosystem supports you, it is difficult to sustain continued periods of work stress. My wife got used to it—she adjusted very well and has supported me throughout the 21 years we have been married. I remember when I was transiting between Tata Sons and Tata Steel in 2003-04, I was completing the pending assignments of Tata Sons such as the joint venture agreement of Tata Sky and the sale of Tata Infomedia, apart from handing over some of the work that I was doing for the TCS IPO to my colleagues. At the same time, I was running the acquisition process for NatSteel with almost no support, as Tata Steel did not have an M&A function at that time. I was also shuttling between Jamshedpur, Singapore and Mumbai. As I was travelling extensively as part of work, my son, who was a toddler, sometimes failed to recognize me when I returned home after a week's travel. He used to stare at me with a blank face, which was a big disappointment for me. I tried to be friendly with him by bringing new toys every time I returned home. At the sound of the doorbell, he would run to the door expecting a new toy, take it, and vanish into his play area. My wife, who is trained as a psychologist, warned me that getting a new toy every time would not help build the relationship because he was only attracted to the toy and not to me as a father. The only way to build the relationship was to spend time with him. Over the next few years, as he grew older and I learned to balance my schedule better, we bonded together with common interests. He is now 18 years old and pursuing a career in medicine. We are more friends than father and son.

Like any other household where the mother is behind the child to discipline him in life and studies, I am more of a friend and accomplice to him. So if I were to reprimand him for anything, he gets upset as if I am not qualified to scold! However, he is a mature boy now and has interests beyond studies, especially in reading and music.

Can you talk about books that shaped your thinking? What are you reading now?

Reading and self-reflection are important and critical to be successful on the work front. We have to develop ourselves as individuals and reading does that in many ways. I generally don't read business-related books as they are very prescriptive. I prefer books on human behaviour, climate science and public policy. Some of my recent favourite books are *Behave: The Biology of Humans at Our Best and Worst* by Robert M. Sapolsky, a well-regarded Stanford neuroscientist, *Minds Make Societies* by Pascal Boyer, *Blueprint: The Evolutionary Origins of a Good Society* by Nicholas A. Christakis and of course books by Jared Diamond and Yuval Harari which are quite remarkable. I am currently reading *The Social Conquest of Earth* by Edward O. Wilson, a pre-eminent biologist and an emeritus professor at Harvard University, and it is fascinating. I also read a lot of journals that help me to be aware of what is happening around me. *Foreign Affairs* is one of them. The more one reads, the wider a person develops the mental canvas and that stimulates ideas and helps form opinions. There is so much to assimilate and learn in life.

What are your other interests and passions? How do you find time to pursue them?

As I mentioned, one of my interests is to understand human behaviour. Behavioural science extends to all facets of life and it is fascinating to study why people behave the way they do and how the human physiology and environment around us influence our behaviour.

The other area of interest I have developed in the last decade has been climate change after I was appointed to the International Integrated Reporting Council (IR) that leads the integrated reporting movement based in London. Subsequently, in 2015 I was appointed to TCFD which was formed by the Financial Stability Board based on the Paris Agreement on Climate Change. This task force is headed by Michael Bloomberg, three-term mayor of New York City, and is doing seminal work on climate reporting and assessing risk and opportunities due to climate change. From my standpoint, climate change will have a phenomenal impact on the world and will not distinguish between countries that are friends and enemies, the level of affluence or where one stays. The Covid-19 pandemic is demonstrating very clearly the potency of an invisible microbe that can enter the human body and can have a fatal impact. Similarly, imagine a hypothetical situation where there is flood across the coastal regions of the world at the same time which can maroon all the coastal cities and populations, or a drought across the world impacting crop cultivation and food scarcity. While these situations seem unreal, if the climate conditions do deteriorate, they may not be impossibilities. Hence, the pace of mitigation strategies needs to accelerate very quickly to save the world and it is incumbent on all citizens of the world to care for nature and help reverse climate decline. These interests allow me to learn and contribute in whatever small way to the public good. In some ways, these are also connected to public policy debates on multiple issues that impact our society, and hence understanding public policy as a subject is very critical. I have a keen interest in the subject of changing norms in society and the emerging debate on the purpose of corporations and their interrelation with civil society. I keenly follow developments in this area, including the Future of the Corporation programme of the British Academy and Said School of Business at Oxford University under the leadership of Prof. Colin Mayer. The outcome of the project will help redefine the purpose of the corporation in the future.

Years ago in 1995/96, I got my initiation into teaching with an opportunity to teach at XLRI. I used to be a visiting faculty in finance and spent my evenings very fruitfully. I spent around four years taking core courses in finance and also finance electives and now feel very happy to see many of my students doing very well in life. To me, those years I spent in XLRI was one of the most fulfilling periods of my life—the time I spent on the campus with the students (many of whom were in the same age group as me), the hours in the library preparing for classes and the joy of seeing students get good placements and move ahead in life was a great experience. The years spent in XLRI were also fruitful years of learning for me in more ways than one—teaching is a two-way interaction and it was an exercise of intellect with a group of 70-odd very bright minds in a class. That was also a very enriching experience for me.

When I moved to Mumbai in 1998, I felt that teaching was one passion I would continue to seek whenever I got the opportunity and I wanted to keep my association with academics and research going. While I have not been able to spend too much time in academics other than giving occasional guest lectures in institutes in India and abroad and speaking in conferences, this is an area I hope I can spend more time in the future.

You are involved in many national and international forums, including on climate change. How do you look at such engagements?

The engagements are a very enriching experience especially when one shares the platform with people who are very knowledgeable in these domains. My engagements both in Indian and international forums, including the IIRC or TCFD or the SEBI Committees in the past, have helped me enhance my knowledge, contribute to the thought leadership and connect me to some wonderful erudite people. Along with work, I think it is important for professionals to constantly look at opportunities that will help nurture their intellect. To that extent, association with either academia or engagement with cutting-edge thought leadership initiatives is important.

Do you get inspiration from anything else? Movies/plays/paintings/travel, etc.? Can you share some experiences?

During my formative years, I used to be very active in many extracurricular activities, including theatre and sports. When I moved to Mumbai, my wife and I used to frequent the National Centre for the Performing Arts (NCPA) for a music concert or a play. I am a keen music listener, especially Hindustani classical music and Tagore's compositions. I am also a keen movie buff but these days it is restricted to OTT platforms. Sports used to be a very important part of my existence in school days, be it cricket, football, basketball and badminton among others. Playing various sports helped me develop the ability to be fair to others with sportsmen's spirit towards life, in general, of taking ups and downs in life with the same spirit, respect the rules of the game, maintain behavioural integrity, and to be a keen learner from failures and mistakes. As a family, we have travelled to several parts of the country and the globe and we unwind and bond as a family when we travel. Photography is the other interest I pursue when I find time.

Who is your ideal/inspiration? How has he impacted you?

My father certainly has been a mentor and a friend to me and helped me shape my thinking as I grew up. He is a self-made person and imbibed a strong sense of values which he passed on to me. He would insist that I give my best in whatever I do and not get either ecstatic or depressed by the outcome. When I was young he used to always tell me to be a good human being first before anything else. These words have been with me and have in some ways been my guiding philosophy in life. The definition of a good human being cannot be relative or be opportunistic—it is absolute under all circumstances. One may have to sacrifice or be denied many things even though it may be fairly due to you, but one has to have the equanimity for situational acceptance and not have any ill feelings towards anyone. At the end of the day, if you are at peace with yourself and can have a good night's sleep because you have given your best, been honest and sincere to people around you, and have been helpful to whatever extent you could, it is enough.

My experience in the Salvation Army Hostel for six to seven years gave me firsthand exposure to how raw city life can be. The day my father dropped me off in the hostel he said, 'Look, this is all I can afford, and if others are surviving, you will have to find your way to survive. Don't do anything that will embarrass me.'

I will narrate an incident from my first day in the hostel. We went by the morning train to Calcutta after which my father left me at the hostel and went off to work. Someone knocked on the door around noon. I didn't know anybody in the hostel yet. I opened the door and found a thin pale person in his mid-20s, standing there with trembling hands wanting to say something but unable to communicate. My first instinct was to shut the door as I was scared. Then I understood he was asking for water so I got him a glass of water. Unable to hold the glass, he dropped it and went away trembling. I shut the door as I didn't know what else to do. Later, in the evening, when my roommate came back I narrated the incident. He and others told me not to worry as that person was having withdrawal symptoms from trying to quit drugs. I had never seen anybody take drugs, forget encountering someone with withdrawal symptoms. You can imagine how I would have felt that day as it was my first day in the hostel! There were many such unusual incidents I went through during my tenure in the hostel. Being one of the younger inmates, I also got a lot of protection from older ones.

When I reflect, I thank my dad for pulling me out of a secluded mindset and exposing me (perhaps not so intentionally) to stark reality. He wanted me to see life up close and develop my ability to judge what is right and what is not. Perhaps, he did not have a measure of what that reality would be. When I narrated my experiences to him later in life, he felt sad about it. But I don't regret that phase as it made me mentally strong and I was able to adapt to different environments and unexpected circumstances much better.

What is the advice you have for a young finance student?

I think at the core of one's development is self-leadership.

> *Life is a journey of experiences and there can be no one prescription on how to live life. But we all need to build the foundation for the future and principles of self-leadership one would like to follow. To me being a good and caring human being is a good point to start.*

There are no shortcuts in life. Therefore, it is best to accept that to achieve anything one has to work very hard and develop a strong sense of work ethics, be it in studies, work or personal interests. The world is full of opportunities but it is important to be focused on which path to follow. Even if one is very good at everything, life is unlikely to be always smooth. Sometimes you will be put through tests in life that seem to be very unfair and people may judge you negatively and develop wrong perceptions. You cannot do anything about it because that is how the world works. If you have strong principles of self-leadership and have stayed on course, you should be fine.

> *To tackle challenges and crises it is important to have clarity of thought and self-belief that you are doing the right thing. There is also an element of self-righteousness and selflessness one needs to develop to live harmoniously in this world and not seek everything for oneself.*

I am tempted to narrate a short story I read somewhere.

> *An old Cherokee was teaching his grandson about life. 'A fight is going on inside me', he said to the boy. 'It is a terrible fight and it is between two wolves. One is evil—he is anger, envy, sorrow, regret, greed, arrogance, self-pity, guilt, resentment, inferiority, lies, false pride, superiority and ego.' He continued, 'The other is good—he is joy, peace, love, hope, serenity, humility, kindness, benevolence, empathy, generosity, truth, compassion, and faith. The same fight is going on inside you, and inside every other person, too.' The grandson thought about it for a minute and then asked his grandfather, 'Which wolf will win?' The old Cherokee simply replied, 'The one you feed' In today's world, the question of which wolf to feed is an important one to answer from within.*

I think it is tough to prescribe or make a list, but do it your way. At the end of the day, if you can have a good night's sleep without any guilt or remorse and can put a smile on someone's face, you are doing well.

> *I always tell my son that whenever in doubt, go in front of the mirror, and you will get the right answer; the mirror never lies. Follow a path not just to succeed in material outcomes but aim to be an honest and sincere person with clarity of thought. Failures are important life lessons and there is learning in every experience in life. Those who learn lessons well through self-reflection sustain themselves better and are happy.*

In hindsight, what is one thing you could have done differently?

I believe life's journey is irreversible so one has to go forward and not backward. Learn from the past and move on in life. Wisdom in hindsight is not very constructive because it lends a sense of self-doubt when you take your next step. In all situations, there will be moments when one can look back and think something could have been planned better or done better. But we don't live in a perfect world and hence the outcomes will not be perfect especially if you reflect on everything. It is very important to judge the situation and contextualize the decision based on circumstances prevailing at that time. I need to be true to myself and be fair to the situation or stakeholders involved. I wouldn't want to compromise on these fundamentals just to drive an outcome that is favourable to me. I have enjoyed what I have done and I have given the best of the capabilities I have. There have been failures and I have tripped multiple times but to me, those were important moments of learning in life's journey and also opportunities to know people better. If these incidents had not happened, I would not have improved my sensibilities and understanding of life in general.

You have received several awards and recognitions. What do they mean to you?

You don't measure life with awards as no one works for awards. I accept them with the satisfaction that the work and path I follow are worthy of recognition. Most importantly, it is a recognition of the consistent contribution of the team that has worked tirelessly and loyally towards organizational objectives. I happen to be in the lead of the team and much like what the American Hall of Fame soccer player Abby Wambach had once said 'I have never scored a goal in my life without getting a pass from someone else', I too feel grateful to the wonderful set of people with whom I have worked over the years. The awards also motivate me to work harder in pursuit of excellence, raise the bar and inspire me to be the best for the team and the institution.

It has been an engaging and eye-opening discussion. Thanks a lot, Mr Chatterjee.

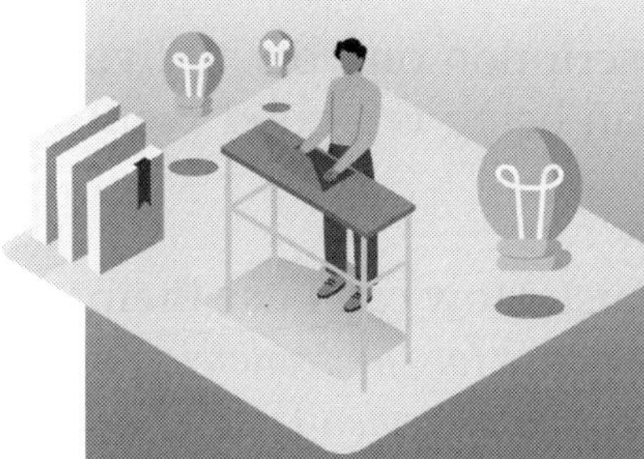

Key Takeaways

KOUSHIK CHATTERJEE

Take 1: You do not need rocket science, just stick to the basics, put in a lot of hard work with integrity and fairness, and enjoy the experience of your professional life.

Take 2: *Sola Nobilitas Virtus* - Nobility is the sole virtue of life.

Take 3: Mental agility and clarity of mind are enablers for human beings to go outside the comfort zone and take on bigger challenges.

Tak**e 4:** Dealing with people's emotions is an integral part of the leadership.

Take 5: When your intent is right, your sincerity is high, and when your objective is clear, things do fall in place.

Take 6: No good thing can be done without obstruction. It is only those who persevere to the end who succeed.

Take 7: Nothing goes to waste in the journey of life. Both good and bad experiences shape your mind and heart for what is to come.

Take 8: If you are passionate, then you will always want to succeed and not succumb to adversity. Our intuitive powers and judgement capability gets far sharper as we go through complex situations.

Take 9: Professional life is a journey of experiences and one can never be trained for all situations.

Take 10: There can be no one prescription on how to live life. Being a good and caring human being is a good point to start.

Key takeaways that inspired me most. How can I use them to change my perspective? (*This space is for the reader to jot down the lessons that they learned from this interview)*

Class 11-12 St. Patrick's School, Asansol, with Teachers (last row extreme right)

Cricket in Jamshedpur in 1990s during SBB stint (front row second from the left). Also in the photograph are Mr Yezdi Malegam and Mr P.R. Ramesh

Early childhood in Burnpur, Asansol

On a family vacation

With wife and newborn son Anirudha

During the thread ceremony of my son Anirudha

With Mr Ratan Tata, Chairman Emeritus of Tata Group

With Mr Ratan Tata and senior colleagues of Tata Steel India and Europe—Mr B. Muthuraman, Dr Tridibesh Mukherjee, Mr H.M. Nerurkar, Mr Phillippe Varin, Mr Jean Sebastien Jacques and Mr Rauke Henstra

Playing the traditional Nagara along with Naren (T.V. Narendran), CEO and MD of Tata Steel, at the inauguration of the Annual Tribal Conclave 'Samvaad' in Jamshedpur

Four generations of Tata Steel Leadership: *(Seated, from left) Mr Ishaat Hussain, Mr B. Muthuraman, Dr Jamshed Irani and Mr H.M. Nerurkar. (Standing, from left): Naren and me*

With Prince Charles in London during the Accounting for Sustainability (A4S) Summit

With Mr Michael R. Bloomberg, Chairman of the Global Task Force for Climate Related Financial Disclosure set up by the Financial Stability Board

Sharing a light moment with Mr N. Chandrasekaran, Chairman of Tata Sons, and Dr Jamshed Irani, former MD of Tata Steel

With Mr N. Venkatram, CEO Deloitte India (left), Ms Zia Mody, Founder of AZB, and Mr Ishaat Hussain, former Group Finance Director of Tata Sons

Speaking at the Financial Express CFO Awards 2019 function

With the Lifetime Achievement award

Speaking on Resource Efficiency at the G20 dialogue in Berlin

Speaking at Challenges of Government Conference 2017:
Bridging the Gap organized by the University of Oxford

Visiting the Netherlands Steel Works in IJmuiden with Tata Group Chairman Mr N. Chandrasekaran

Speaking at a discussion of the Global Task Force on Climate-related Financial Disclosures (TCFD)

Extra Shots

Koushik Chatterjee

Sola Nobilitas Virtus

When we reached out to Mr Chatterjee by e-mail to help us with his story to draw life lessons for aspiring finance professionals, we got a response within 30 minutes. It said, 'If it helps young and aspiring finance professionals to draw lessons to shape their journey ahead, I am up for it.' Given his large portfolio of responsibilities, it was a pleasant surprise to see him forthcoming with his time. Once we went through his story, we saw that he is also a dedicated teacher (read about his XLRI experience in his interview), apart from being a CFO. He believes and lives by his school motto *Sola Nobilitas Virtus*, meaning 'Nobility is the sole virtue of life'. By the time we finished writing his interview, by our guesstimate is that he would have spent over 30-40 hours helping us rewrite and edit the best possible content.

We still remember the day we first met Mr Chatterjee. We were waiting to get into a large conference room and saw several people walking out of the room after what seemed to be a very intense discussion. We thought that he would need some time to reorient. We could not have been more wrong. As we walked in, he greeted us warmly and started almost instantly with his full attention. One thing you notice about him is his calm aura and pleasant demeanour. You instantly feel at ease with him and he has a way to make people feel comfortable. Several other people we spoke to later also described Mr Chatterjee as a person who can maintain his calm even in the most difficult situations.

As we heard his story, we noticed how he has always brought a calm and effortless temperament to otherwise intense and stressful situations. His story and experiences made us see simplicity and fairness in otherwise complex business situations. His focus on people, relationships and the greater common good in pivotal business situations stays with us as a guiding light.

We were also lucky to have free access to him on most weekends to know more details on the life lessons he shared. This was during the Covid-19 pandemic situation and considered high corporate stress times. In all those conversations, he never missed asking about our wellbeing, was focused only on things that we planned for our call, and never got distracted by the hundred other things he may have on his plate.

Learnings in Action

Nobility is the sole virtue of life became an additional imperative for us as we looked at our business situations. 'Fairness to all stakeholders' is something that we learned from Mr Chatterjee. Surprisingly, this lens enabled us to find much more optimal solutions easier to execute than earlier.

Calmness is a state of mind that is infectious. We could not help but get impressed by Mr Chatterjee's overall calm approach to business issues. Based on a few lessons that he taught us, we realized that we are not able to handle complicated or stressful business situations calmly. The situation may not have changed, but our response has become a lot more thoughtful and measured.

Can you think of a stressful situation that you could have handled better and with a lot less heartburn? Do you think considering fairness to all stakeholders as a dimension improves business solutions and overall business impact?

Raghava Rao

CHIEF FINANCIAL OFFICER
AMAZON INDIA

With more than 25 years of experience as a finance professional in the fast-moving consumer goods (FMCG) and e-commerce industry, Mr Raghava Rao is the CFO of Amazon India. He has held various positions across finance and accounting, the supply chain, mergers and acquisitions, treasury and general management. After his B.Tech in computer science from IIT Bombay, he got his MBA degree from IIM Calcutta. A career with Hindustan Unilever (HUL) saw him complete assignments at seven locations and three countries, before he took charge as the finance director and CFO for Amazon India. In February 2019, he was promoted as Amazon's first ever vice president for finance outside the US. A frequent speaker at various leadership and finance events and an occasional blogger, Raghava Rao is today regarded as one of the most influential finance leaders in the consumer tech and digital industry in India.

For him, it was a case of 'been there, done that', which inspired him to move from the FMCG industry and HUL to head Amazon India's finance function. 'In the e-commerce industry, I saw a once-in-a-lifetime opportunity to use the skills already honed in FMCG to shape the growth of a sunrise industry that will forever alter the way customers shop in India,' said Mr Rao, who started his career in 1994 as a management trainee at HUL. 'It was a clichéd but an irresistible opportunity to work hard, have fun and make history!' In his current role, he is at the centre of India's hottest industry, and a senior leader in a team building Amazon's customer franchise in the hotly contested e-commerce battle.

Fireside Chat

Can you please take us through your life's journey?

I am a south Indian from a Telugu family, but was raised for a substantial part of my childhood in north India. My parents hail from a small village near Vijayawada. My father, an engineer, had humble beginnings and was sent to Madras (now Chennai) for higher education by his elder brother. He then joined TI Cycles. My mother is a homemaker, and I have a brother four years younger than me.

When I was two years old, my father's job led us to relocate to Ludhiana in Punjab. Picture us, a middle-class south Indian family in Ludhiana, in the heart of Punjab—a very ostentatious, prosperous and outgoing society. It was a paradigm shift in terms of language, culture, food and lifestyle.

My childhood was a unique fusion of Telugu at home and Punjabi outside it, and was anchored to an incredible degree of attention to education. My parents ensured we spent our vacations at our native place. My mother worked towards making us comfortable with both north Indian and south Indian cuisine. This unique dual cultural influence and exposure in my formative years made me culturally and mentally very flexible. Later, in my youth, I would see many students finding it difficult to adjust to a change of culture, food or location. I took to this north–south fusion with relative ease, thanks to my background. That said, my core has typical south Indian middle-class values centred on simplicity and emphasis on education, hard work and family.

I studied in Sacred Heart Convent School, easily Ludhiana's then most well-regarded school. It was also a magnet for students from prosperous and influential families. Convent education cemented a strong comfort with English as a language, and my parents inspired me to wholly commit myself to academics. I had the unique distinction of being a school topper consistently from Class 5 to Class 9, and was a strong favourite among many teachers. I had an intense ambition to be the district topper for Ludhiana in Class 10. In a bitter blow to me, I was unexpectedly pipped by another student for the topper's rank and became merely a district second ranker. For many years, until wisdom dawned and the passage of time gave me a more mature perspective, I would very naively quote this academic setback as the biggest disappointment of my life.

Ludhiana's Punjabi culture is famously flamboyant. Here I was, a conservative middle-class south Indian, growing up with friends from highly affluent families. A friend, I recall, was gifted a Maruti 800 on his 16th birthday, and another's affluent family owned a fleet of petrol pumps. In this childhood context, education got subconsciously positioned as my ticket to, perhaps, a similar prosperous future. Hard work in academics was the theme that shaped my growing-up years.

My parents, particularly my mother, instilled in me very middle-class values based on frugality and hard work. Today, when I look back, what my parents ingrained in me is what I refer to as the marshmallow test. The marshmallow test, made famous by its Stanford association, refers to a test wherein children are asked to choose between having one marshmallow immediately or wait for 15 minutes to get two marshmallows. For children to opt for the latter choice, they need to have internalized the concept of delayed gratification and self-control, and according to the study, this group does well later in adult life. Work hard today, and you will get the reward later in life is what my mother would have simply called it!

An interesting collateral benefit of being the favourite student of my teachers was that somewhere on the way, I was nudged to participate in debates, extempore contests and public speaking. I took to this comfortably, and the ease with public speaking turned out to be an asset I could leverage in my subsequent professional life. For several years in Ludhiana, I had an unbroken record of leading my school to the top prize in interschool and interdistrict public speaking contests. Somewhere on the way, I also built a good track record in quizzes, creative writing and poetry. As the years passed, the affinity for poetry faded away, but the knack for creative writing survived and finds an occasional expression when work demands that I put a pen to paper, or finger to keyboard. The mix of my academic record as well as public speaking, creative writing and presentation skills formed a set of core skills during my student life that I think I still draw upon as part of my leadership style.

I am a hopeless introvert when it comes to social occasions. But drop me into a team, give me a task, and I seamlessly morph into leadership.

Resuming my life's journey, my father was transferred to Delhi and it coincided with my higher secondary school phase (Class 11). I was admitted to Sardar Patel Vidyalaya, one of Delhi's elite schools. Situated in Lodhi Estate, it was popular among children of the capital's bureaucrats and was run by a Gujarati trust in a rather Indian traditional style. Academic standards were distinctly high. Along the way, a passion for science and engineering was ingrained in me; it was around this time that the ambition to 'crack' the IIT entrance examination was instilled in me.

The pursuit of a ticket to the IITs led me to adopt a highly disciplined approach in Classes 11 and 12. Looking back now, I tended towards an ascetic avoidance of any kind of distraction, be it movies or television. The hard work paid off and a fond memory I have is of standing in a crowd of students peering at the just-posted results on the bulletin board and reading out my scores—I had topped the school in Class 12.

The IIT JEE results that followed was the icing on the cake, and an All-India rank of 151 helped me to gatecrash an offer in the coveted computer science stream at IIT Bombay. It was here that I found myself surrounded by some of the most gifted and innately brilliant minds of my age group, and honestly, I now struggled to maintain an on a par and median performance. However, I actively participated in extracurricular activities. I made a hash of a student election for general secretary, and famously messed up an inter-hostel performing event competition my batch will cringingly remember as 'Moonstone', eponymous with an organization disaster and indelible memories of comical incompetence on the stage. I managed to graduate with a very average 7.5 score, made respectable only when compared with Chetan Bhagat's fictional but memorable *Five Point Someone*. The student election for general secretary was one failed episode where the introvert in me struggled to relaunch myself into an avatar of a candidate and went about canvassing for votes. Some of these experiences were painful and unsuccessful, but I never regretted them.

Most IITians beat a path to the US for higher studies, and it's often a ticket to a better life. But oddly, with a family tree that had no presence on foreign shores, and a recently acquired aversion towards a further pursuit of technical education, I tilted towards the IIMs. Deep within, I was perhaps emulating my father, who thrived in a managerial role. Cheesy as it may sound, Manmohan Singh's historic budget speech of 1991, where he heralded the liberalization of the Indian economy, seemed like an inspiration call for the engineer in me seeking a calling in India's corporate world.

I received interview calls from all four IIMs, and chose the final offer from IIM Calcutta. Unlike the IITs, where I struggled to keep my head above water, I thoroughly enjoyed my life at IIM Calcutta. I was enthusiastically active on the extracurricular front, including hosting, for instance, an intercollege quiz that went on to be a hit. I had a respectable academic track, and recall being ranked in the top 20.

Was finance a conscious choice, or did it just happen?

Finance was clearly a choice I made and, in retrospect, worked well. I had an engineer's comfort, though not the accountant's predilection, for numbers. As an introvert, I instinctively avoided specializations that I thought leaned on relationship building skills such as marketing and sales. Subsequently, of course, I became wiser and learned that relationship building comes with leadership roles, and has less to do with any specific function. But I stayed comfortable with my choice of finance.

Can you take us through your career journey and experiences in some detail? In retrospect, what do you think are a few of the important choices you made, and experiences you had, that shaped your role as a CFO?

When at the IIMs, I had an internship offer from Hindustan Lever Limited (or HLL, subsequently known as HUL). I absolutely fell in love with the company, its leaders and business. The placement week, at the end of the second year at the IIM, is intense and stressful. Graduating MBA students compete for offers with the best employers across back-to-back and stressful interviews. HLL was the first company I was interviewed for. By the end of the first hour on the first day of the placement week, I was fortunate to have a confirmed job offer from them.

My love for HUL was shaped in my internship, where I had the experience of working under a charismatic person. He made me see HUL as a breeding ground for shaping and growing leaders like him running large businesses. That summer internship sparked an admiration in me for HUL, and that led to a career lasting nearly two decades. The admiration and respect for HLL (now HUL) lingers even today.

The 20-year tryst started with training stints at the Shyamnagar factory situated on the outskirts of Calcutta (now Kolkata), Nasik, Delhi, Bangalore (now Bengaluru), and subsequent roles in Bareilly, Pondicherry (now Puducherry), Pune, Bombay (now Mumbai), Singapore and London. The exposure and experience at different geographical locations, spread around the country, laid the foundation for what I am today.

My first role, lasting two years at the Bareilly factory, deserves special mention. I was posted to an almost run-down factory at Bhojipura, on the outskirts of Bareilly in western Uttar Pradesh (UP). HLL had acquired this factory as part of the Kissan (the brand of jams and ketchups) acquisition from Brooke Bond in 1993.

As a 23-year-old, I was designated as the finance head of the factory that had an annual output of about Rs 40 crore, and employed about 200 workers and managers. I was heading a team of employees who were in the age group of 50–55 years, and whose experience in the number of years at that factory alone exceeded my age. Instinctively, I sensed I had to first win their trust and respect; later, I realized this also meant winning their affection. Given the age difference, merely outranking them in hierarchy was insufficient for me to succeed in the responsibility entrusted to me to strengthen controls, help scale up the factory, and integrate with HLL's culture and ways of working. It was here that I learned basic interpersonal and leadership skills. Common sense sometimes has to be learnt and can't be taught. I learnt it helps to forget hierarchy and adopt a polite and respectful approach while handling subordinates much senior in age. Earning trust and respect through interpersonal skills is basic, and getting the relationship right with your team is the first building block for any leader.

The IIMs don't teach you the importance of addressing a Shukla or Gupta as a 'Shukla*ji*' or 'Gupta*ji*' in western UP; it's a pretty basic part of Indian culture to respect your elders. This politeness, however, needs to be married with a certain firmness to maintain the subtle assertion of authority. Getting this balance right was key for me in my first role as a 20-something leader.

Factory operations, including procurement, inbounding and storage of raw materials, plant machinery maintenance, shop floor operations, control over finished products and—the most important—the administrative supervision of factory workmen and the team of officers leading them, were under my purview.

For me to be an effective finance head, I had to intimately understand the physicality of factory operations. To comprehend them, you start by understanding what actually happens in a shift on the shop floor. It was fun for me in finance to come for the occasional night shift and chat with the shift officers. A key initiative being run at that time was to improve productivity and reduce machine downtime by making the machine operator take ownership of machine maintenance instead of depending on a separate maintenance crew. This seemingly simple initiative meant a big change in culture and training, and involved negotiating with the factory union to get the concept across. As the plant's finance leader, I was closely involved with the union negotiations, and was on first-name terms with the key leaders. All this made me emotionally invested in the factory and the team. Sundays were about playing cricket together with the factory personnel and there were frequent visits to their home for an invited meal. Family get-togethers with the factory team were frequent and thoroughly enjoyable in that culture.

In terms of core functional skills, the on-the-job learning was about hardcore accounting concepts such as analysing the balance sheet, trial balance, account receivables and payables, month-end closing of books and so on. All these were due to the interactions with the auditors and accountants. As an engineer-MBA, I didn't have a chartered accountant's (CA) functional familiarity with these concepts, but the job made no relaxation for this ignorance. I had to simultaneously learn and supervise such accounting aspects, manage field auditors' visits and defend the scrutiny of books. By the end of the second year, I felt confident as I was on par with any CA on this aspect of the job. Since then, I have never felt disadvantaged in the company of chartered accountants when discussing accounting matters.

An unexpected and challenging crisis occurred with the introduction of excise duty on the factory's products in the government's finance budget. Almost overnight, the government officials from the excise department landed at the factory gate and suspended factory dispatches until the excise registration was secured. Suspending factory dispatches had the effect of halting the factory operations—a critical setback during the peak manufacturing season. The entire factory team looked to me as their finance leader to secure registration and resume the operations.

As a straightforward and naïve youngster at the beginning of his career, I had zero experience in working with government officials. Completely committed to the HLL ethical policy of dealing with government officials, I found myself in a deadlock, and frustrated over some delaying tactics adopted by the officials in granting excise registration despite us completing all paperwork. Our factory manager then came to my rescue by handling the excise officer tactfully but ethically. We got our registration done over lunch with the excise officer at one of Bareilly's better restaurants, and nothing more. This experience showcased that a firm's ethical tone needs to be blended with humility, relationship-building and generous gestures offering respect when working with government representatives.

Another episode pertained to detection of a fraud carried out by an employee handling cash. This incident taught me the importance of close monitoring of cash at the cash handling points and how one must 'trust but verify'.

My next assignment in Bangalore was in a role that called for supply planning and logistics. I was part of the core business team at the head office, and the fulcrum between the demand team comprising sales and marketing and the supply team comprising factories purchase and transportation people. Managing a national demand-supply planning network required working with the IT systems. This, in turn, involved the science and art of managing forecasts.

My next role was as a purchase manager, where I handled procurement of a raw material portfolio of about Rs 50 crore annually. I quickly learnt my portfolio had a wide spectrum of purchase baskets, involving very different approaches. On one hand, there were a certain class of raw materials—commodities—where one had to be very tactical in buying and stay deeply connected with industry trends. But on the other hand, there were specialized items where I had to forge strategic and long-lasting relationships with carefully vetted vendor partners. This taught me negotiating skills, and the importance of seeing a deal from the eyes of the vendor. I learnt that to negotiate the price of PET (polyethylene terephthalate) bottles, one had to keep an eye on crude oil prices, the timing of Ramzan, onset of the monsoons and supply-demand mismatches in the soft drink bottling industry. This role had the added satisfaction that I was directly impacting the profit and loss (P&L) than just being involved in bookkeeping and finance administration alone.

After that, I was transferred to the Pondicherry factory, a much larger factory than the Bareilly one. There were many challenging situations in this stint, including handling a hostile and militant workers' union, an unfortunate factory accident resulting in the death of a factory worker and the consequential dismissal of a fellow manager for a control lapse leading to the unfortunate accident. The latter episode was followed by an overhaul of the factory safety systems. Unfortunate as it was, the learning I got from the remedial actions on the overhaul of factory safety systems was tremendous. This was because preventive, detective and auditing systems for ensuring physical safety at a factory have a close similarity with financial control systems that are intended to prevent fraud and strengthen controllership.

In 2002, when I was 31 years old, I became a full-fledged CFO at Kimberly Clark Lever, a 50-50 joint venture (JV) between HUL and Kimberly-Clark Corporation (KCC). This role involved signing the balance sheet and the annual report, filing the income tax returns, managing the board meetings and other tasks, besides driving business and financial strategy. I was indeed a full-fledged CFO but for a small company. I had to handle two sets of investors—HUL and KCC—each with a different perspective and culture. Being a 50-50 JV and a marriage of equals, it was essential to maintain parity protocols between both the investors, a key skill learnt in stakeholder management.

A particular episode on how we responded to a competitor has stayed in my mind. We had until then enjoyed a strong market share for our Huggies brand of diapers, and had a history of successfully fending off competitive launches. Towards the end of my tenure, Procter & Gamble (P&G) made yet another attempt to gain the market share by launching a new variant of diapers with very competitive pricing and innovative product features. Lulled into complacency due to our successful prior track record of defending our Huggies franchise, we were slow to react. We ruled out both a price drop and a revamp in our product. While subsequent developments panned out after I left, the complacency from our side cost us dearly. Our market share plunged subsequently as P&G succeeded in this launch. In our smugness, bred by the past successes, we had made the cardinal mistake of taking the customers' needs for granted, and we had to pay for it.

The disruption happened because P&G launched imported products, which were technologically superior. For instance, P&G brought in a particular design innovation in the making of diapers, which wasn't possible with our machinery. We hesitated to innovate on the product because we had a sunk cost in the existing machinery that couldn't be upgraded, and matching the new product features would require a different set of machinery. We were not ready for this massive investment, as it would affect profitability. All this cost us our market share and subsequent actions, initiated on the realization of the full extent of the impact, were slow; clawing back the market share was exceedingly different. It was a fantastic lesson learnt on how short-term thinking and lack of clear consumer understanding can damage the long-term value of a business!

Overall, the long-term profitability of a business is built on the twin pillars of deep consumer understanding and regular competitive benchmarking, a truism I experienced as the finance leader of this JV. Therefore, the four years at Pune were a significant learning experience. I doubt whether such learning would have been internalized if I had a shorter stint.

I think, right from my initial years, these roles taught me the importance of accounting and basic controllership as necessary prerequisites for a finance role. The value you add in a finance role comes from simultaneously improving both efficiency and effectiveness of operations, and contributing and influencing strategic thinking.

Accounts' bookkeeping and financial controllership are hygiene issues, and can derail delivery if absent. We have to ensure the foundation is strong in terms of controllership, accounting hygiene such as reconciliations, segregation of duties, making sure the books are clean, audit issues are taken care of, and of course, its compliances, tax and regulatory. Improving the effectiveness and efficiency of operations can range from raw material purchase to negotiations, or identifying wastage in logistics or manufacturing. It is important to note that financial controllership, through hygiene in accounting, is a prerequisite, though excellence in that area alone cannot ensure excellence in delivery as a CFO. I have personally witnessed finance leaders lose their jobs because of acts of omission, beside acts of commission, leading to misreporting or control breakdowns.

Strategic business-finance partnering in FMCG requires finance to play a role in brand pricing policies, determining short-term and long-term financial and non-financial goals, making calls on resource allocation, tracking competition and the industry ecosystem, monitoring performance, contributing to cost saving initiatives and partnering on strategic plans that can impact market share.

To succeed in business partnering, the secret sauce is getting intimately familiar with all the functions and to deeply engage with business leaders in discussions on their own turf. I often refer to a fly-on-the-wall test to ascertain if someone is a good finance partner. In this test, imagine a fly on the wall listening to a corridor conversation between a finance partner and a business partner for 10 minutes. At the end of 10 minutes, the fly is unable to identify who the finance partner is and who the business partner is among the two. That's because both finance and business seamlessly speak of business issues, and business issues are intermingled with finance metrics. The finance partner should learn and advocate business matters, and equally deeply embed finance frameworks into their business partner's mind. When you have passed that test of being intimate with your business partner's domain, and have simultaneously and reciprocally infused finance metrics into your business partner's thinking, in my books, you have passed your test as a good finance business partner!

My tenure as the executive assistant to the then CEO of HUL, Doug Baillie, was a tutorial on how to be a leader of leaders. I had the great opportunity to shadow Doug, and observed his leadership style to run a Rs 40,000-crore giant business. There was valuable learning in just observing his personal habits and discipline that enabled him to operate as a CEO of a business of that scale. For instance, at first, I found it amusing and then interesting to observe he carried a stationery kit with him, and frequently edited printed documents using pencils, erasers and coloured highlighters. Shadowing him, I learnt what it truly meant being a leader of leaders. He had exceptional emotional intelligence; he once told me within minutes of entering a meeting, he could easily gauge the pulse through sensing the body language, tone of voice and choice of words used by other members of the leadership team. He used these signals to steer the discussion away from potential deadlocks, or towards consensus, and knew when to push for a timeout on a decision. Basic discipline in time management and crisp verbal communication skills were deeply ingrained in him. This was my first ringside view of the theatre of a leader of leaders.

Change management was the need of the hour at HUL, as it was going through a lacklustre period from 2000 to 2009 that many referred to as 'the lost decade'. This necessitated reorganization, and Doug Baillie took the initial steps. Later, Nitin Paranjpe succeeded him and continued from where Doug left it to elevate the performance trajectory. As part of change management, Doug wanted to conduct quarterly workshops for the top 100 leaders. I was assigned the responsibility to conduct this series of 'leadership offsite'. The main theme for this series of offsites was to get the leadership team to co-create an energizing vision for the future, and an operating plan that would speak to this vision.

In this role, I had to coordinate with the other directors, prepare the agendas for the board and other leadership meetings, and communicate the outcome of such meetings effectively to all concerned. I learnt the critical skill of dealing with conflicts, and dealing with them dispassionately on the merits than getting caught in the politics of the situation. This required walking the delicate balance between helping other senior stakeholders achieve their outcomes, and impartially representing the CEO's office in my staff role as the executive assistant.

The next stop in my professional journey was Singapore. This was exciting because it was my first international assignment and taught me the experience of leading a finance team comprising people from different nationalities. The role involved working in matrix structures across geographical and national borders for a large multinational organization like Unilever. It helped me understand and track competitors on a global scale, observe their execution across different countries, detect patterns in their strategies, and anticipate their next moves on a global chessboard. All of this while simultaneously planning our own strategies with marketing communication, brand pricing and product innovation as key levers. These were also interesting times during 2008–10, when the global recession was all around; staying ahead in this volatile market was important.

I was responsible for the laundry product range of southeast Asia, which included countries such as China, India, South Africa and Turkey. As an Asian–African regional team, we were responsible for long-term goals, target setting and control of the three-year innovation and marketing road map for the countries in our region. The respective country heads were vested with the responsibility of actual in-market execution, using these innovation and marketing levers through a fusion with their own go-to-market local strategies. The organizational design needed us to be comfortable with the constructive tension between strategic priorities that we had as a cross-country global team, and the tactical compulsions that the individual country leaders espoused in advocating their country's local interests.

My next stop was at the London head office, which brought a separate set of challenges for me. I had to work on a finance transformation project to bring productivity to the finance function on a global scale. Put bluntly, we had to give a blueprint for cost reduction through headcount rationalization, and do this while improving efficiency and without causing any loss of morale. I was working with five very senior leaders reporting directly to the global CFO. Each of them had varying perspectives on the problem statement I was expected to solve. While the productivity objectives of the project were delivered through the blueprint, we underestimated the massive change management needed. Progress on getting these big leaders to commit to the blueprint was slower than expected. This was a stint where in hindsight, I think I could have done much better in driving consensus and change management.

After this, I came back to India as head of treasury and mergers and acquisitions (M&A) for HUL. This role called for constant interactions with the external bankers, and I had to keep myself abreast with the financial markets—money market construct and metrics, forex markets and their interlinkages, Reserve Bank of India (RBI) policies, economy news, likely policy interventions and matters regarding the finance ministry, global financial policies, US Fed rates and so on.

We were involved in M&A transactions, and I worked on some strategic disposals of business units. This required me to work very closely with the government, investment bankers and others. During this time, I learnt the importance of corporate finance and deal-making. In M&A, deal pipeline success is low and typically only one in 20 potential deals actually fructifies. This can be frustrating if your only measure of success is a consummated M&A deal.

In this context, I recall some advice offered by an investment banker when we were trying to work through a difficult transaction. He said that for an M&A deal to fructify, magic needs to happen, sequentially, through what he abbreviated as P-C-M. First, the physics or the structuring of the asset underlying the transaction has to make sense and be agreed between stakeholders; second, the chemistry has to work between the buyer and the seller, only then the maths or the financials have to be closed.

I had a memorable 20-year stint at HUL, but at some point, it had to end. That's when the Amazon offer came my way. I am glad I accepted it because it gave me an opportunity to work with Amit Agarwal, Senior Vice President and Country Manager, and bring my experiences to help the Amazon India team solve some exciting and complex problems. Amit's words during my interview with him echoed for long—he said that to win in India, Amazon would need to invent in India and for India. On a separate occasion, he also mentioned his mission was not just to launch Amazon in India, but *be* the Amazon of India. Years later, I realized this was my own desi version of Steve Jobs' iconic pitch when inducing John Sculley from Pepsi to get hired, *'Do you want to sell sugar water for the rest of your life? Or, do you want to come with me and change the world*?'

I joined in March 2014, just nine months after Amazon made a low-profile India launch in June 2013.

I was acutely conscious I was leaving an established company after 20 years, for one that was a mere start-up in India at that time. I expected adjusting to differences in work culture between both the companies to be my biggest challenge; I may have to learn certain things and maybe unlearn a lot of other things. Getting the right mix on what to unlearn, and what not to unlearn, would be important for my success.

There were many similarities between the organizations, both being multinational companies (MNCs), in the performance culture, emphasis on value systems, processes, a very complex matrix organization, the role of finance and the expectation that finance would play a strategic role. Both the companies follow a merit-based culture and are customer-centric in their DNA.

Amazon, however, has its uniqueness which I picked up soon after I joined. Amazon is a digital and data-driven company, working with data being a core competency. Meetings involved senior leaders frequently scrutinizing data across rows and columns, identifying aberrations, and linking them or seeking insights to these observations. Culturally, it is completely accepted for a junior employee to challenge a senior leader on their decision, if they feel the data supports the challenge. Amazon expects—and encourages—its employees to have the backbone to disagree boldly if something is not right, and if they have the right data to back it up. Another unique leadership principle at Amazon is that the company expects everyone to be vocally self-critical. This means reviews are expected to call out areas not going well, or mistakes made, thereby often seemingly coming across as defect focused. These leadership principles are documented, and all the leaders demonstrate them through their behaviour. The way people are hired, assessed or promoted, and the vocabulary used to justify these decisions is entirely based on these leadership principles. Meetings revolve around a written document, described as a narrative, rather than PowerPoint presentations.

Also, Amazon has a high appetite for mistakes and failures; this is just another side of the coin for driving a high pace of innovation. The culture is not to penalize people for failures, but to learn from it. For instance, a certain team discovered that due to a technical bug, payments were being incorrectly made as commissions to associates for driving customer orders to the website despite the orders getting cancelled. The bug was identified as a discrepancy, an analysis was run to unearth the cause and why it missed detection thus far, and the lessons were documented and circulated globally so the teams elsewhere could learn from this defect. We keep reminding ourselves that it's still Day One, and there is plenty of opportunity to invent more and better stuff for our customers.

True to Amit's declaration when I was hired, Amazon has been inventing at a furious pace in India and for India. A necessary insight I was careful not to unlearn was that in India, the ecosystem has frugal and innovative entrepreneurs. Multinationals can drive synergistic growth by forging the right partnerships with such entrepreneurs. The supply chain team forged an India-first low-cost fulfilment model to leverage the ubiquitous *kirana* store to supplement Amazon's middle mile, and make the last mile delivery to the customer's doorstep for a small fee. In another example of an India-first innovation, the seller-facing team innovated and introduced the seller flex model. The seller can leverage Amazon's fulfilment network and warehouses and thus take their business online with reduced effort.

When you work with a seller or an Indian partner, his return on investment (RoI) is the most important financial metric he optimizes for; often, he prioritizes this financial metric over an absolute percentage profit margin or absolute profit amount. This is because in India, the sellers and entrepreneurs are often constrained on financial capital. The capital is quite fungible and benchmarked to the RoI adjusted for a risk they get when the same capital is deployed to alternate productive options such as real estate, stock market, lending or cost of borrowing. You cannot, therefore, make an assumption they will drive for higher topline growth. Instead, they will often optimize for their percentage return on investment, and you have to factor this into how you engineer your partnership.

At Amazon, another dominant mode of thinking is that a business is best managed by defining the controllable inputs which drive outputs. Business reviews, then, focus on the health of these controllable inputs. These inputs are almost defined in a customer-relevant manner, thus ensuring the business is truly centred on the customer.

Of the many priorities I set myself, when I took charge as head of the finance team in March 2014, right at the top was to build a finance team that could scale the business in India. When I came in, we were about 15 in the team and half of us were just a few months into the role. Having had the experience at HUL of small and big teams, I had a clear view of the division of responsibilities with the team members.

A simple organization design principle I followed was that the finance organization structure should mirror the organization structure of your partner.

As we hired to scale with rapid growth, the trick was to maintain the balance between growing previously hired people into larger roles and hiring bigger leaders laterally from outside to lead a now larger business.

The second challenge to be tackled was to influence the 'mental model' (a peculiar Amazon phrase) of the business leaders to steer their business over the next several years.

Amit and I coined a goal for Amazon India: 'Get Big, Get Fit and Get Close'.

'Get Big' means to work on the inputs and thereby increase the sales to gain scale;

'Get Fit' implies an improvement in unit economics to systematically strive towards breakeven and subsequent profits;

'Get Close' means to drive loyalty and accelerate engagement among the customers.

Another priority was to embed performance management; to get the mix right between experimenting with different business models and evaluating the results to make changes. It is a mix of telling people, 'Hey, wake up and smell the coffee', or 'This emperor has no clothes' to bring them closer to the harsh reality; and yet sometimes be a cheerleader for the team to keep pushing ahead, and say, 'Okay, don't worry. We will cross this bridge later.'

'We need to get big fast. To do so, it's important for us to think and act like cowboys. We will not be afraid to take risks, and we are not afraid to fail.' These were Amit's words, which echoed Jeff Bezos' quote to the team and Amit. 'I don't need computer scientists in India. I need cowboys.' He further

> *added for good measure, '"Fire, fire, aim" is sometimes better than "Aim, aim, fire".'*

Jeff wanted the Amazon India team to take risks, move with speed, make mistakes and learn from them.

> *'Don't make the same mistakes twice, he said. Just make sure you make new ones.'*

In conformance to India's regulations, we follow a business model very different from that in the rest of the world. I had to partner to give shape to that mental model. And, yet at the same time, finance had to hold the bar on controllership and be able to say no when required. For example, in the US, doing business on credit involves a lower risk, given the high bar on contract enforcement. However, in India, tracking down a delinquent seller or a shopkeeper is difficult; realizing receivables from wilful defaulters can be expensive and uncertain. So, in such situations, despite an overall mandate to take risks, exercising control on the credit transactions is important; this goes back to the Amazon principle of having a backbone.

Also, it was a challenge as a finance person to call out to a business partner that a certain project was not yielding the expected results. Innovation requires investment of tremendous emotional energy by a business partner, and calling out a failed experiment or proposition at the occasional time can often sound like someone calling out to a parent, 'Your child is an ugly child.' Doing this correctly requires the right balance between Amazon's two intentionally, seemingly self-conflicting leadership principles that direct one to 'Earn Trust', yet simultaneously 'Demonstrate Backbone'.

CFO Office Demystified

In your view, what are the top priorities for a CFO and the role of finance in business?

I would put down three priorities.

First, ensure controllership and governance. A minimum of this is non-negotiable and must be embedded in the business.

Second, ensure that the right culture is set and capability is built for delivery. Mechanisms or processes must be designed and operated to enable decision-making. Resource allocation and performance management must conform to a pre-agreed strategic framework that creates long-term value. In Amazon, that framework is indeed long-term value creation; decisions optimize the net present value of long-term cash flows as opposed to optimization for accounting profits in near term.

Third, build a high-quality finance team that can scale with the growth of the business. Good people in the team attract good talent, and this raises the bar on performance. When the team starts performing well, this attracts even better talent and feeds a virtuous flywheel between people and performance

I spoke about the first objective earlier. To emphasize it further, controllership is a bare minimum and a hygienic condition essential. Putting in place controllership and governance doesn't get a CFO praise, but failure to do so will get the CFO fired. The second and third priorities are where you create real value.

Let's talk about a framework to embed long-term thinking in the organization—a part of the second priority I mentioned. First, define the long-term goal. If you recall what I said, for us this is 'Get Big, Get Fit and Get Close'. We have a certain long-term ambition for the business, defined in terms of the customers we want to serve, the depth of engagement and hence the size of our business, and a certain goal on profitability. This has been agreed with business leaders in a process facilitated by finance, and the leaders own their long-term milestones: 'Get Big, Get Fit and Get Close'. The long-term ambition gets refreshed every year in the form of a long-term planning exercise. The plans not only adapt to what we have learnt recently, but also renew the commitment to long-term goals.

We use tenets, tools, mechanisms and mental models to ensure these priorities stay embedded in the immediate plans. Let's take tenets. Tenets are rules that govern decision-making, often when there is a conflict. One of our tenets is we will not penalize the customers based on today's cost when we know the cost might be lower in future. If we have a piece of reasonable high-confidence calculation, which says in three years' time, this is what our costs would be when we reach a certain scale on volume, and we are confident about it, we would not take into account the current cost but the one three years hence, which is a reasonably good horizon. To make it simple: if it costs Rs 150 for something now, and costs Rs 50 according to our high-confidence forecast after three years, then Rs 50 could be what we consider for customer-facing decisions today; finance keeps us focused to this North Star.

Let's talk of tools, and how they are embedded into decision-making. Data is a resource for us. We build tools and capabilities that help us organize and mine this data to get insights; translate these insights into action, and use these actions to make predictions. Finance and business work very closely with machine learning on data mining. We have good tools, but it's still Day One, and we have plans to get better.

Let's take an example to see how data, tools, mechanisms and capability come together. Consider a situation where different customers in Delhi have ordered a mix of products, all of which are available in, say, Bengaluru. We need to move these products from Bengaluru to Delhi. You have a choice to move them by road or air; road being cheaper today than air. A conventional finance framework would optimize for today's costs and P&L, and ship everything by road because that's the cost that the P&L can afford today. However, we have data that tells us when certain class of products are shipped faster, they disproportionately delight the customer. This delighted customer, then, returns more frequently to shop online. In short, we can build rules that tell us two of, say, five products should be served by air. This is because it predicts that the higher cost incurred in air shipment will pay itself back in terms of the high-confidence future cash flows; for those two items, the customer is likely to respond to faster delivery speed by returning more frequently to shop at Amazon. The incremental cost of shipping those two products by air versus road is justified by the incremental net present value of the future cash flows. The cash flows are associated with the predictions that the customer will transact more often with Amazon if a decision is made to ship those products faster by air. Remember, this decision has to be made in a fraction of a second by an algorithm that runs millions of times every day when a customer browses the website. Also, this is a tricky issue—how you consider air shipping costs today, or those in the future, and how do we know what cost to assume. So, in reality, it's a lot more complicated than what I described. But it probably gives you a good example of how finance can work with the business to evolve tools and capabilities to embed such decision-making into rules that get executed daily.

As you can see, to get the above equation right, one needs finance people to be embedded in the core of the business, to help discover and invent these decision frameworks. Once finance is embedded in the business, you also discover the opportunities for finance to invent further.

Another role the CFO plays is in the allocation of resources. It always helps if we are in sync with the business partner; sometimes one could tell the business partner to wake up and smell the coffee, or as I said earlier, to point out to the emperor who wears no clothes. But before that, internalize the framework for resourcing. Take innovations, for example. Amazon follows the concept of self-contained teams. Jeff Bezos invented the 'the two-pizza team' concept wherein he said the individual teams working on an innovation should be self-contained, but should not be larger than what two pizzas can feed. We can develop more meaningful relationships, and maybe come up with new ideas and inspiration in a smaller self-contained team. With that as a context, the CFO should play a role in allocating resources to the right teams that need resources. These resources are often headcount or money budgets. Do your right projects get the right headcount? We've driven a decision framework where we handle a technology-related headcount different from a non-technology headcount; a typical CFO has to evolve, agree and embed heuristics for sensible allocation of resources, including headcount.

The third priority I mentioned earlier was hiring, retaining, developing and growing the right talent for the finance team.

What are the things you look out for when you hire a person? Many young professionals would be interested to know the qualities and criteria to be a part of finance in Amazon.

Like with all the hiring decisions in Amazon, we ask three questions when we hire someone: Will this candidate fit into our culture as expressed through our leadership principles? Can this candidate grow to the next level? Is this candidate better than 50 per cent of the incumbents in the current talent pool at that level?

We strive to maintain diversity of the finance talent we hire, and need to do better. We seek diversity in terms of gender, companies where candidates have worked, industry they are drawn from and their educational qualifications.

What are a few of the talent requirements in finance, and how has this evolved? How do you see the talent landscape changing for you?

First, we need finance people who are comfortable with handling data. One of our leadership principles is 'Dive Deep'—the person must be able to deep dive into data and draw insights. Depending on the complexity or seniority of the role we hire for, the key questions are a mix of the following: Can this person handle data? Does this person show an appetite for peeling the onion? Does this person have numerical proficiency? Can they frame a problem statement? Can they handle situations when data is insufficient, or there are data conflicts? Can they drive conclusions? Can they use these conclusions to drive decisions and actions? Can they use data to drive a change in thinking?

One of the challenges we have is the finance talent pool we hire from India. These finance people are not conditioned or skilled to handle data extraction, manipulation of processing by themselves; they often need an additional team member, say, an analyst to do the initial data crunching or extraction. They are, however, good at analysing data once served to them. In contrast, the finance talent in the US is perfectly comfortable in writing Structured Query Language (SQL) queries to retrieve data from data warehouses. In India, the finance people are very comfortable and sharp at framing a query or analysing and interpreting data; fetching data is something they expect somebody else to help with, as this skill set is not readily available. What we have tried to do is hire people with Excel skills and upskilled them to learn SQL. Another option, which we have found working well, is bringing together a team with different skill sets working in coordination. Fortunately, in India, it is easier to hire a junior person with SQL skills and make them work in coordination. This has worked well from a cost point of view.

Another key skill set required is the ability to build financial models. It is very different from any other consumer packaged goods (CPG) company. For instance, if you are a business finance person at the shampoo profit centre in a shampoo manufacturing company, a lot of time and energy goes in understanding how much a shampoo bottle costs. Let's say it costs Rs 100, and is being sold for Rs 200. The business finance person coordinates with the marketing department to understand why the selling price can't be higher than that. Then, we go into the cost break-up backwards and see how the cost can be brought down; it, of course, depends on the market response, brand positioning and customer affordability. Then, we try to go backwards into the supply chain and find how to reduce the cost price by reducing the raw material price and so on. I call this transaction economics, and this is where a major part of our finance energy is often spent on. Even a rupee saved goes a long way due to the volume of sale of consumer goods such as shampoo. That's how you create value because the firm values it at that number.

In digital companies, because we have excellent data, a lot of our time goes into the decisions where we use data to predict what the future customer action will be; then, we shift the allocation of our spends and investments to measurably demonstrate we are getting the maximum RoI on customer actions that may happen in the future. Getting this right needs skills in data handling, financial modelling and predictive sciences to come together. We need finance talent that can have the skills to do this as a second nature.

Around the time I was leaving HUL, it was very topical to talk about 'Big Data'. It's an interesting observation since I joined Amazon, in conversations here, I hear the word 'data' a lot. But I rarely recall hearing the phrase 'Big Data'. The Eskimos, they say, don't have a simple word for 'snow'; instead they have 14 different words in the Inuit language to describe 'snow'. Data for finance in the Amazon is what snow is to the Eskimos.

A connected question: How do you manage and retain talent? What is that makes talented people stay?

Two fundamental reasons why people leave is either they get disenchanted with their line manager or leaders, or don't see a path to professional growth. A key reason I have stayed for seven years at Amazon is because I love working with Amit and the leaders around me here. Amazon is a great company, with an inherently positive culture that keeps all of us energized and constantly motivated to work hard and make history. People are respected, by and large.

So, it's as simple as that. Employee retention is a marriage between the right leader and right culture. Simultaneously, we should be able to guide people in the team towards career growth. The journey starts from how you hire.

While I was serving my notice period at HUL, after putting in my papers and prior to joining Amazon, another senior member of the finance team at HUL had quit with an intention to join one of Amazon's competitors. Knowing he was well-regarded, I had a conversation with him and asked if he would be interested in joining Amazon. I steered him towards the Amazon interview process, which he cracked. He ended up joining Amazon two weeks before I joined after serving my notice. We later moved him to a very challenging role, where he delivered well. Very interestingly, a few months later, the same opportunity was repeated yet again. Another finance person, similarly well-regarded and someone I knew, quit HUL with an offer to join the same competitor. Yet again, we were able to intercept and motivate the person to switch options and join Amazon instead. Today, both have grown as leaders and remain two of my best hires.

Yet another memorable hire involved a person, who impressed us in our hiring rounds but subsequently declined our offer because he had accepted another offer. While I was disappointed by his rejection, we were impressed by his integrity and I kept in touch with him. A year later, we were able to persuade him to reconsider and join us. These were all memorable hires—and hiring the right people is the first step in building talent.

I am not an extrovert, and quite likely, come across as an intense person. But I strive to set a high standard on governance—right from setting annual goals to performance appraisal. This hopefully reassures my finance team they are boarding a well-captained ship. Also, overall, I think finance is well respected in Amazon. People tend to stay if they feel their function is well respected, the organization is a good place with good culture, and their leader is someone who they can look up to for values.

What kind of a boss are you?

Let me do one thing. I will read out the extracts from my peer feedback. We have a process every year in Amazon where the peers give your feedback on the IT system, which is captured in the system, then is accessible to the line manager and is later released to you. Obviously, when it is released to you, it is released anonymously. I think it is quite interesting if you read it, as you see patterns of consistency in what the peers think of you.

(It was fascinating to go through the feedback Raghava Rao received and he shared with us. We are reproducing a select feedback that brought a perspective of his style)

'He is the charioteer, patiently and determinately steering the entire business towards the profitability destination by expertly reining in a large number of wild horses, threatening to run away in different directions. His ability to constantly take on increasing breadth and complexity with the same high standard, and add value with his good judgement and perspective that extends beyond his immediate area of responsibility.'

'The ability to leverage his expertise in the space continues to influence the team to think about the long-term sustainability, ability to write narratives in a thought-provoking manner, having the backbone to challenge popular opinion, attention to details, and passion for participating in the cross-functional areas to raise the bar are his superpowers.'

'Raghava is a genuine builder and shaper of the business with the right blend of situational understanding. Business acumen, caring for people's development and the backbone to make tough calls.... He brings in a very balancing voice and direction in discussions. Raghava has been a persistent advocate of "Get Fit". He shows the backbone and tenacity in driving home this message, and strong judgement in knowing which area "Get Big" makes sense in and where it does not. Raghava indexes very high on ownership, and displays this on multiple occasions during the year.'

'.... All the leaders look after him to get his feedback on how to strike the right balance between "Get Fit" and "Get Big". Raghava has a very busy schedule overseeing many different businesses. But I feel businesses, which are not in the direct span of his control, can also benefit from his guidance.'

Can you share with us one life-changing experience, good or bad, that changed your perspective; something which is very close to your heart, something you cannot forget?

Yes, there are a few very important events; seemingly minor but they cast a shadow or illuminate a path across time. It was in 1991–92 when I was doing my engineering. I remember listening to Manmohan Singh present his future-defining finance budget, where he kickstarted liberalization. I recall being fascinated by that event, especially as an impressionable engineer who had set his mind to pursue an MBA. So, that was an important moment for me.

The other was in IIM Calcutta when I got selected for a summer placement at HUL. It was a fantastic project. I met a person who I thought was a great role model as a leader. He was charismatic, had excellent verbal skills, could frame a problem statement very lucidly and was fearless wading into conflicts. By association, I developed an admiration for HUL that could produce leaders like him.

Another memorable person at HUL, during the same time, was my then boss and commercial manager. He was a great thinker and had an exceptional intellect; most importantly, he had great empathy and was a humble person despite his stature in the organization. He was based in Bangalore. I recall when he visited Bareilly for our first meeting, as was customary, he first went to meet the factory manager before he met me. I received word he had arrived, and was invited to meet him at the factory manager's office. I was pretty junior to him, and as a young man was in the first few weeks of my first assignment. I went to the office to meet him. When I entered the office for my first meeting with him, he got up, walked towards me and shook my hand. For some odd reason, I found that gesture very memorable and it later occurred to me why.

> *You see, it was the first time in my life that somebody more senior than me had got up when I walked into a room. It might be a small gesture from his side, but it moved me and affected me a great deal.*

Another incident, probably minor, demonstrated deep empathy from the same boss. It was January, and my finance team and I were struggling for long hours to close the books for the year. The office infrastructure was very poor, and western UP was going through what was described as the worst cold wave in a decade. But my team commuted long distances at night and braved the cold in and outside the office to work through nights and close the books on time. When all was done, my boss sent a congratulatory mail from Bangalore addressed to all as to how the Bareilly team had completed its tasks working through the hostile winter conditions. I was surprised how he knew all this since we had never discussed the weather. I was deeply moved by his incredible understanding. Despite being in Bangalore and heading wide-ranging teams, of which my team at Bareilly was just one, he knew about our difficult physical working conditions. It was a tiny gesture that touched me deeply and told me how fortunate I was to have a leader who had empathy for his team. He was such a down-to- earth and humble leader—with an awesome intellect. To this date, he is one of the best bosses I have ever had and I am still in touch with him.

One more memorable moment at HUL was my experience working at the Bareilly factory, where I was leading a team of people much older to me, a few of them nearly double my age. I would have been around 24 or 25 years old at that time. After a two-year assignment, came the day when I had to leave office for the last time to take up my next assignment in Bangalore. When I had to leave the office, every single person in my team came out to escort me to the car in a procession. I still vividly recall how the entire team, in a deeply moving gesture, walked alongside the car to the factory exit gate. It is a nice feeling to have people look up to you as a leader, and made me very emotional.

Getting Personal

What does the day in a week look like?

I get up typically at 7 a.m., go through e-mails, read the newspaper a bit, then come to the office at 9 a.m. I maintain a timesheet to have a check on the time spent. I know the time slot for each meeting. Most of my meetings are with Amit. Then, there are business review meetings with business partners, which take about 40 per cent of the time. Each meeting and its discussions could deal with totally varied topics in comparison to the others. So, it is necessary to keep shifting the mental framework according to the situation. I hardly spend time at the cabin alone. Mostly I am with one or multiple persons discussing or reviewing something. I also spend time with my direct reports or skips to know how my finance team is functioning, how things are working with them currently, compared with their last meeting with me. Most of my meetings are according to the schedule and regimented, with rarely any time for social conversations.

I am a big fan of the book *The Five Choices*. For the last two years, I have been making a conscious effort to call out my priorities to myself at every quarter, and schedule time for fulfilling them. It's not perfect, but I feel I am more purposeful now than I was before I set this discipline.

The good part is my home is close by. So maybe three days a week, I go home for lunch. I do not skip lunch, but keep an hour for the meal. It takes about 15 minutes to walk down and walk back, but that's time well spent.

How do you spend your weekends?

I spend about an hour or more in some physical activities, either at the gym or running. I read a lot online. I am neither a TV person nor am I into social media. I do sometimes watch Amazon Prime or Netflix, where you can pick up and choose what you want to watch. I am also not too keen on watching cricket and restrict it to just the World Cup. I spend time catching up on e-mails, and tasks that require long and uninterrupted attention spans. Then, of course, I try to spend some quality time with my family, go to movies or dine out.

Can we know the kind of books and journals you read, the content you consume? What is it that you typically use on a daily or weekly basis? What do you like to read, what do you do?

I read newspapers. But I have noticed, over the years, the time spent on the print edition has decreased and most of my reading happens online. I am not a big fan of local national media because I see them lack in-depth analysis. I find time spent on *The New York Times'* online edition well spent. There are a couple of apps such as Quora and Pocket that I use, which governs many of my reading habits. Pocket is quite user-friendly, where we can read the saved articles even when offline. I spend near zero time on Facebook.

On books, I have not been much of a voracious reader but a thorough one. For the last couple of years, I have been trying to focus on building productivity. Some of my favourite reads are:

- *The 7 Habits of Highly Effective People* by Stephen R. Covey
- *The 5 Choices: The Path to Extraordinary Productivity* by Adam Merril, Kory Kogon and Leena Rinne
- *Getting Things Done* by David Allen

I have also read some books on emotional intelligence. I used to read a lot of fiction earlier, and that largely helped to strengthen my writing skills. I have read P.G. Wodehouse's works multiple times. My favourite authors in fiction are Michael Crichton, Jeffrey Archer and Ken Follett. Of late, I have developed a taste for Indian historical fiction. I loved R. Venkatesh's *Gods, Slaves and Kings* about the siege of Madurai and the life of Malik Kafur, the dreaded general of Delhi Sultanate ruler Alauddin Khilji.

Do you get inspiration from movies, plays, travel or anything else?

Long-distance running is something I am trying to build my capability for. I have a long way to go to realize my dream of running a half marathon. But I tell myself that it's still Day One for me!

Thanks a lot, Mr Rao. A very unique story indeed!

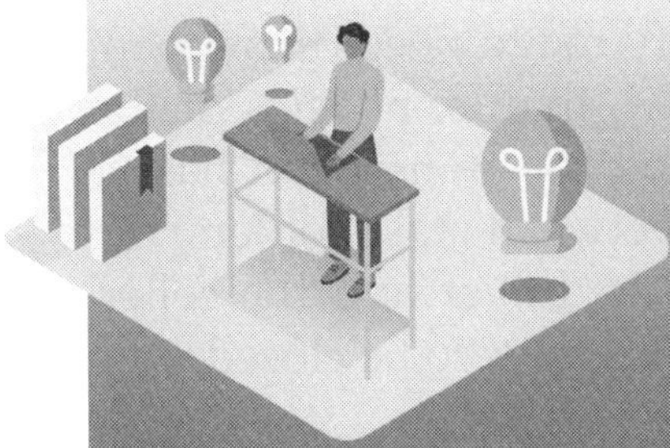

Key Takeaways

RAGHAVA RAO

Take 1: Get big on scale. Get fit on unit economics and get close to the customer.

Take 2: Common sense sometimes has to be learnt; it helps to forget hierarchy and adopt a polite and respectful approach while handling subordinates much senior in age.

Take 3: 'Fire, fire, aim' is sometimes better than 'Aim, aim, fire'.

Take 4: Don't make the same mistakes twice. Just ensure you make new ones.

Take 5: 'Earn Trust', yet simultaneously 'Demonstrate Backbone'.

Take 6: Never take customers' needs for granted.

Take 7: Data for finance is varied and integral like snow for Eskimos.

Take 8: Always take the fly-on-the-wall test to ascertain if you are a good finance partner. In essence, it means that a fly on the wall listening to the conversation should not be able to identify who is the finance partner and who is the business one.

Take 9: Deal with conflicts dispassionately on the merits and avoid getting caught in the politics of the situation.

Take 10: For an M&A deal to fructify, magic needs to happen, sequentially, in the form of P-C-M, that is, **p**hysics or the structuring of the asset underlying the transaction has to make sense and be agreed upon between stakeholders; the **c**hemistry has to work between the buyer and the seller, only then the **m**aths or the financials have to be closed.

Key takeaways that inspired me most. How can I use them to change my perspective? (*This space is for the reader to jot down the lessons that they learned from this interview*)

With parents and brother

With mother and brother

New Beginnings!

With wife

With parents, wife and children

Selfie time while trekking

During a team outing

Receiving the 'Most Influential CFO' award from CIMA

Receiving the 'Man of Substance' award in April 2017

Speaking at the India Leadership Day 2019

Fireside chat with Prof. Bhagwan Chowdhry at ISB

As a special guest on CNBC–TV18

Extra Shots

Raghava Rao

Fire, fire, aim!

When we initially started, we were focusing only on home-grown Indian companies and their CFOs. However, we realized that there is a larger start-up ecosystem developing in the country, and we should bring in a representative from this community who can talk about the life of a CFO in a new economy business. Amazon India started operations in June 2013, which gave us a perfect opportunity to talk to a CFO handling a high-growth environment.

Post the initial discussions on call, the meetings with Mr Rao were scheduled. As we marched to the Bengaluru office next to a popular mall, the general vibe of the office was that of a start-up. The first conversation extended a bit beyond the scheduled time. There was a knock on the conference room door, a young employee coolly walked in and said that she had booked the conference room for a meeting. Mr Rao looked at the time and we went hunting for another room. There was not even an attempt to throw the weight of the CFO around. *We have flat organization structures and everyone is equal,* came to life, right there.

The story of long descriptive notes is quite popular about Amazon and when we met up with Mr Rao, we understood why the CFO got a standing ovation globally when he presented the India plan. He has a unique way of articulating a thought that there was no other possible inference that can be drawn from the conversation. It is as detailed as it needs to be, not a word more. It seems he has applied the P-C-M method to our conversation as well.

First, the physics of the underlying 'purpose' was confirmed. He wanted to give back to the larger student and finance community by sharing his life lessons.

The chemistry was checked. We had a long introductory conversation and luckily for us, there was instant trust from both sides.

The maths, 'the content', was closed only after the first two aspects were taken care of.

Learnings in Action

'*Fire, fire, aim*!' is easier said than done. When there is a situation that demands action, speed is everything. But more often than not, we get stuck in deliberations and fail to act. The ability to accept that we can be wrong and then proceed irrespective of initial failure is a quality missing in even senior leaders. They are in the 'Aim, aim, fire' mode.

In March 2020, we all witnessed this firsthand in our jobs. Till then, 'work from home' (WFH) was 'aim, aim, fire!' There were numerous discussions on the advantages and disadvantages of WFH. Organizations evaluated the pros and cons, deliberated on risks and mitigations. Then the Covid lockdown happened and all organizations moved to WFH. Like many, both of us were very confused about how this would work. But then we had the new lens to think through given to us by Mr Rao. Act on a couple of aspects that seem to have a fair chance of success and then readjust after the results—'Fire, fire, aim!' It worked very well as suddenly we were in action mode rather than in an analysis paralysis. We knew for sure what works in the given environment and context rather than guessing what might. Adjusting and recalibrating was a lot easier and impactful than putting together a plan that had less errors.

Then it emerged that this equally applies to most areas of our lives, both personal and professional. Act and take a chance on yourself, calibrate later as required. Let's take our careers. Are we overthinking the impact of a different role in a career? Are we saying, 'Yes, enough? What is stopping us from taking the next step? Why not try it and see how it goes?'

R. Shankar Raman

GROUP CHIEF FINANCIAL OFFICER
LARSEN & TOUBRO LIMITED

A qualified chartered accountant and a cost accountant, R. Shankar Raman is the Group CFO of Larsen & Toubro (L&T) Limited, one of the largest and most respected conglomerates in India.

In the past 35 years, he has worked for India's leading corporates in varied capacities in the field of finance. He joined the L&T group in November 1994 to set up L&T Finance Limited, a wholly owned subsidiary. Over the years, he has assumed responsibilities of overseeing the entire finance function at the group level, including functions such as risk management and investor relations. He was appointed as the CFO of L&T Limited in September 2011, and subsequently elevated to the group's board on 1 October 2011. He was the chairman of the Confederation of Indian Industry's (CII's) National Committee of CFOs in 2017–18. He was also a member of Uday Kotak's Committee on Corporate Governance constituted by the Securities and Exchange Board of India (SEBI). He is also on the board of management of several companies within the group.

He has won several awards, such as Best CFO of Asia in the industrial sector in a survey conducted by the prestigious New York-based *Institutional Investor Magazine* and Best CFO Awards from *CNBC TV18, Financial Express, Business Today* and YES Bank.

Fireside Chat

To start with, can you take us through your life journey?

It was a very modest and undramatic beginning. I belong to a south Indian middle-class family based in Madras (now Chennai). My father owned a printing press, and my mother was a homemaker. I have two sisters and a brother.

Running his own business and having to support a family of six, my father had to work hard. I used to see him work 18 hours a day. He ran a printing press, but it did not have the current data processing technology. It used the old treadle machine technology, where people used to compose sentences, letters and so on manually. My father used to print question papers for schools and I recollect how I used to proofread the question papers during my summer vacations. I watched at close quarters the amount of hard work he put in and the modest money he was making. We did not have a car or an air conditioner. Much later, we got a television. All the money Dad made went into maintaining the family and giving us a well-rounded education. All four of us siblings got into good schools, but we were not scholarship holders so he had to pay the fees.

I suppose all his efforts taught me that there is no shortcut to success. You have to work hard to succeed. Secondly, it also taught me, very early on, not to be unnecessarily swayed by the add-ons you can do without. Even today, I remember my father saying, 'Your thinking should be high, living should be simple.' We imbibed the values of not taking any resources for granted and not to seek something we could not comfortably own. We shifted houses to make sure my father was living close to the workplace, with the printing press on the ground floor and our residence on the first floor. Therefore, the commute time was exactly 10 seconds from his workplace to home, and vice versa. Added to this, there were other infrastructural challenges in Tamil Nadu those days. Our business relied on electricity, which meant that we had to struggle for our water and power supply. People would fix marriages or other functions, and commission invitation cards for printing. This needed time-bound execution, so we could not make excuses, saying there was no power and hence we could not honour the commitment. We had to deal with those situations, making me realize that electricity should not be wasted. Water came in the taps for only certain hours in a day, so we had to finish all the work in that period. We washed our own clothes as there was no luxury of a washing machine. If I tell today's children about all this, they will think I am out of my mind!

I learned to be on my own, fix my own things, manage my timetable and work within certain constraints, to make the best out of whatever little opportunities came in. These are some of the fundamental things I carry to my job even today. Those values resonate throughout life and a person who follows them tends to be balanced. My advice is not to throw away money just because you have earned profits for some time, and at the same time must not avoid necessary investments because you are stingy. I learned the balance between what you need to earn and what you need to spend early in my life.

My mom was a homemaker and did not have much say in the economic affairs of the household. It was not an easy life for her either, with four children, and all the constraints, such as uncertain power and water supply, as I mentioned earlier. What I learned from her example was how she maintained a very even temperament. Even today, I am known in the organization as somebody who does not lose his cool. I do not shout at anyone or throw my weight around. It is just my style of working and living right. There are people who are required to do a lot of shouting, especially at our project sites. If you behave the way I do, nobody will turn and look at you. You have to shout, throw things and do all the drama to make sure you get your way done. It might be true for that situation, but as the CFO, you live with conflicts and demands of several businesses—each of them has its own logic that may not always tie in with the corporate logic. You need to do a fair bit of conflict resolution and balancing. I think I can do it effectively as I possibly imbibed restraint from my mother. In some sense, I feel that many experiences you pick up in the first 10 to 15 years of your life shape the way you approach any life situations.

My schooling was at Padma Seshadri Bala Bhavan. I was an average student at school, with decent scores, but nothing to suggest I could reach a position of this responsibility. I stayed in the middle of the class, and was happy with that positioning because if you are at the top of the class there is visibility and pressure. The number two is always trying to get number one, and number three is trying to get number two. It creates a bit of tension and high visibility with the teacher. If you are right at the bottom of the class, everybody ridicules you and knows about your position. So, in a class of 30, I figured somewhere between 12 and 20 is a good place to be in. And as things happened, I landed up in that range, changing a few places here and there. Since I was in the safe middle, people could neither write me off nor could they treat me as the brightest student. I always preferred to keep a low profile. That, in a way, defines my personality. I have never been high profile or aspired to be so. I prefer to stay that way because I think it takes away distraction from the equation, big time.

However, when I got into Class 10 and then Class 11, I realized I had to excel. I couldn't stay at the middle of the road any more. I also had to make a conscious effort to make sure I didn't get into difficulty for my further education. In those days, we went through the 11+1+3 education format. We had the pre-university and the degree. I slogged in the matriculation year, and did reasonably well, much to the surprise of all my teachers. That was possibly the first instance where I discovered that if you bend your back, results do come. It is just that I had never cared to do it till then. I am mostly an outdoor person and actively participated in sports, especially in cricket. I used to represent my school at various levels, such as representing the state of Tamil Nadu at the sub-junior level. I also represented my college, and was in the running for the state selection process in the university.

I went to Vivekananda College to pursue the B.Com course. I had good enough marks to get into a science college, but I chose commerce as by the time I finished school, I realized I would like to explore the commercial route rather than the science one. Possibly, this was because of the experience I had during summer holidays when I wrote invoices for Dad, drew delivery challans, and helped out in other matters. It was exciting to see the entire cycle of paper rolls getting converted into cut sheets, printed cards, dispatches and so on. Inadvertently, I ended up developing a liking for the commercial domain. However, I did not have the courage at that time to say I would be an entrepreneur and do something on my own.

I scored very well at the pre-university exams, and also earned my degree with good scores. After I got my degree, confusion arose when the college management tried to persuade me to continue my studies in the college and go in for a Master's in commerce so that I could play for the Madras University. The physical education director of my college had high hopes for me, as I was the top run scorer for two years consecutively. But I decided against it as I did not think my future lay there. It didn't look very sustainable to me beyond the age of 30 years. Let us say, you are 18 or 19 when you start, it gives you just another 12 years, assuming you are successful. What are you going to do beyond that? I did not have a clear answer at that point. My father did not encourage any discussion on cricket as a full-time career, and I don't think he was very happy about me spending so much time on the field. It was time-consuming. I would get up at 5 a.m. and be out on the grounds by around 5.30 a.m. Then, I would practise till about 8 a.m., rush home, shower, grab breakfast and run back to college for the attendance roll call at 9 a.m. In his mind, I was getting up and running away to play every day. I think that while he was man enough not to come in my way, he was quite relieved when I made a choice not to pursue cricket as a full-time occupation.

I have always thought things through before taking decisions. They may or may not have paid off. I did not have the maturity to evaluate the pros and cons, but I went with whatever made sense. The insecurity of life after 30 years of age in a cricketing career made me go against it. Knowing the kind of immense challenges we are faced with, right from school admissions to jobs, I had to take responsibility for my life. One thing was very clear in my mind—I could not do anything that would let my parents down. They had done a lot to get me where I was. I obviously could not do something which would make them feel disappointed. Therefore, the choice was, in a way, simple. Their non-interference allowed me to make my decision and stay with it. Possibly, they would have interfered had I said that I would ditch studies and play full time. However, I could never test that hypothesis.

Actually, it is very amazing that all four of us managed to do something with our lives with zero pressure from our parents. Not even once did my father dictate to us on any terms such as persuading us to become doctors or engineers. All he insisted on was that education was important. I was not interested in the family business because I had witnessed the limitations associated with it, and the hard time my father had. Eventually, he decided to wind up his business when neither me nor my younger brother were interested in continuing with it.

My father kept saying that he wished me to be 'triple' qualified. I do not know where he got that idea. Those days, you were either a doctor, an engineer or a CA combined with a cost accountancy degree from an Institute of Costs and Accounts (ICWA) and a qualification as an assistant company secretary (ACS). He was fascinated by this triple qualification. The subtle pressure of having to qualify for all three disciplines was always there in the background.

Coming back to my studies, I passed matriculation in 1975. The pre-university and university degrees came in 1976 and 1979, respectively. The triple degree concept stayed in my mind, and I decided to take up studying chartered accountancy full time. Enrolment to cost accountancy and company secretary courses could be taken up part-time.

It so happened that my classmate's father, who lived in the neighbourhood, was a partner in a reasonably well-known CA firm called Brahmayya and Company. When my classmate joined the firm, I also applied. My scores were good enough to secure admission in the process instituted by the firm and I went in for the three-year apprenticeship programme.

I look back with surprise now at my way of thinking at that age. During my apprenticeship, I did not spend my time getting into the micro nuances of audits. Many of my batchmates found it fascinating to open up client books, make extensive notes, and query the practices followed. They took to auditing as though it was a full-time employment. In contrast, I used to go to audits with my study material in hand, although this may sound unfair to the firm and the client. Nevertheless, I found time for studies alongside work as I had only one aim—to clear the examination. Those days, the pass percentage in CA exams used to be just two per cent. Since I did not want to lose the opportunity, I traded off auditing experience for the exam preparation—and it worked. I cleared the exam, though I was nowhere close to the first 50 ranks. However, I became a qualified CA at the age of 24 years. Those days, we had to do an apprenticeship for three years without which we could not appear for the exams. Today, I guess there are no such rules; one can be a CA at 21 now. Parallel to that, I also enrolled for the cost accounting course and cleared the examination in 1986.

The next crucial step was to find employment. After completing my studies for the B.Com degree, I appeared for the Reserve Bank of India (RBI) officers' exam, just for the sake of it. It so happened that I got a call for the interview three months after I finished my CA examinations. It took them three years to shortlist candidates and call them for an interview.

I was not sure about the opportunity to go for an interview because I had appeared for the selection exam as a B.Com graduate, and now I was a CA. But my father asked me to give it a go. I appeared for it without any preparations as such, and to my surprise, I was appointed. I became an RBI employee in 1982. I was expecting my results soon, so I asked my father how to go ahead. He asked me to hang in there. After the results, he asked me to inform the RBI of my CA qualification just in case they would give me a career break based on the additional qualification.

To my dismay, during my stint with the RBI as a coin and note examiner, I had to wrap a handkerchief around my nose, and do currency checks on all the notes, including soiled ones that came from all over the country. Each one of us as coin and note examiners was given a certain number of chests. We were expected to count the notes, remove the ones not fit for circulation, and make bundles of 100. The RBI workforce also had productivity norms. If I started my work at 9 a.m., I used to finish by 11 a.m. and could leave the premises by 3 p.m. although after 11, one could do nothing but hang around. I do not know why the cutoff was at 3 p.m. and the office hours were till 5 p.m. I followed this routine for a month. Then, fortunately, the

CA results were announced and I passed. I then approached the supervisor concerned and told him that I was now a CA. When he asked, 'How does that matter?' I told him that since I was a CA now, I deserved to do much better work than counting old notes. He told me to continue doing so and if I did the job well, I would be promoted as the chief note and coin examiner, the one who supervises the people counting the notes. I was disappointed and told my father that I intended to resign. As always, he allowed me to make my own decision. In about two-and-a-half months, my stint with the RBI ended.

Then I joined a company called Best & Crompton in Madras, an outstanding company just like L&T today, with a turnover of about Rs 100 crore in 1984. At that time, it was a large turnover for a diversified company. It was a professionally managed company spearheaded by M.K. Kumar, an extremely capable leader. It was into multiple businesses such as lift manufacturing, pump manufacturing, industrial electrification, financial services, information technology and real estate. Financial institutions held about 40 per cent of the company's stocks, the rest being widely held by others. There was no promoter as such, just like L&T. Fortunately, through a reference, I got into the company as an internal auditor with a salary of Rs 750, which went up to Rs 2,400 in six years, after which I left the company. During those six years, I was first employed in auditing and then moved to corporate finance in the company's financial services subsidiary. Being a financial services company, money was the raw material. I was generating resources, and the company was deploying them.

I often had to undertake work-related trips to Mumbai (Bombay then). I used to walk around the streets of Nariman Point and Fort, calling on banks and introducing the company since it was a relatively new one. This is where the marketing person in me was born, as I had to handle the task of selling the company, and myself as the representative of the company. I believe, as a finance professional, the ability to communicate and influence are key attributes. Nobody teaches this skill to you in any formal way. Mumbai was such a happening place and when I went back to Chennai, I missed its pace. This motivated me to make Mumbai my next destination. Obviously, Mumbai has its own challenges, such as the local commute, which was a major put off.

Around this time, my senior at Best & Crompton quit and joined Lloyds Steel Industries, a growing company in the 1990s. The early 1990s was a period of Non-Banking Financial Corporation (NBFC) boom. ITC got into the NBFC business, as did Best & Crompton, while McKinsey was advising L&T to get into it too. Wipro as well as many other companies also got into financial services. My senior, Y.R. Rao, gave me a call urging me to join him, and as I pondered over whether I should or should not, the prospect of living in Mumbai lured me to accept the offer. My dad was unhappy about this decision. This was one of those rare times when he said, 'Should you?' I said, 'Yes,' and was very determined. I packed my bag and set off to Mumbai. I was about 28 years old, and not yet married. My dread of the daily train ride to work made me negotiate with the company for a car and paying guest accommodation in South Mumbai. Fortunately, I got a place 15 minutes away from Nariman Point, and a pre-owned car that moved. So, that's how my working life in Mumbai began.

I spent about five years with the Lloyds Group. Before we realized it, we were running a loan book of around Rs 400–500 crore, which was significant at that time. So, the company became large quickly. I had never seen a profit after tax (PAT) of Rs 10 crore from financial services until then—in the financial services division of Best and Crompton, we used to make Rs 1–1.5 crore at most. Moreover, this company was making a double-digit PAT, so it looked much larger. The job portfolio was much larger, and I was excited to be part of it all.

I was then asked to manage the other side of the business. The promoter trusted my thoughtful use of resources, and asked me to try my hand at lending operations. I was now raising and deploying money. I ran both the wholesale and retail business. My job became more travel intensive; four days a week, I was travelling to different cities and states in India. Soon enough, I completed five years at Lloyds. The company was successful, and my designation and salary increased as the portfolio expanded.

As a part of the growth story, the company got listed on the stock exchange in 1991–92. However, I was a bit apprehensive about potential-related party transactions, and the challenges they would create in a highly regulated industry like financial services. We were raising retail deposits and debentures in Lloyds and public accountability in a family majority-owned enterprise got me thinking, as I was the authorized signatory. This made me look for a different work environment.

It was around this time a colleague passed on information about L&T starting a financial services company and said he had some contacts there. His qualifications did not fit the requirements of the job, so he referred my name to the recruiter. I collected and updated my information about the company and then appeared for an interview with the consultant. He advised me on the expected dress code, which was an alien thing for me, coming as I did from a company that accepted informal attire. After some grooming sessions, I appeared for the interview at L&T. But before I continue about that, let me narrate an interesting anecdote.

Around the time of this interview, I got married. It was an arranged marriage. My wife was raised in Jamshedpur because her father worked for the Tata group. She always tells me the main reason she agreed to marry me was because I lived in Mumbai, which meant that she would not have to stay in Chennai, where her parents had decided to spend their retired life. She, somehow, could not develop a liking for Chennai.

Finally, my interview with L&T was fixed. I went for the interview in the suggested professional attire, which was a dark blue suit. Post the interview, I went in the same blue suit to pick my wife up from the railway station. She was returning from her Chennai visit. Keen to pick her up at the earliest point (I was still new in marriage), I stood at the exit gate of the Dadar station. Catching sight of my unexpected blue suit that resembled the attire of ticket inspectors at the exit gate, and not glancing up to see my face, she mistook me for the ticket collector and handed over the ticket to me. The impression I sought to create with my professional look took a completely different turn, one that I did not particularly enjoy!

My business background gave me an advantage in succeeding at L&T. As a businessperson, I like to invest in growth and guaranteed returns. Typically, the finance function tends to play safe and is more focused on securing the base; the willingness to take risks is much less. We were also aided by the fact that we had a very aggressive, risk-taking managing director (MD) and chief executive officer (CEO) in A.M. Naik, and a very supportive boss in Y.M. Deosthalee. This suited me, as there were no internal battles for me to fight.

A CFO needs to create value, not by hoarding cash or keeping profits safe, but by reinvesting and sharing the returns with the shareholders. The businesses are preoccupied with their survival in every quarter, and do not find it easy to reflect adequately on new opportunities. Banks and accounting firms are constantly on the move to buy or sell assets. Finance functional heads become the front-end touchpoint for all these intermediaries to come and refer proposals. In such situations, one does not have to start from scratch—some homework is done for us and produced in booklets given to us. Finance officers in companies have to keep themselves in a position of access, and present themselves as officers looking for a good opportunity and not be seen as blockers. People do not want to lose time meeting people whom they think are unresponsive. To stay relevant for them, there has to be some ownership of what they bring, some honest attempt to understand and evaluate whether the officer's proposal will bring results.

I think, at the end of the day, unexplained decisions are always suspect. So, the efforts based on rejection should be much more than acceptance. It tests our conviction and understanding of where the business needs to be. It is important to keep the connection going with the external marketplace.

Similarly, we need to position our business well. One of the areas I spend a lot of time on is investor relations (IR). The detailing of the road map became a very important aspect of building credible investor IR practices. We have been repeatedly winning pan-Asian level awards as the company with the best IR practices on the polls conducted by funds, analysts and brokerages. I think the realization of the need to reach out to external participants, have a communication road map, and walk our talk were very important steps in my career. What builds credibility inside builds credibility outside. I represent a brand that is phenomenally important for India's growth, so we need to present it well. The company immensely supported the IR effort through the travel cost budget in dollars, as we travelled extensively to Singapore, Hong Kong, Europe, the UK, the US and other countries. The company realized the benefit behind it based on the number of research reports written on the company—the more the number, the more the visibility. This was in line with Mr Naik's game plan because for capital raising, it was important that a credible platform was created and it was not as though we had a template for these things.

I think this ability to pick up something as it was and make an opportunity of it is a very important attribute any professional should have; more so finance professionals because they constitute the bridge to the external finance world.

A major reason for my success is that I was fortunate enough to have supremely able team members, who saw my goals as theirs. This, I feel, is the success of a leader. Insecurity may sometimes be a hindrance to this goal, but my attitude of not fearing failure came handy. L&T is blessed that the employee turnover has always been comparatively very low.

When the stock market regulator was evolving its listing regulations, people started talking about the expanded role of the audit committee, and its scope of work. To L&T's credit, about 20 years before all of this became mandatory, it had an audit committee as well as a nomination and remuneration committee. All this was possible because we were widely held, and a professionally managed company. We always sought comfort in the collective or committee approach. There was comfort in collective decision-making because everybody felt they should not risk the company's fortunes based on their individual decision-making. We are not one person's company, but a people's company. To that extent, it was always better to have two people signing off a mandate rather than one.

These committees started looking at various risks to the business, and we realized we would have to integrate their efforts. The task was assigned to me to put a risk-management system in the company. The firm had grown significantly, and every day we were bidding for jobs across businesses. In some, we were succeeding and in some, we were failing. People who were empowered at the business level were committing the company's resources and balance sheet on a daily basis. But their understanding of the consolidated balance sheet of the company was inadequate. It was very important for the company to get a sense of its risk appetite, but there was no specific formula to calculate this. We needed to scrutinize the balance sheet, structure of the company and the value at risk it can take, then try to define that appetite, and allocate the risk to businesses depending on growth aspirations. Those who were growth-oriented got a higher risk allocation.

We created a structure and brought in a chief risk officer's desk. A first-of-a-kind dashboard to monitor the identified risks was set up. We also engaged risk-management consultants to create a framework for assessing risks. We have come a long way since then. Today, most of the decisions go through a risk management process. We have created the authorization and governance structure at various levels, going all the way to the MD and CEO, and we have a pyramid that maps the risk the company takes. The whole idea of doing all this is to make sure we know what awaits us. While businesses deal with risks, it is important to aggregate them to decide on the risk/reward strategy. The biggest risk involved in our business is that it takes at least five or six years to assess whether the business effort was successful or not. By that time, it is often too late to make amends for not succeeding. The profits that stay with the company come at the end. Meanwhile, the project personnel could change or get replaced or other unforeseen situations could occur. If there is an adverse outcome five to six years after bidding, it has to be handled by the company—which is why risk management is absolutely essential. More important than knowing what to do is to know what not to do. Here again, I was blessed with a highly experienced team that helped me build the right framework and acquire credibility in enabling decisions. Some had a business background, which was also a great advantage. In addition, there are some non-negotiables, but in that case, we walk out of those contracts irrespective of pressure from businesses who look at these as great opportunities.

You mentioned niche areas of finance such as investor relations (IR) and risk management. What about other factors, such as financial reporting and similar things? In your experience, how have finance organizations evolved? How are you handling the reskilling of workforce?

Financial reporting and governance of financial reporting are getting automated and routinized. Earlier, people did these tasks, but now machines are doing them. Today, software can produce the returns as long as you know how to tag the transactions, which means that the function has evolved, and what earlier took 80 per cent of the time can now be done in 20 per cent. The rest of the time can be deployed for other purposes such as finance strategy, capital allocation, resource optimization, cost management, IR and risk management, among others. In the past, we have spent time tallying the trial balance with a team of highly qualified finance professionals. The responsibility vested with me was to reskill them, and make them realize that generating a report was no longer their responsibility. According to me, this transition is still a work in progress. We have several engagements with the team and expose them to programmes conducted by universities such as Harvard or business schools such as Wharton in our management development centre. We have a leadership development programme, where we take 25- to 40-year-old people, place them in batches and try to expose them to concepts such as valuation, business finance and other aspects. This is to make them understand that merely reporting financial results is not where the future job lies.

Since it is tough to get this perspective across, we created a shared service centre in the company. We realized that duplication of this work in several pockets, just to keep several people engaged, is not an efficient way to work. At the same time, transaction processing had to be done. Hence, the shared service centre we created had to be a hub-and-spoke model. We have about 450 people working in shared services, and are now trying to reduce it to 250 through process re-engineering and digital initiatives.

We also did not want documents flowing all over the place. Auditing needs to be done where documents and scanned images are adequate for recording transactions. This gave us the idea to create centres of excellence. We have four or five of them in the company today, where purchase-to-pay, subcontractor processing, payroll and employee benefits processes are handled. We created islands of excellence, and started reallocating experienced resources into these functions. What it helped us to do was to bring some domain expertise into shared services because machines have to be programmed and algorithms validated. We have decided there is no point in seven people authorizing a transaction. We cut that number drastically down, and started using these experienced people to do what we call forensic validation. The work should move on, and not wait for authorization, but whatever gets authorized and passes through the system, has to be validated at the backend for exceptions. Exceptions need to be captured, and worked on, so the experienced staff started working in the areas of exception reporting rather than straight functional reporting.

Many of our individual businesses have grown from Rs 7,000 crore to Rs 20,000 crore. We run around 600 sites. Every site needs an accounting team on-site, storekeeper, administrator and other personnel. Some sites are then grouped into clusters, and each cluster has a finance incharge responsible for the outcomes. A group of clusters becomes the business vertical headquarters and the group of business head verticals becomes corporate headquarters. All this created career opportunities for capable and experienced resources.

Towards right-sizing the organization, we also gave the option of voluntary retirement schemes (VRS) to some employees, while we helped others to find other opportunities. We have allowed people to retire, but without replacements. Nobody was ever sacked overnight; we gave them ample time to leave. We realized that the more we depend on machines, artificial intelligence and embedded validations, we need less people for routine functions.

We are now onboarding more subsidiary associate companies for the shared services and adding more processes. We are in the process of adding record-to-report processes to our shared services. Earlier, it was transaction processing, receivables, payables, salaries, retirement, travel, provident funds (PF), medical benefits and so on. Now, we are trying to get more complex processes going. Slowly, I think we will keep muscling this up because we want the business finance personnel to be a lean team that works with business analytics. I want business enablers to operate the business. I want the exception reviewing to be done at the mid-level. The bottom of the pyramid will be machines and artificial intelligence, and all processes will be digital. Whenever a business presentation is made by any of the site/cluster/area incharges, we insist on knowing what their role is in promoting digitization. Every year, we formulate a theme and our key result areas (KRAs) are around that theme. The theme in the current year is digitalizing finance and accounting (F&A) processes. Wherever possible, digitization has to set in and we need to junk processes that are not necessary.

The persons involved can be taken care of. I want them to increase their productivity, otherwise we cannot keep pace. We will get redundant, since decades-old organizations are always more vulnerable to this kind of obsolescence than new-age ones. The past performances can give a sense of false security, but we have to evolve for a better future.

We are in that transition period, so it is very exciting. I keep telling myself this opportunity is similar to the one that the Y2K coding of computerized systems meant when the year 1999 changed to 2000. Therefore, this transition is an opportunity to shift from manual to lean digital, and we have to encash it. It is essential to be open to change and evolve. I do not know what lies ahead. Definitely, things will change; flexibility and adaptability to go with the flow are the required attributes to be able to function well. Let us see—only time will tell what happens to us.

There is a lot of buzz around transformation and digital finance. How do you see that shaping your industry/company? Do you see a changing talent landscape with this disruption in finance? How are you handling that change?

I do not think we have come to a point where we can say we have fully evolved digitally. A lot of time today goes into mapping what to do with the legacy systems, and convincing ourselves to ditch a service that has served us well over the years. When you transit, you would not like to map every single process into machine learning because it makes the throughput less effective. As we are trying to get more automated, efficient and productive, we are trying to redraw processes. Does a particular process require several approvals beyond the first approval or does it become automatic? As they say, 'Work should not flow, work should get done.' Why should it flow through so many desks? What is the value added? Somewhere, we will have to revisit processes, and that is the stage of evolution we are currently in.

We are one of the first companies in Asia to adopt systems applications and products in data processing (SAP) for our enterprise resource planning (ERP). I am talking about the mid- to late 1980s. But having said that, are we doing everything completely digitally? Is there no manual intervention? Far from it. I think the level of digital maturity is very business specific right now. You don't get cut-paste opportunities in our business—every project is unique, all equipment we manufacture for a project is unique, not commodity manufacturing. In commodity manufacturing, you can afford to somewhat replicate things; in our case customization is very heavy.

We need to actually take the transactions out of these situations, and try to map them differently. We can automate all of the banking processes today, but we cannot easily do this in project execution. In the digital evolution, what we are trying to do is get all the low-hanging fruits out of the way.

Risking redundancies is another challenge. Digitization makes people insecure about their jobs and roles, so if we require their cooperation and participation in this process, we need to upgrade their roles. Then comes the part where they have to unlearn what they were doing and learn the new processes. Unlearning and learning is a big challenge. It doesn't come very easily to people—although they want to learn, they struggle to unlearn. Beyond a point, it is a bandwidth issue. Capabilities of people involved differ, especially with digitization. The veterans in the organization may not be able to relate to it since they have been doing work differently for the past 20 or 25 years, but the newbies might upgrade themselves fast. Does that mean we let the veterans go? It involves a lot of thinking on human resource (HR) intricacies, and introducing this process should be in small digestible doses.

We are trying to handle the situation by mapping those people whose skills can be upgraded. For example, with 130,000 people in the group, we have scores of people pouring over travel claims and authorizing medical reimbursements. We have tried to machine learn the whole thing, so that a few people can look at exceptions that get thrown out, study patterns and feel comfortable analysing data rather than generating it.

The big change we need to condition ourselves to is that our jobs do not end at generating data. Analysis and interpretation are more critical and are open to challenges, and criticisms or differences of opinions. This skill is still developing in most finance professionals. In the earlier days of my career, tallying a trial balance was champagne time. Now, it is all automated and people are hired as financial data analysts. No matter what the nomenclature used for the management, all that matters is that the performance report of the business/division should be available by the end of the month, with some credible forecast of the future and some scenario analysis thrown in for good measure. It is not a miracle any more. So, what the organization is looking at is more value-added information on what lies ahead. This is what is happening in most organizations, and everyone is grappling with this transition.

Today's generation finds it easier to fit in. Companies that have existed for seven or eight decades believe they have been successful in the past, and will continue to be so in the future. To unlearn this belief, and to realize the past does not guarantee the future, calls for a change in mindset.

We are trying to convince vertical finance teams to make computers the base of the pyramids; the layer on the top will be the value-added analytics' guys and the top person would be a business enabler; they will have skin in the game as much as the CEO has, because these two people will have to chart the path ahead for the business ultimately.

I can give a very simple analogy. Banks used to have relationship managers just to contact customers. Today, automated telephones and internet-enabled bots are the relationship managers. Your front-end interface with the bank has disappeared completely and you only have product specialists. If you have decided you would like to examine a particular product or an offering, those specialists come and talk to you. So, the first level is eliminated.

Secondly, for any mechanical manufacturing, if you have robotized the manufacturing process, the robots work 24x7 with no expectations whatsoever. Accordingly, while the products and services, say, in the infrastructure space, could still be the old world in our case with non-digital offerings, the manner in which these are offered would completely change. For example, even the construction industry has moved beyond the concrete mixers, and gone for the pre-fabricated structures with dressed-up glass façades. The frontline supervisors, responsible for concrete mixers, have been eliminated.

These are interesting times. Actually, in the next five years, in my opinion, there would be a lot more changes that we may not be able to visualize today.

In the banking industry, one of the complaints we keep hearing is that the business has moved to digital processes very fast; therefore, finance function has to adapt as well. In manufacturing, will finance go digital first, and then the business will follow? Or, is it a parallel run?

In banks, customer convenience is given more weight. Hence, they are introducing changes in their processes to make banking easier. They want customers to save time and handle their banking with just their gadgets, and reduce their cost to serve as well.

In our case of a project/manufacturing business, the world is the marketplace. We might have temporary issues like everybody has regarding economic barriers, tariff hikes, trade wars, all of that. But I do believe it is a passing phase. Globally, I think the market economics and dynamics cannot be short-changed by somebody saying the local demand is sufficient. This approach cannot be sustainable. In a very integrated marketplace, every person for that opportunity needs to be taken very seriously. There is no sustainable protection possible.

Secondly, people's preference for a vocation is changing rapidly. Earlier, people were ready to work at the client's site, staying in makeshift cabins for years, away from their families. This is not the preference any more. The options and opportunities available to the engineers today (and when I say engineer that is just a matter of reference and is true for anybody) are multiple. So, why would an engineer opt for a life like this, a nomadic life exposed to elements, and constantly being under pressure to deliver? Very few people would, and this is why the cream of technical talent from, say, the IITs, who used to work in such jobs are no more here in India—they are all in the Silicon Valley.

The next rung of people in the pyramid upgrade themselves and fill this gap, so constant training of people at the lower level is essential to make sure we deliver to the customer's expectations. Therefore, the customer does not have to compromise in any way; on the contrary, for the same price, functionalities are increasing. So, since you need superior brainpower to work with, it is inevitable we find ways to automate.

From a banking perspective, it is customer preference that has led to the growth of digital working. Here in our industry, it is a question of survival. The skills need to be preserved. If I have to run 600 sites, and I can use automation and digital processes, I need to have 600 good leaders more than 600 good teams. That's a whole world different—600 good teams mean every project has at least about 20 critical positions in a project—with personnel involved in planning, procurement, scheduling and so on. It is very difficult to find 600 good teams. If I have a good leader at the project helm, I can automate a lot of this process and centralize the processes. Then, the chances of errors reduce.

Secondly, given the competitiveness of the industry, you have very little headroom for mistakes or reworking, among other things. You have to get it right the first time and only an algorithm will get you there at first. Human effort will not always get it right the first time.

Thirdly, we are not willing to compromise on growth. If today we are a $20-billion company, we want to become a $30-billion company, then we want to become a $50-billion company. So, the market space is expanding. If it is India today, tomorrow it is some other country or continent. To manage these projects or customer expectations in all these places, we need consistency of performance, which automated solutions and digital interfaces can provide.

We try to take output data from the various machines and equipment we deploy at sites regarding their performance, and feed them into a central system. We can hire a few people in a centralized location, and they could control site productivity based on the on-site data. This affects the cost dynamics, and this is where the role of the finance function comes in. Finance needs to analyse the cost–benefit and risk–reward to enable a winning bid. Finance function starts its work as soon as an opportunity is mapped or cited. It starts giving the numerical values to all those technical specifications of the opportunity. Then, we start working on the acceptable cost and provide for reimbursements and contingencies if things go wrong. Only then is the bid submitted for an award.

Thereafter, you will have to walk that plan and finance is intimately involved there as well. Continuous monitoring of several thousand line items in a particular project or manufacturing process and allocating costs to every one of those line items is essential. There has to be a rational way to allocate costs. Sometimes, bids are lost because we allocate costs wrong.

So today, for us to be successful on the technical side, finance needs to pull its weight, without which the technical outcome will remain unsuccessful. At the end of the day, we are a commercial organization. We are judged by what value we create for the stakeholders and it comes from what value we have been able to create from the resources deployed.

How can finance be the key enabler for business and create that value?

Finance plays the role of enabling a business to foresee the costs of a project, which will be valid for at least five years in terms of labour, materials and so on. Therefore, a finance professional acts as an economist, too, as he is expected to build cost curves and factor in eventualities too.

Finance helps to make contracts and bids successful. In every contract, we have an opportunity to seek customer reimbursement if the costs increase beyond a particular tolerance. Finance comes into play to provide these insights. Today, I see a blurring line between the role of finance and business in either a project or manufacturing or services businesses. Business and finance can be equated to two sides of the same coin; they have to roll in the same direction to avoid chaos. Hence, alignment is very necessary. Business is usually aggressive whereas finance is inherently conservative. Finance needs to have a certain business orientation to strike a balance.

We need to believe that to win business is the priority, controllership is secondary. Controllership should be in terms of allocating, monitoring and extracting the value from the resources deployed. Today's language has changed; nobody accepts a 'No' for an answer. If it's 'No', we are expected to provide a solution for it. For instance, the best way to deal with credit risks is to ask for letters of credit or guarantees—but the client would not usually provide that.

If I am going to be straightjacketed and say, 'Look, we do not want to take credit risks, take guarantees from each customer,' then actually the business does not need us. We provide an assessment of what the risk appetite of the organization is, whether for a particular client, sector or country. We identify the thresholds and manage them. How do you manage if the thresholds keep on increasing? It is a task finance teams face because ultimately, if the account turns bad, it is the finance people who will have to defend provisioning with auditors, management, board and outside investors. So, the accountability of the finance function has gone up multiple notches, and the minute we started accepting global funds, accountability has also become global. There are some funds sitting in Boston or Frankfurt investing in the company, based on our commentary on how the businesses will stack up. Therefore, there is a representation warranty issue here as we represent the company in a certain light. You cannot do it for the sake of short-term price improvement in the market. You have to go back and stand in front of the same investor.

One of the reasons why investors like companies such as us is because for the last 20 years, we have been standing in front of the same investor year after year, giving the right picture, good or bad. Any kind of misrepresentation can cost us this hard-earned reputation. Therefore, the public accountability of the finance function has also changed. In addition, the credit rating of the company is supposed to be the turf of the finance people.

We will have to manage our balance sheet in a manner that ensures the credit rating is satisfactory. Balance sheet management ranges from the inventory policy to asset acquisitions. Businesses believe that unless they invest money, they would not get returns while finance people believe returns with a minimum investment is the way to go. The minute a project is sanctioned, payback is forgotten. Finance has to again play a responsible role by creating a what-if scenario for resource constraints. The business cycle can change, and in such a situation the finance department has to be proactive, simulate situations, and be capable of using statistical methods and mathematical accuracy to account for risk. We have come a long way from simple double-entry responsibilities. We have to keep moving up the value chain, and there is no shortcut to success.

We have to carve our path and work our way up. It is a function of individual preferences and comfort levels, but you should not stay in the same place; be ready to move to a position of discomfort zone. Everyone hesitates to come out of the comfort zone. It requires a lot of courage. We try and enable that within the finance function.

With youngsters, a repeated complaint is that their role is not diverse enough or does not grow fast enough. They want to know what should they do so that their leaders get the confidence to keep adding to or evolving their role.

'Never say no' is an attitude I have imbibed, simply because refusing opportunity means denying growth. If we are getting a chance to create an impact and add value, we should use it. I do not believe in the work–life balance, but firmly believe that work is a part of life. Instead of prioritizing your schedule, you should schedule your priorities. For me, there was never any reason to complain.

This is also possible only when we have full family support. I am blessed with a wife who is very supportive. Being a CA herself, she has also had a very hectic schedule during her working years. She has multitasked managing work and home beautifully. We do not have children, so in a way, we just turned this into a point of strength as well.

I had an ideal platform for growth—a very aggressive CEO and an enabling immediate boss as well. I, too, believe in empowering everyone under me in decision-making. It might be tempting to take all the decision-making responsibility on oneself, and feel important, but I wish to empower those under me. This helps work to happen at a faster pace. Today, the ease with which we are able to close, consolidate and present 160 or so individual unit accounts every 90 days, is only because there are many people who assume responsibility for what they are doing. However, this is a challenging task and some may not be able to cope. So, I guess it is a personal trait that helps you to cope; it is also how you respond to a challenging situation.

In 1983, I qualified for and continued to work in financial services until 2000. Then, I was asked to join a group to look after corporate finance, accounts, taxation, insurance, none of which I had experience in at that scale. I felt L&T was taking a bigger risk than I was. I could have easily opted for the financial service sector such as the banks. But at that point, it was just gutsy on my part. Had I not taken that decision, we would not be having this conversation. Sometimes you just have to make a switch, and believe it can be done. Success is then inevitable. One of the main reasons people can't switch easily is their fixed and long-term commitments due to loans and mortgages such as equated monthly instalments (EMIs) on houses, properties, vehicles and so on. These commitments cause insecurities and fear of job loss. Some are hesitant to take chances, while some take it as a chance to leap.

Every success story has 100 failures behind it, which nobody is interested in. This what the world is all about. So, I am not at all surprised at the way I started this journey, and what I am now, almost nearing checkout time. I worked my way out of several situations.

Commitment, hard work, self-belief, perseverance and a positive mindset have helped me along the way. Young professionals should take a long-term view of life and make those initial sacrifices, stop making comparisons and unreasonable demands on themselves. If they are lucky enough to find platforms or a workplace like I have been able to find, the future turns out to be bright. An ability to look at a glass as half full is so crucial in making our professional lives worthwhile.

When you recruit for some key positions, what do you look for in a talent?

The main aspect I look for in a candidate is attitude—positivity and being proactive. I look for the ability to influence people, being articulate, being able to disagree with dignity and possessing problem-solving skills. If these traits are there, I think we can groom that person. Base-level technical competence is also essential. I just try to explore these facets in the conversation, as my interviews are very conversational and not question and answer sessions. I try to walk through some experiences with the candidates and see what comes out from those. The downside is that my interviews take at least 90 minutes, with follow-up conversations, because of this approach.

In every industry, there are common themes or qualities or traits you need to be a CFO, but is there something unique about this industry, say the infra-complexity of being a CFO, one of which you mentioned to be cash allocation. Any others you would like to share?

Yes, I think the ability to work through policy decisions is very important because CFOs are working in public spaces. A simple public interest litigation (PIL) can upset your entire cash flow programme or plan; any work in public spaces means dealing with public policy and government policy. If you want to be a successful CFO, you need to know the law of the land. It is not easy because it is sometimes State-specific or Centre-specific. A project may be multilaterally funded, so it takes an international colour. Any programme like, for example, a bullet train, will be funded by multinationals. So, the policy framework, within which we need to work even as an engineering, procurement and construction (EPC) contractor, could be subjected to the international governance of that contract. My job as a CFO is slightly different in that regard compared with anything one does within the enclosed spaces of a factory. That needs a different set of skills. I think that would be the most significant differentiator between working in an infrastructure company and other places.

Also, you need to have the ability to look through and identify risks that may happen six to eight years down the line; it is a guesstimate only. If you get it right seven out of 10 times, you are lucky.

How do you improve your guesstimate? Does it come from your intuition or is based on years of experience?

Yes, repeated experience. I think you learn from experience. So, we try to create portals where we capture our mistakes. It is very difficult for a business to say it made a mistake last time which could recur, and hence set a price for it. The business will say it made a mistake last time, but have learned the lesson, so will not price it—instead, it will do it better. This conflict about risk-pricing is a constant struggle in the infrastructure space. Just because it happened last time, it need not happen this time or vice versa. Generally, you need to be aware of what could go wrong. Over time, I have realized there are a set of no-nos, and you do not negotiate on those. If you are able to have the maturity to say when not to bid, you will survive. Otherwise, all businesses want orders; they won't let go of any opportunity. In any case, one is not winning everything one bids for, but will win one of four or one of five. So, the tendency is always to keep that five as large as possible to improve the probability of one's winning.

Getting Personal

How do you interact with other CFOs or finance professionals? Is it through forums or some other way?

You get to know these professionals over time, but the initial interactions were all through forums. Last year, I was heading the Confederation of Indian Industry (CII) National Committee for CFOs, which is an opportunity to chair a committee of almost 40 CFOs. The interactions are all through official channels, but some develop into friendships lasting a little more than normal acquaintances. For many of the client companies, it is useful to know their CFOs. It is easier if you have an existing relationship to resolve issues.

What is the role of a mentor in one's career? Can you share a few of the life lessons instilled in you by your mentors?

Yes, I did have the good fortune to be guided by a few very good mentors. While I was working in Best and Crompton, the marketing manager was Mr Jayaram. He was the first one to introduce me to the nuances of marketing and always took me along when he went for client visits. He taught me to speak fearlessly. Today, irrespective of who is in front of me, I can make my point clear. The lessons learned from him during those precious days have been a critical part of my growth.

Then there was Ramakrishna Rao, who introduced me to handling responsibility. He was the MD and CEO of the financial services firm set up by Best and Crompton. He was an ex-ICICI general manager and was also a statistician; everything he did was based on data and statistics, so my penchant for being data-driven comes from him. I was part of a four-member team responsible to set up the company. It was this experience that helped me set up L&T finance from scratch. He did meticulous planning despite not being a computer literate. Since I got to work with him in close quarters, I learned a lot in terms of planning.

The third person I worked very closely was the Lloyds Finance MD and CEO, G.C. Garg. He taught me the art of risk-taking. I was responsible for the profit and loss (P&L) of Lloyds Finance. I learned from him the ability to develop a nose for risk, and put money where instincts are. I made mistakes but it helped develop the ability to take risks. The ability to take a view on investments is something I also learned from him.

The fourth person I should add is Y.M. Deosthalee. I think I learned the art of navigating large organizations and people management skills from him. He taught me the art of putting processes ahead of personalities. He also finetuned me, in a manner of speaking.

I also had the unique opportunity to work with A.M. Naik, who taught me to be strategic in thinking. The ability to correlate financial parameters with business outcomes was his specialty. To be able to work in his team meant being on top of data and information and the stint with him made me a lot more thorough in what I did. 'When you go out to hunt a deer, prepare as though you are going for a tiger hunt' was his motto, and that has stayed with me quite like a mantra.

I was very fortunate to learn from all these capable persons. Even now, when a situation arises, I think about how they would have dealt with it. All of them have retired and Mr Ramakrishna Rao and Mr Y.M. Deosthalee are no more. The others, I think, are getting on with their years out of active employment. But I owe a lot to all these people for being the professional I am today.

If you just look back, is there anything you could have done differently?

Some things did not go as planned. I wanted to build a top-class financial services business for L&T. However, I myself was involved during the first five years, which was largely an incubation period. Today, it is a successful business, but the only role I play is being L&T's representative on the board. Not that I have any misgivings about any alternate opportunities that have come my way. Fortunately, so far things have gone okay.

There is always scope for improvement. I know should have spent more time with my parents when they were around, but now they are no more. I should have been more supportive of them. I could have been more efficient, more entrepreneurial. Nevertheless, honestly, I am very thankful for where I am, what I am and I am contented with that.

What does your typical day look like during weekdays?

I wake up at 5 a.m. I either go for a game of badminton or for a walk or do some yoga until 6.45 a.m. Then, I get ready and reach the office by 9 a.m. The day passes with a series of pre-decided internal and external meetings, and this goes on until 6.30 p.m. Then follow-ups are done on what transpired during the day, making plans and monitoring, dealing with whatever is necessary. This goes on until 9 p.m.

Between 9 a.m. and 6 p.m., I need to be available to work for the business. Sometimes, I might get an empty bonus time slot and use that to clear my backlogs. The slot between 6 and 9 p.m., when most people are not in the office and the phones cease to ring, is my most productive hours. Invariably, I have a spate of missed calls during the day as I do not carry my phone to meetings at all, leaving the gadget in my room because when I see people midway in a meeting being dragged into another task by someone's phone call, I find it disrespectful to the person sitting across.

My journey back home is to return all these calls. This is how the day is spent.

Do you plan your weekends differently?

The weekend for me is just Sunday. I try not to work, but focus on getting organized for the week ahead, which takes almost half a day. The other half of the day, I try and watch some sports or indulge in reading. I am not much of a movie buff or a television watcher. On Sundays, my waking up time is the same as weekdays. I like to have extended sports sessions, either badminton or running, on Sundays. I try running around 10 km during Sundays; this I feel is very important to keep my toxic levels under check. If there is any travel scheduled on Monday, I prepare myself on Sunday. Honestly, there is very little time to idle. On some weekends, we spend time catching up with siblings and select friends. I think it is important to have some friends at the workplace also; as we go up the ladder, it does become lonely and it is essential to be able to communicate with a friend.

I am also very active in my housing society. There are only half a dozen people who put their hands up for anything of common interest. I chaired the managing committee for eight years. Mumbai is very unkind in some ways, as it does not give you time to socialize that easily. So, pretty much, Sunday is my day. I do not really find time to spend on my own interests on other days as much.

Could you talk a little bit about your better half, and the role she has played in your life?

Oh, there's plenty I can say about her. Ours was an arranged marriage. I always believed I should never do anything that would bring disgrace to my parents or their beliefs. I was keen she should be educated and independent because I sort of knew that by the time I got married, I was going to get busy with work. Her father was also an employee with a leading corporate house, so she knew the struggles involved.

My wife is a CA and a cost and works accountant herself. She was chosen as the all-India best cadet in the National Cadet Corps (NCC), and was part of the Indian Youth Exchange Programme in 1980 with Canada. The best cadets were picked to spend three months in Canada with a Canadian family, and likewise live for three months in India with an Indian family, along with Canadian cadets. She got a lot of exposure from being on her own in a foreign country and a foreign household. So much so that she even ate chicken to survive there, though she came from a strictly vegetarian family. All this seasoned her into an independent and strong-willed lady.

She always took the decisions at the home front. Initially, I used to feel a little worried that she did not have to depend on me for anything whatsoever, be it purchasing something for the house, or anything bigger. However, I got used to it and accepted this was the way it was going to be, and it continues to be so till today. The best part about her is she is one of those people who never gives up. She is very good-natured and helpful. She has been a very silent teacher in my life, but I have not told this her because she will laugh it off. I think I have picked up the finer aspects of life and human interactions from her. Secondly, she allowed me to be what I am and gave me the bandwidth to operate. She is my lucky charm and always let me go forward in my career without worrying about anything else. She is a very active outdoor person, and also very well read. You can learn many things from her in just an anecdotal conversation; she is multifaceted as a person.

Since the last 10 years, she has left the corporate world and has gone the social service way. She is a brand ambassador of Pinkathon, organized as a women's run for a cause, and works to empower women and educate them about the importance of health and self-care. She organizes events, weekend runs and other activities, saying that ill-health brings along dependency. She is very gifted musically and can pick up any instrument and play. Even today, she sometimes turns words into a song and uploads it to her friends on WhatsApp. As is very evident, she is leading a much more interesting life than I do.

What are some of the things you take inspiration from like travel, movies or anything else?

I am not much of a movie buff. I would rather spend time playing sports or watching sports channels. What inspires me is all these sportsmen and women who actually defy many odds to go after their ambitions. I am always amazed by their endurance, conviction and the will to succeed. They have a 'never give up' attitude, and enjoy the moment in spite of all the pressure and challenges. If we see every problem as an opportunity, we will enjoy dealing with it. I am 60, and getting old. My motto is to make every day enjoyable. At the end of the day, we should never feel it was spent wastefully.

Within sports, cricket, of course, is my favourite and I have played at multiple levels.

Unable to find time for cricket, I also play badminton nowadays. I like to watch tennis, badminton, cricket and athletics. I have taken to running to maintain fitness for the last few years. If I am able to spare time, I would rather get out somewhere to do any of these things than be glued to a TV or read a book. I am not much of an avid reader now, but in school, I used to read a lot of books.

Any favourite books from back then that inspired you?

I think all of us have gone through Enid Blyton and P.G. Wodehouse, Alistair MacLean, James Hadley Chase, among others. I liked *The Godfather* by Mario Puzo and books like that. Another book I remember is *Iacocca: An Autobiography* by Lee Iacocca that has many useful nuggets on turning around a business.

I can pick up anything and read a few pages, but I am not someone who has to read a book every week.

What do you read to stay updated on current events and industry happenings?

Nowadays, a lot of research papers by Harvard and Stanford have caught my interest. I am trying to read up on digital processes because that is something I do not have my hands around fully. I would recommend a broader view of global developments, a view that may be biased at times, but which gives us the maturity to decide what information to seek. All the newspapers, I think, often carry motivated stories, sometimes sponsored, but I feel most of their reports spread misinformation and there is no worthwhile content beyond the headlines. I do not think they add great value, with some exceptions once in a while, of course.

I would suggest people read material based on the business they are associated with, apart from general reading. We do not read enough about benchmarking, competition, reviewing strategies of peer sets and so on. I think those materials would be more useful for people in their careers than reading general stuff. It is a very intelligent way to stay relevant.

Thank you very much for your time!

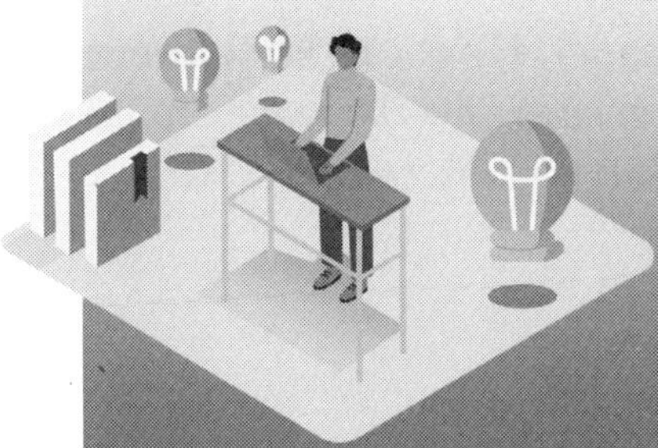

Key Takeaways

R. SHANKAR RAMAN

Take 1: Choose a situation as it was and make an opportunity out of it to succeed.

Take 2: You need to work hard to succeed. If you bend your back, results do come.

Take 3: A CFO needs to create value by reinvesting and sharing returns with shareholders.

Take 4: Never say 'No'. Refusing opportunity is denying growth.

Take 5: Speak fearlessly. Never be afraid to make your point clear

Take 6: Prepare intensively and extensively. 'When you go out to hunt a deer, prepare as though you are going for a tiger hunt.'

Take 7: Work should not flow. It should get done.

Take 8: Put processes ahead of personalities.

Take 9: The ability to see a glass half full is crucial for making professional lives worthwhile.

Take 10: Past performance can give a sense of false security. Evolve for a better future.

Key takeaways that inspired me most. How can I use them to change my perspective? (*This space is for the reader to jot down the lessons that they learned from this interview*)

With wife at Dubai Flower Show

At Lord's Cricket Stadium, London

L&T in the service of nation

Delivering a speech to L&T employees

Recipient of Financial Express Best CFO award in 2017

At the Tata Mumbai Marathon

Extra Shots

R. Shankar Raman

Overprepare and bend your back—results do come!

There was an air of excitement when we went to meet R. Shankar Raman as he had been a CEO as well during his career. He had built a company from scratch in the financial services sector. We were looking forward to some stand-out insights from the CFO who had faced the unique challenges of a CEO.

We met him at the L&T Mumbai office. We were ushered into the conference room where R. Shankar Raman joined a minute before the scheduled time. He did not carry his mobile phone, so was never disturbed throughout the session. We did ask if this was the normal practice for him or if this special treatment was just for us. What he said changed our approach to meetings forever. He said that he considered it a mark of disrespect to the attendees if after committing time to them, he engaged in responding to calls or texts instead of paying attention to them. If the news was important enough, it would reach him. Otherwise, he was 100 per cent devoted to the meeting until it finished. If a Group CFO of a massive conglomerate like L&T showed that discipline, what stopped us to make people feel special and do what seemed right?

R. Shankar Raman comes across as a very serious person when you meet him, and honestly, a little intimidating. He is very measured in his responses, weighing each word before he speaks. After an hour of talking to him, he seems like a completely different person. Warm and easy to relate to, he has an understated humour. He is the epitome of a person belonging to a middle-class family making it to the pole position through sheer hard work, grit and determination.

Learnings in Action

We keep hearing that there is no shortcut to success and it was the one theme that resonated throughout this interview. *Overprepare. 'When you go out to hunt a deer, prepare as though you are going for a tiger hunt.' If you bend your back, results do come.*

We were both doing reasonably well in our careers but reached higher levels as we started putting in some additional hours either to sharpen a sales pitch or introducing an additional round of quality checks before we delivered a work product. This learning of being overprepared completely changed our win ratios. In the longer run, it was a time-saver rather than an additional investment.

Take, for instance, a sales pitch. We started thinking through all the possible scenarios in mid-sized opportunities when the company expands. We started laying out the future in phases for the finance organization pitches instead of restricting it to the current requirements. We laid out the industry dimensions over the functional aspects to expand the impact on other functions due to the current transformation that was under consideration. And this, we saw, started differentiating us from the competition. Our win rates skyrocketed and we also saw a significant increase in follow-on requests to build that future. Similar results occurred as we put in more hours to detail out the business plan or delivered a new product or hired a new candidate. The list goes on. We invested more time, which saved more time and got us results.

Examine your actions. Are you overpreparing to perform on your key result areas? Do you see a case to invest more time in overpreparation and will it help you get to the next orbit in your field? Does this thought get you excited to jump in right now and start the process? These are the questions you could ask yourself as you go further on your planned path.

SRINIVAS PHATAK

CHIEF FINANCIAL OFFICER
HINDUSTAN UNILEVER LIMITED

Srinivas Phatak is the Executive Director and CFO of India's largest fast-moving consumer goods (FMCG) company, Hindustan Unilever Limited (HUL). One of the youngest CFOs in our list, Srinivas joined HUL in 1999 as a commercial manager and has held multiple roles in the company at various locations. In his own words, he has charted a highly unconventional path to the CFO's chair, facilitated by his desire to deliver a sustainable business impact over everything else.

Our favourite quote from the interview is 'Never waste a crisis'. We were also lucky to be able to ask him the 'First 100 days as CFO' question, as he was a recent appointee to the post at the time of this interview. Srinivas Phatak is a chartered accountant (CA) by profession.

Ever smiling, Mr Phatak is the proverbial swan who maintains a Zen-like calm on the exterior, while relentlessly paddling towards his goals. For his contribution to sustained business delivery, and landing the value-accretive acquisition of GSK Consumer Health Care India, an associate of GlaxoSmithKline, UK, with iconic brands such as Horlicks and Boost, Srinivas was recognized as the CFO of the year by the *Financial Express* in 2019. He was also awarded as the best CFO in the FMCG category by the Institute of Chartered Accountants of India (ICAI).

Fireside Chat

Can you please take us through your life's journey?

My father is from Maharashtra and my mother from Andhra Pradesh—both of them were bankers. Progressive, unconventional and ahead of times in many ways, theirs was a love marriage in the 1960s.

With quintessential middle-class values and upbringing, I lived and learned in many cities in India, including Hyderabad and Lucknow. Early exposure to different parts of India enabled my sister and me to gain a very deep appreciation of different cultures, lifestyles and habits. As a close-knit family, we learnt early the importance of building connections and relationships.

Given that both my parents had full-time jobs, my sister and I also learnt how to be independent and take charge of our education and day-to-day lives. I completed my graduation from Nizam College, Hyderabad, a very old prestigious college, and went on to do chartered accountancy.

Both of my parents came from rural backgrounds and large families, but they progressed through hard work. For example, they had to walk for more than five kilometres each day to even reach their school. My parents taught me the importance of a good education and meritocracy, and gave me the freedom to take my career and life in the direction I desired. So, my early life was all about diverse experiences, doing well by doing the right things, and building a balanced life.

HUL has the soul of the 'middle class', and this helps us serve the everyday needs of our consumers. This great company and people have had a huge role to play in my development as a professional and a human being.

Did you always want to take up commerce, or was science ever an option as well?

With an imaginative mind, I would come up with plenty of ideas and options when I was really young. There was also a brief period when I chased the thought of joining the defence services; actually, there were quite a few of us thinking in that direction. I never really relished physics, chemistry and biology. I used to find (and still do) mathematics and commerce very interesting. This led to a natural inclination towards finance. So, I did my BCom and then CA.

So, you had a clear intent to do CA while in college?

Absolutely. By Class 12, I was clear I was going to pursue CA. I found finance and accounting quite fascinating. I wanted to be a good CA, and to me it sounded quite cool. In today's world, young students and professionals are fortunate to have very good exposure and appreciation of career options, and alternate routes to unlock them. Back in the day, most of the conversations used to be about pursuing medicine or engineering; for some reason, everyone in Hyderabad was planning to move to the US for higher education. A few of my friends, with some understanding of finance, helped me shape my thinking.

During my college days, I realized I was wasting a lot of my time. So, I decided to take up studying at the Institute of Cost and Works Accountants of India (now known as the Institute of Cost Accountants of India) in parallel while setting my sight on CA. I completed both the CA and ICWA courses in 1996.

Another important aspect was the choice of the CA firm—a smaller firm gave you time to study, while a larger one came with exposure. In hindsight, perhaps one of the best decisions I made, with help from a friend, was to join Lovelock and Lewes (now PricewaterhouseCoopers [PwC]), Hyderabad. My experience at PwC was fantastic—I learned a lot about large and diverse businesses, developing a good appreciation for the finance function and quality corporate governance.

It is not as if in life you are always clear about the path—it was not clear to me anyway. It is only a bit later in your life that you start to discover your purpose, potential and where you can go.

And in the firm, it was mostly audits?

I spent only half of my time in audits. For some strange reason, I spent the other half on special assignments deputed at the client's organization and solving some real problems for them. Honestly, that was the part I enjoyed a lot more than I ever enjoyed audits.

I still vividly remember the work we did to transform accounts receivables of a financial services company, investigations we undertook to uncover fraud in a fertilizer company, and crafting the end-to-end financials systems and processes of an exports business. There were a lot of interesting assignments with the ITC Group across their various locations.

That seems like a lot of rich experience during the early days.

I was fortunate to have had exposure to statutory audits wherein I gained a lot of understanding of controls, risk management and financial statements. Working for clients on various projects gave me an exposure to how decisions are made from a company's point of view.

On reflection, was it all success or did you have any failures? If so, what did you do and how did you put the pieces back together?

This is where I have to share with you that I did not clear my CA final examination in the first attempt. I had a brain freeze during one of the papers and before I realized it, the game was up. At that point, it felt like a lot of things had come crashing down. But, then you realize that life gives you plenty of opportunities and you need to be ready to seize them.

> *The point is not that you failed, the question really is, how do you respond to failure and setbacks? The right outlook can take you on the path to success. I had to pause, reflect, recommit and go about earning my stripes.*

It was helpful to look at the bigger picture in life. I had done well till that time and had confidence in my abilities. The life journey of my parents was always something to look up to as they did incredibly well despite constraints. So, I began by being resilient and unwavering as I worked towards my goals.

The second aspect that helped me is my optimism. I have always believed that if you really need to make fundamental shifts or changes, large doses of optimism and huge amounts of energy are a must.

Very inspiring. Did you get your first job from the campus?

No, there was no campus in those days. The campus was just about getting created. In fact, I think it was in 1996 that they instituted the first campus. ITC carried out its own recruitment, and those who wanted to join had to apply directly. I went for my regional interview to Madras (now Chennai), while the final interview was at Calcutta (now Kolkata), after which I joined ITC. My experience of working in its various businesses through audits and special assignments helped me make the cut. I was not in contention for HUL; for HUL, you had to be among the top 50 CAs from all of India to get a call for an interview. Incidentally, that criteria remains unchanged at HUL, that is, at the inception, you should have demonstrated yourself as among the best and brightest. We will not dilute that. HUL gives people subsequent opportunities once they have learned from different experiences and have delivered a business impact.

How are HUL and ITC different in terms of induction?

In HUL, young finance talent is recruited under the Unilever Finance Leadership Programme (UFLP), where recruits spend 12 months on key projects with tangible delivery across the various functions of the company. They are exposed to our social responsibility agenda, and gain international experiences with Unilever. In ITC, post a strong induction programme, we joined internal audits for about three years, which again built very strong fundamentals. I think the end objectives are similar in both the companies, while the routes are different. I must admit I do not know what ITC does today.

Can you tell us more about your ITC experience?

The whole experience was fascinating. We had classroom induction for one month, where key business leaders presented the business strategy. We then spent about five months in the field. I doubt if there is any other company which invests so much time and effort in building talent from scratch. And, that too, a very different order of learning. People from businesses and functions come and talk to the young talent during the classroom induction. Post the initial training, the young executives are deputed in turn to the various business units.

We spent a month in a factory followed by a couple of weeks in a branch selling cigarettes and understanding the sales system. The next two weeks were in a hotel, where we practiced handling not just finance, but different functions of the hotel, such as shadowing the front office, going inside the kitchen, shadowing housekeeping. By shadowing operations, you are not only there to learn about the controls or the functions or finance and so on, but get an understanding of business. So, when you flip back to internal audits, you are looking at the totality and not doing a finance audit alone. More importantly, you are doing a total business audit right from strategy to governance down to, let's say, manufacturing operations and statutory compliances. In ITC, you also learn how tobacco is grown and procured. There is no part of the business you do not touch.

Apart from being a fascinating experience, you also make fabulous relationships, which are again a big currency, something you can encash all your life. At that point, we had about 30 people in audits. When I now look back, everyone has done very well in some industry or the other. The alumni network continues to be invaluable, and most of them are a phone call or WhatsApp away.

In ITC too, I had exposure beyond audits. After the first year in audits, I was seconded into their international business as a stop-gap to handle commodity hedging, forex management and the treasury. After about a year, I came back to the internal audit. Then, just when I was finishing my audit stint to get posted in an operational role, HUL came calling. I joined HUL in September 1999.

What was the motivation to leave ITC?

HUL was and still continues to be an aspirational company and a premium stock. So, it was the excitement of joining HUL and serving the day-to-day needs of the consumers as well as learning about varied businesses and delivering an impact as a finance professional that was the driver. Interestingly, I don't think my father really understood, or was convinced about, my rationale for leaving ITC.

Having said that, while I worked with ITC only for three years, and that too, about 20 years ago, the company and people have left an indelible impression and positive impact on my growth and thinking. I have a high regard for their governance standards, robustness of processes and care for their people. I have a lot of fond memories of my time there, and a lot of affection for my erstwhile colleagues and friends.

If we look through your career so far, is it your optimism which has kept you learning and picking the best out always? Everywhere, you saw that as an opportunity of learning instead of complaining about the long hours, incessant travel and multiple tasks.

On the topic of learning, it is multiple things. You need to have interest and willingness. Brands, consumer products, among other topics, fascinated me. Hence, I stayed away from merchant banking, a big craze in the 1990s. I had to be a part of solutions, and hence enjoyed operational roles more than audits.

Right from my CA articleship, I have had long days and nights. I still remember crashing overnight at office, or working non-stop for 36 hours. Learning is hard work, but how can you even complain about things you really enjoy? I find connecting with colleagues and learning from them to be very energizing compared to sitting down with books. New and different experiences are refreshing; rehashing the same things over and over again is draining.

HUL had a red carpet laid out? Tell us more about it.

With HUL, it was baptism by fire. I was asked to join the yeast business (part of their chemicals division) based in Chiplun, a city in the state of Maharashtra. For starters, I did not know HUL was into the chemicals business, and could not even locate Chiplun on the map of India. Suddenly, the allure of Lux and the warmth of Brooke Bond seemed like a distant dream. My line manager told me to take a 250-kilometre car ride from Bombay, and I landed in Chiplun.

I joined a HUL joint venture (JV) with Dutch partners, which was called Lever Gist Brocades. Yeast, as you may know, is a key ingredient to make bread; this was our backward integration initiative, having acquired Modern Foods from the central government earlier. I had to start from scratch, that is, from manual accounting, learning about technology, commercial and factory operations and regulatory compliances.

We were four managers and we gave all we had to get the business on fire. We had a host of issues, which included getting the right product quality, managing competitive pressures, putting in right systems and processes across the entire business. But while doing so, we built some very strong bonds and enjoyed our camaraderie. We were the early start-up in every sense, selling a very interesting proposition of dry yeast to customers, which was tough as that market was fresh, faced mounting losses and had lots of cash burn. I had to ring-fence cash to pay monthly salaries, convince both partners to repeatedly infuse cash and in doing so, increased the share capital and even raised external commercial borrowing.

At the end of 18 arduous months, we made a recommendation to exit the business and eventually did that. I give a lot of credit to the senior leaders at HUL finance, who recognized my potential and gave me an opportunity to move into the exports business after Chiplun.

During this stint, I would wonder many a time if I had done the right thing by joining HUL. I was working at ITC for three years, doing well, and, as I mentioned earlier, was about to move into an operational role there.

In all this, I learnt two interesting things:

The world view of Chiplun was amazing as it is about halfway between Bombay and Goa, and next to a river. Living in a small town with limited resources was tough. So, the perceptions and reality can be very different and it is imperative to learn to manage them.

The only opportunity you have is the one in front of you, and all you can do is to make the most of it. It is very easy to think of greener pastures and walk away; it is more difficult to stay put and say, 'What can I do with what I have, and build a better future?'

How did your career at HUL then progress?

By HUL standards, my career journey is quite unorthodox. When you look at my career, I was in Chiplun for 18 months handling the yeast business and then moved to the exports business to handle commercial (buying, logistics, finance) and quasi-business development. After that, I moved into the treasury where I spent four and a half years, the first two dealing in forex and bonds, and the remaining time setting up a global treasury centre to handle forex and liquidity for countries in Asia and Africa.

So, I was nine years into HUL, but still had not handled FMCG customer development (sales) or marketing. In 2008, I got an opportunity to lead finance for foods and refreshments; our second largest business and about 20 per cent of HUL's turnover.

In that sense, I came from outside, did all the roles which many people traditionally would not do, and still came in as the head of finance for foods and refreshments. It could have been easily possible for someone to say I did not have the requisite skills and capabilities to handle finance for foods and refreshments, so I give full credit to D. Sundaram, the HUL CFO, for taking a risk and giving me the opportunity to do the job.

Post the foods and refreshment stint, I did investor relations for a year. In 2012, I moved to London where I did global category finance for deodorants and oral care. After two years, I moved to Switzerland to handle supply chain finance for North America and Latin America, one of my toughest assignments. After a successful and eventful stint, I moved back to London to take charge of financial shared services for Unilever. In November 2017, I took over as the CFO of HUL and Vice President, Finance, for South Asia.

My choices have been about how you can really contribute, and where it really adds value to the organization. I am not sure if anyone (at least in HUL) would follow this template, but I was very comfortable.

> *So, for me, you define the job; the job does not define you. Pick up diverse experiences, do well and success follows you.*

Can you talk to us about your stint in Switzerland? You said that your role there was one of your toughest ones.

I was based in Switzerland for about two and a half years, and the first 12 months were one of the toughest in my career. With a centralized business model structure, we were running the supply chain and supply chain finance for North America and LATAM from Schaffhausen, Switzerland. Effectively, all the core supply chain activities, strategic planning, centralized operations and performance management were handled from Switzerland. We were in the process of rolling out systems, applications and products (SAP) in data processing across 23 countries, and had significant challenges. Volatility in LATAM arising from macroeconomic factors as well as location and time differences created multiple challenges in getting our costs right.

For nine out of the 12 months, we did not see a turnaround. Just when we had sorted out one issue, we hit another low, over and over again. However, we did turn it around after a year, and started to see stellar results thereafter.

A few learnings:

Many times, we organize ourselves for expertise and efficiencies, and this leads to functional silos. What we need to keep in the forefront is the end-to-end view; not just what is best for the vertical market.

Resilience and self-belief make a huge difference. I had to believe we could turn the situation around, get the team to believe it, and get them energized. As a leader, you can be vulnerable but should not allow the shoulders to droop.

Paint a picture of eventual success and sell it to the larger organization. Have clear tools to measure progress. This becomes important, especially in the case of a challenging business environment and getting the organization to patiently wait for a turnaround.

Have the courage of conviction to make tough choices whether on business issues or people. For example, in due course, we changed the business model for LATAM to make it fit for its purpose.

Overall, it was a very fulfilling experience, in practicing leadership as well as technical skills. I proved I could deliver in a very different environment and away from India. I believed I could rewrite my own possibilities, and my delivery enhanced my 'personal brand'. I can say I discovered a new me, and it was no surprise that the senior leadership took notice very quickly. To use a stocks analogy, I got rerated.

We see that you led many interesting roles within Unilever. When do you start looking for that change or how does that opportunity present itself?

There is a certain beauty about this company, and you will have to give credit to the leaders. This company, by design, starts to move people every two to three years to give varied experiences and bigger responsibilities. You are as good as your last role, and then you start all over again. For instance, in 2012, when I moved to London, it did not matter what I did in the previous decade. I had to deliver a business impact and prove myself again.

I still recollect my treasury days, when my predecessor CFO, P.B. Balaji, was my line manager with a headstart of a year and a half from me. I had to learn from scratch as I had no idea about bond trading, yields, market risks in a fast-evolving environment, and yet had to keep pace with a high-IQ boss. I would come in each day thinking of how I could make a difference, and go back feeling quite miserable. I realized that the only way was to put my head down and learn; I started by saying I don't know anything about this, but I will be getting there soon.

> *I have realized the first three months in the job are going to be miserable because you must reset yourself. You start from a space you do not know well. If you have a mindset affirming that you will learn from anyone and everyone, you are in good place. Be comfortable and let everyone know you are willing to learn. Then, it all falls into place.*

I have been very fortunate to do a plethora of roles, and have always been excited to really pick up every role and do it well. It could have been easily possible for me to play safe. Instead, I always asked myself, 'What is going to add value to the company and to me?' In due course, it was all about creating an impact on the business and people.

It is interesting to note that when a new opportunity presents itself, you do not spend much time deliberating but pick it up if it makes sense. What makes you confident that it is the right opportunity?

It is quite simple actually. I ask myself if the opportunity will make a positive and differentiated impact to the business and people. Then, 'Will the opportunity enable me to either build and/or develop new facets?' If it is a yes, go for it. The way I look at is that you are only betting on yourself. In such a situation, what is the downside? You will succeed or fail, but either way you will come out better than where you started. Set a goal and go for it. If you don't have a goal, you can never score.

As I have progressed on my journey, living my purpose has become an important dimension.

> *The moment you get a frame of reference for making a fundamental impact to the business and the people, success will follow.*

I am totally convinced one needs to be ready to fail a few times. Playing safe, hedging bets, will mean you will never realize your full potential—the organization will see through this and your progress will stall. So, over the years I get excited about big goals and have become comfortable dealing with ambiguity.

Where does your positive energy come from amid the negative energy around?

It is slightly difficult to answer. A part of it is DNA that I cannot really explain. But the other part is how I have conditioned myself over the years. To tap into opportunities, one needs to have a lot of energy. It is not dissimilar to what is driving a young and vibrant India. What also helps is having the ability to switch the mind off and find some quality time with family and friends.

I get a lot of energy from people, and therefore, I actively seek out people with positive energy. For example, tomorrow morning I am going to have breakfast with about eight new employees at the company, and I am quite confident I will come out feeling refreshed.

While I do discuss many things with my wife, and she helps me a great deal to manage my emotions, I like to leverage different sets of people for very different things.

> *I think I picked up the concept of a personal board of directors in a training programme, and I find it very appealing. My advice is: set your personal board to work for you.*

Your personal board will comprise a set of people who help with your different needs. For example, some people will give you intellectual stimulus but not necessarily friendship—that is when you reach out to a different board member. EQ, the emotional quotient, will come from elsewhere. Don't look for a common set of people for everything you need, for your needs are not equal, they vary.

Do you do something in the mornings to generate energy?

It is about different things at different times. I try and get some good sleep and exercise at least three to four days in a week, be it early morning or later in the evening. When I was in Switzerland, I would calm my mind by focusing on nature, my breathing and some meditation. Weekend cycling trips into the forest was again a great way to recharge.

How do you orient yourself working for experiences rather than the next promotion or raise?

There is no disconnect here. When you accumulate different experiences, you build your arsenal and get a multiplier effect as you keep progressing in your career. You gain subject knowledge and expertise and are, therefore, better equipped than others; you learn to live with ambiguity.

In addition, to navigate today's complex, modern and large-metrics organizations, you also need to build and nurture right relationships, need to have a connect with key stakeholders. So, I do this consciously. Strong delivery and connecting with people who matter must go in sync to succeed.

First, do a good job and then pull together that story in an engaging and captivating manner. It is a relative comparison as much as it is your absolute delivery.

How do you manage relationships within different teams and within finance, given the reality of conflicting priorities?

First things first, it is always primacy of business, consumers and customers. Individual functional metrics cannot be greater than the business. We are committed to driving growth, which is consistent, competitive, profitable and sustainable. Be objective, authentic and do the right things; if you build your credibility, people will trust you.

Play the full range of emotions, that is, be generous with your appreciation, be supportive, challenging, indulgent and very tough. All these qualities have a role to play and when you do the job well, you can manage people and conflicting situations effectively. In all this, there are non-negotiables that will always remain non-negotiables.

Second, in large organizations, you will need to get people inspired with the vision and strategy, excited by possibilities, and you need to galvanize them to bring in the collective force. I have often heard our senior leaders talk about a mindset: '*Ambition* has to be greater than *Resources* (A>R).' I found it fascinating and very energizing. With my experiences, I have brought in *Resilience* into the equation, and my equation now goes something like (A>R)*R.

Another important aspect would be to get your teams to dream big, to focus on output/outcomes. You also need to create psychological safety, that is, create a safety net and have their back when results don't measure up to the stretched goals. I deeply care for my team and would love to create big leaders.

Staying on the people topic, how important have mentors been for you and who are they?

It is important to have a connect with various leaders; it helps you pick up different facets. In your career journey, you will need coaches, mentors, advocates, sponsors, etc.—all these have a different role to play. So, I don't have one mentor or one role model. I was fortunate to have worked with some wonderful leaders; some of them were my line managers, while others were pure mentors.

I published an article titled 'Ode to My Masters' on *LinkedIn* to capture the essence of what I gained from some such leaders, namely, V. Kannan, D. Sundaram, Sridhar Ramamurthy and P.B. Balaji. Each of these leaders was very different in their style, strengths and outlook on various aspects. However, there are two factors which are overarching—the passion for putting business and people first, that is, to do it right for both the business and the people.

Some tips on mentoring and coaching:

> *You will need a coach at every stage of your life; not just when you commence your career. Think of it like this—what does Roger Federer not know about tennis or has not done or achieved in the game? Yet, he still has a coach, and every new coach has got him to scale a new height.*

> *Be clear and sharp about what you are looking for. A sponsor is different from a mentor and is also different from a coach. Outcomes of engagement are very different based on a sponsor or mentor.*

> *For each of these engagements, go prepared. In my case, the preparation time is, more often than not, more intense than the actual conversation. Clarity and preparation help me get a lot out of the engagement. You need to get your return of investment; a casual 'coffee conversation' approach does not help in a discussion with a coach, mentor or sponsor.*

The company has given me a formal coach now based out of the UK. I get external and independent perspectives and some brutal feedback, which is super helpful in shaping all aspects of my leadership.

I am quite picky about whom I mentor or sponsor. Currently, I am a mentor for two of our emerging talents in India, and a sponsor for two strong women finance leaders based in Europe.

CFO Office Demystified

One thing some of our readers would like to know is about the first 100 days as a CFO. Given it will be fresh in your memory, can you take us through the experience?

First, India is a critical market for Unilever; therefore, a very rigorous process was adopted for the selection of a CFO. There were assessments, which were both internal and external. The final shortlisting decision was made by the business CEO and the global CFO. This is very important because a rigorous assessment meant I entered the place with a strong wind beneath my wings. Soon after I took charge, the first thing I did was to spend a disproportionate time with the business heads in understanding the business and its nuances. One assumption you should never make is that you know the business well because you have spent your entire working life in the organization. The world is changing at an unprecedented pace, and so is the business.

Second, I spoke to as many stakeholders as I could—whether they were internal or external—to get diverse perspectives, and then build a point of view of my own. I tested my hypothesis and ran it past as many people as I could. However, the important thing here is to finally distill the hypothesis down to three to five aspects you would focus your energies on for the next few months, then list the next three to five things that will follow thereafter.

Third, I crafted the finance strategy along with my leadership team. We called for three key pillars in our strategy:

a) Win business because business comes first.
b) Create leading capabilities for the business and the function.
c) Create a team of amazing people.

One softer aspect here is that while thinking, your mind needs to be in the fifth gear. It is important to create a sense of urgency and paranoia within you to understand as many things as you can. But at the same time, you need to be slower in actions to make sure you carry the team and the different stakeholders with you.

Fourth, I spent some quality time with my entire team in Jaipur. We had our annual finance conference, and the timing coincided with my joining. This gave me an opportunity to connect with more than 170 people in two days and celebrate good work by the team in the previous year.

Finally, use the first 100 days to establish your brand and get the organization to recognize it. In my case, I had just joined and begun to play the role, when the Goods and Services Tax (GST) Council reduced the GST rates from 28 per cent to 18 per cent at a very short notice. This impacted nearly 50 per cent of our portfolio and there was no clarity on what was supposed to be done. So, I worked along with the CEO, customer development team and supply chain team to devise our strategy and how to communicate the same. We had a clear plan within three to four days of transition. We started implementing it immediately and decided to keep the government updated proactively.

Within 15 days, we had a complete proposal in front of the government, which included paying about Rs 160 crore as it was practically impossible to land the reduced priced products in the market at that short notice. So, we stuck to our principles of doing the right thing, and then deposited the benefit that accrued to us in the interim, that is, till the new products with lower pricing were in the market.

I have always believed in never wasting a crisis, for these situations give you an opportunity to reshape many factors and stretch out to take things head-on.

> *Never waste a crisis. That is another thing that you learn in life. I repeat, never ever waste a crisis.*

Can you please guide aspiring CFOs on what stands out during the selection process?

Prepare well and be ready to satisfy different stakeholders who come from very, very different points of view. As I went into the selection process, I worked with many stakeholders, senior leaders and colleagues. This helped me to have a clear perspective on the business priorities in dimensions of up to 12–18 months and beyond. Along with this, I have a very sharp and clear point of view of what I bring to the table to support the business agenda, a clear articulation of what makes me distinct, and a clarity on what the cutting edge is *versus* anybody else.

While many people will test out different aspects, I think one should really focus on a few. If I were to summarize: you need to demonstrate a growth mindset, an ability to bring the outside in and deal with ambiguity and uncertain situations, a strong resilience and finally, give confidence to the CEO and the real stakeholders that you will uphold the highest levels of corporate governance and risk management.

One other aspect will be your ability to work with people to nurture them, care for them and guide them—challenge them when required and show a mirror to their actions. As the CFO of the business, you will not only look at the talent for today, but will also be focused on creating winning talent for tomorrow.

Five or ten years down the line, how do you see the finance function transforming? What will be the role of the CFO then?

The role of the CFO is transforming rapidly. I think the pace of this change is only going to increase, as we keep moving into the future. In fact, I don't see the need to wait for five or seven or ten years for it to happen. In my opinion, the three critical elements with respect to the future CFO will be:

First, to assess how you are as a strategist enabling the business to win consistently, competitively, profitably and sustainably. This will call for a complete rewiring and reinventing of the business model into the future. Here is where you need to work with the CEO, management committee and many external stakeholders, to drive this change. In our industry, the biggest shift will come from channel transformation as well as portfolio transformation enabled by digitalization and, therefore, the future CFO needs to understand these changes and be a growth enabler and catalyst.

Second, to create leading capabilities for the broader business and function. There should be a huge focus on how to leverage data and analytics. It starts from crafting the data strategy by sitting along with the people who handle various aspects of the business, be it first party, second party or third party data. The other focus area should be to look at new, differentiated business models and leverage partnerships. Once you are able to do all this, you can create pools of growth areas and capabilities, which will help us drive the business and function forward.

Third, to build talent for the future, if a business that is going to be 2x or 3x of where you are. You need to get people with very differentiated skills. It could possibly mean a third to a half of the functional talent could come from a data and digital background without any understanding of finance or accounting. I think you need to get ahead of the curve, and start to drive this change to leverage the full benefit.

The results are announced every quarter and there is a lot of buzz that everyone sees as a follow through. It will be interesting to get a peep into how the result day looks.

What happens on the result day depends on how well you are prepared to go into the event, how well you have thought through the various aspects because it is an intense day; you spend a lot of time with the board, the audit committee and the external sets of people. Therefore, a rigorous preparation, a clear articulation of what messages you want to land, and how you want to handle the questions become very critical.

Typically, our day starts around 9 a.m. with some board committee meetings followed by an audit committee meeting, and then the board meeting. So, we spend a lot of time deliberating on the various aspects of the business and the results between 9 a.m. and 3.30 p.m. At about 3.40 p.m., immediately after the market closing hours, we declare our results to the stock exchanges. Then, Sanjiv (Sanjiv Mehta, CEO) and I go on television to talk about the results and land key messages. We then do a few interviews with news wires and print media. Around 6 p.m., we get into an investor call with our analysts, where we again present our results and answer questions coming from different stakeholders. This call lasts for about two hours, after which we call it a day. It is a very intense but a super critical day because you really need to be at your best and bring your 'A' game to the table right through the day, from 9 a.m. in the morning to 8 p.m. in the evening. These are the moments that matter.

We are sure there are exclusive events that need to be orchestrated. Are there factors beyond numbers?

That is true. The conversation goes beyond numbers. It revolves around the changing environment, consumer behaviour, our strategy and so on. And then, there are exclusive events which have a human angle, along with the financial angle. Take for instance the Kerala floods.

During the floods, we made our products available to the affected people and contributed to the chief minister's flood relief fund. We also worked with the non-government organizations (NGOs) in restoration work, and contributed funds for the construction of about 75 houses. From a business angle, we supported our partners completely. Right from taking back all the damaged goods to supplying credit till they bounced back to their normal condition, we were at the forefront, living our values of doing good. This made a huge difference and HUL was able to bounce back much faster. All this comes with a cost but must be weighed with the long-term benefits.

Does digitization help to solve a few of these number crunches? How have you approached digitization in finance?

I have a bifocal approach to digitalization in finance. To me, it is very clear that the role of finance comes in two pillars—the first one is what you do with the data and digital capabilities across the organization, and the second is what you do from a functional (finance) point of view. The projects which are integrated, broad-based and cut across multiple functions, often lead to higher growth and profits, transform marketplaces, and enable the development of different business models. In the case of HUL, the CEO runs a digital council, in which I, along with some key members of the leadership team, partner to build, structure and land business projects. For instance, the finance team led the project called Livewire—we created data lakes and made information available across many data sets to the organization in a manner which is visual and has drill-down capabilities. This has been a huge unlock because in the meetings and moments which matter, everyone has the information at the click of a button, and, therefore, all the conversations are focused on landing and making decisions.

Specifically, when we talk about digital processes in the finance function, my approach is centred around three ideas:

First, how do we get more from the core systems? Many companies have bid sizable investments into the core systems, be it SAP, Coupa or Concur. Thus, it becomes very important for us to leverage and utilize these systems to the best. Personally, I believe there is about 15–25 per cent of untapped value there. One should first target that.

Second, is to drive intelligent automation. Focus on simplification, elimination, automation (using robotic process automation) and offshoring processes. Use the unlocked capacity to move up the value chain by using artificial intelligence, natural language processing and other technologies.

Third, is the element of developing industry and applications (I&A). It is the journey from information to insights to interventions. We need to start leveraging the wealth of data sets and use algorithms to find insights. They should then be used by the finance team to make active interventions in the business. I&A can also help to strengthen controls by enabling the finance team to move beyond a rearview mirror view. You could use data analytics to crack through controls by picking out hotspots and outliers. And as we learn, we want to move the needle further, and get into predictive controls.

What are the key skills you would look for when recruiting, say, a 20-year-old finance professional?

When I am recruiting, apart from academic excellence which they possess when applying to HUL, I mainly look for three to four qualities or skills.

First, individuals absolutely need to have hunger, ambition and aspiration. They should have fire in the belly to make a difference.

Second, I test people on how broad-based their knowledge is. Many will cut through by the time they come to me from a functional standpoint. But having a broader understanding of macroeconomic developments, and perspectives on how different aspects correlate or link, is super critical because when you finally end up in a business situation, the people who are able to connect the dots between different information sets do well. Often, I try to see if people can think on their feet and stretch their imagination. Typically, for any question, people prepare for the first answer option and maybe for the second one. This is where I push them to look for option three, option four and option five. People who do not give up and continue to examine different aspects are the ones who can make a difference.

Third, the other quality I am absolutely clear about, and look forward to in people, is their value system because HUL, and Unilever as an organization, always believe in doing the right things. Hence, it is important for individuals to have value systems which measure and align with ours.

Lastly, I look for people with diverse viewpoints, those willing to speak their minds and not get cowed down by what is politically right, because these are the people who will lead the business and function into the future.

How do you retain finance talent and keep these people motivated?

You have heard me talk about the amazing pillar of people being a key thrust for us. Therefore, the whole thinking around attracting quality talent, building their skills and capabilities, and giving them opportunities to be the best they can be are the three elements to articulate our approach. As an organization, we move our people from one role to another in two to three years. This could be in India or outside, and covers diverse aspects of finance and business. You could be in a factory, working on brands, or managing the treasury, among other tasks. Therefore, giving people different experiences is a big enabler towards building and motivating talent.

The second aspect we focus on is every team member's individual development plan. Each one in the function has a development plan customized to his or her requirements. It starts with the 'PURPOSE' statement, followed by capturing aspirations/setting horizon goals, working backwards and defining development plans in the medium term (one to five years) and lastly, setting the agenda on what one is really going to do in the immediate 12 months. I think having different horizons help us customize the development plan, and support people to make that happen.

The third element is about diversity and inclusion. You need to create an atmosphere where different viewpoints are heard and respected. There is an equal opportunity for people to present their points of view, put forth and support their ideas, and take them forward to really drive a business impact.

Lastly, we have designed our rewards and recognition system around recognizing people for their effort and not only successes and failures. We recognize people for their stellar efforts even if the results don't turn out to be in line with the expected results. This allows people to stretch and deliver what they can. In the last six months, we have worked hard towards creating psychological safety for our people so they can take on bold and audacious goals, and not worry about the consequences because they know we have their back.

What would be your advice to finance professionals who want to achieve success in their career?

First and foremost, I would urge you to find and understand what your true calling is. In Unilever, we have articulated it as the 'PURPOSE'. Purpose is your guiding light, something which excites you and gets you going. And if it is linked to a greater good, it is always helpful.

The second piece connected to that is to figure out what you want to do in finance and the aspects of finance you want to build your career on. Finance has many interesting facets from accounting to core finance and expertise areas to business partnering to strategy. Similarly, each industry is different, whether you want to be in FMCG or manufacturing, or financial services, or venture capital. What is important is that you need to be really focused on what area excites and energizes you. Identify that, then fix your focus on it.

The other advice is to try to broad-base your experiences, pick on different things to do and areas to focus on. I think everything you do to broad-base your experiences in the initial stages of your career, will help you focus and build a great career.

Finally, my last advice is always this: be the best person you can be, the best finance professional you can be, the best leader you can be, and do everything you can to give yourself the best possible opportunities. You need to have the right connect with the stakeholders. You need to build, navigate and orchestrate networks, and be ready to succeed. In many cases, you need to be prepared to fail—this is when you pick yourself up, bounce back and get going.

Getting Personal

Apart from your work life, maybe even in the work life, what are the hobbies/other interests you have that you basically pursue beyond your work and to de-stress?

I believe there are three important aspects to manage your personal self—manage energy, emotions and time. A right balance between the three can help you succeed in your personal and professional life. From a physical well-being point of view, I love to play sports, especially racquet-based ones, such as tennis, badminton and squash. Between playing sports and making it to the gym, I try to get exercise at least three or four times a week. This not only keeps me fit and healthy but also gets rid of a lot of negative energy one tends to pick up.

Other than sports, I have a keen interest in travelling, music and reading. My wife loves history, culture, people, nature, and I think it has had a big rub-off effect on me. We really enjoyed our stay overseas, particularly in Europe, where we managed to visit many countries such as France, Spain, Italy, Greece, the whole Scandinavian set. We didn't travel with any rigid plans; instead, we went around meeting people, understanding different cultures and learning the history of each place. Music is something I continue to enjoy; I find it very relaxing and rejuvenating. On reading, I am very selective. My wife and friends are voracious readers, and keep suggesting a book or two from time to time. However, I like to maintain a balance between what is required from a work point of view and what gives you fun and energy.

The last piece is the ability to digitally detox, whether it is during the day or the evenings. One good change we made a few years ago was to watch very little of television. I think if one is able to reduce the amount of time spent on digital devices, it helps one find time to pursue many interests. Another habit is to avoid beginning the day with a gadget. This habit can cause anxiety. If you get to that important email at about 7 a.m. or 7.30 a.m., instead of immediately after waking up, what do you lose? To me, it is again a big balancing act. When we were young and there were no gadgets, we would wake up at 5.30 or 6 in the morning, the newspaper would come to the house and we would spend time reading it, and enjoying quality time with the family. I try to do the same now.

How do you plan your day during weekdays and what do you do on weekends?

Over the years, given that I worked in different countries and time zones, I had to be quite adaptable in the way I function. Some of my jobs used to start very early, whereas some of the others involved me working till late at night. What really works for me, and I have now made it a habit for the past year and a half, is a model of starting very early.

I try and get to work by 7.30 or 7.45 in the morning, and use the time between 7.45 and 8.45 as my pure thinking time. I like to describe it as my 'three by three'. What I mean by this is that I use the time to think about what I will focus on for the next three days and the next three months. This framework helps me keep my mind very sharp and get the right balance between the immediate needs and longer plans. As the day kicks in, I try to get a good mix of what I do internally in the organization and what I can do externally. For instance, when you look at my day today, I am discussing the business strategy for one of the verticals in the morning, followed by an operational discussion on data and digital processes. In the afternoon, I am addressing a group of people on the changing role of a CFO; I am meeting a few of our emerging talented people over a cup of tea in the evening. Not all days can be so well structured, where I am able to touch some elements of all my priorities, but I am certainly working towards increasing the proportion. To this effect, I have started to spend 10 to 15 minutes each day looking at my calendar, and working with my assistant to make some choices.

The other habit I have started with is to put a firm stop on work and leave the office at 6 p.m. I use the commute time to catch up with a lot of people, the team, some younger managers in the function. I think that really helps me get the pulse of the function and the organization. Once I reach home, I try to get some exercise to unwind, followed by a good night's sleep. This allows me to be more focused and productive.

One of my mentors recently told me, 'There is no way you can finish the amount of work this job will throw at you; to be honest, we are running a Rs 40,000-crore company with the ambition to make it a Rs 80,000-crore company. Therefore, it is critical to make choices in terms of where you invest your time, and how you invest it. The additional mantra is to make sure you have top-quality talent; empower these people, help them build their capabilities and trust they will get the job done. This is the only way you can create the time and space.'

Over the weekends, I try to completely switch off from work and spend time with my family and friends. I catch up with friends, preferably with those who are not connected to my work life. We just head out, catch a train and go somewhere for a chit-chat. I also use my weekend to read, pursue my interest in sports and other things. The last 12 months, my wife has been operating out of London, and I have been in India. Hence, I have also spent many weekends visiting her to spend some quality time. Even though I am there only for a few days those days are very dear to me. I try and get about half a day a week, typically Sunday evenings, to plan my week's agenda and, therefore, get more productive for the forthcoming week.

You mentioned you like to read in the evenings. Can you share your reading list and some of your favourite authors?

My reading habits fall in two areas of interest. One is to keep myself abreast with the latest developments and happenings in the world of business or broader macroeconomic fundamentals. The second is something that expands my horizons. On a day-to-day basis, I start my day with a quick read of the *Economic Times*, *Bloomberg* and *Bloomberg Quint*. I turn to the *Economist* and *LinkedIn* in the evenings to read some interesting perspectives and articles. I complement these with some selective reading in functional areas, such as data and digitalization, development of the accounting functions and so on.

Apart from work-related readings, some of the interesting books I have read in the last year were:

a) *Factfulness* by Hans Rosling. The author uses facts to explain how the world is a much better place than what we make out of it, given the biases or the lack of objectivity we have.
b) Another interesting book is *The Hundred-Year-Old Man Who Climbed Out of the Window and Disappeared* by Jonas Jonasson. I liked the narrative and how it is written; the clarity with which the whole picture has been painted. It's a very inspirational account of the lead character, which explains that if you are really willing to stretch yourself and give yourself

the full opportunity to develop, you can achieve whatever you want.

c) Among a few other books I liked are *21 Lessons for the 21st Century* by Yuval Noah Harari and *Bad Blood: Secrets and Lies in a Silicon Valley Startup* by journalist John Carreyrou, which is the story of Theranos, the multibillion-dollar biotech company that claimed it would revolutionize blood testing but turned out to be a fraud.

d) Then, there is always the quintessential Agatha Christie. I always enjoy reading her novels. I think Hercule Poirot is an absolute inspiration and these mysteries are something I continue to read because as the author says, 'It's a good test of your little grey cells.'

Can you tell us more about your better half?

My wife, Sumita, is a vitreoretinal surgeon by profession. I met her in Chennai through a common friend who was her colleague at Sankara Nethralaya, the charitable eye hospital, and my wife was her roommate. Since then there has been no looking back—we have been together for 15 years now, and going strong.

As a person, she is very positive and has an infectious energy. She has always been a pillar of strength and has helped me traverse the ups and downs of life easily and smoothly. While in many cases, she is my biggest support, she is also my harshest critic when required. She has been a significant contributor to my overall career and development. Working in a company like Unilever has meant that I have changed roles and locations every two to three years including being based out of London and Switzerland between 2012 to 2018. Therefore, she was never able to manage a full-time career in one organization. She used these opportunities to add new skills to her career, and her role as an Ophthalmologist. I am grateful to her for some of the sacrifices she has made and for giving me the freedom to pursue my opportunities. I don't think my success would have been possible without the big role she took on and contributions from her side. She is my grounding force, who keeps me balanced. I really value her as a friend, and rely on her in everything I do.

Leaving your modesty aside for a second, if you were to talk about yourself, what do you think are the top three, you know, things that distinguish you from your peers?

There are two drives that get me going. The first one is to create a sustainable business impact and the second one is to build people, to make a difference to talented ones. Everything I do really comes down to these two pillars, and what follows is a natural progression.

Think big, dream big, achieve big is my motto—the ability to really think big, think with the mindset of ambition, which is greater than resources. I do not fear to set up an audacious goal and then encourage my team to work towards it. In fact, I don't believe in playing safe. I think once you craft a big picture and strategic vision, and work that through, you make the change; you ensure a very clear point of view of where you want to go, whether it is within the function, or from a business point of view.

Second, my ability to move into an ambiguous territory and come back to pragmatism is a distinguishing character. The ability to deal with ambiguity, insecurities, potential failures, not only for your own self, but to help the team navigate through these changes works for me. I think I do a good job in backing the team to the hilt, especially when the chips are down. It starts to create a psychological safety, encouraging people to put their best foot forward.

One aspect I have learnt over the years, and I credit Russel Reynolds, the management consulting firm, for this framework, is about the 'AND' aspects of leaderships. The framework calls out for four elements a leader should be: a) risk-taking AND reluctant b) connecting AND galvanizing c) disruptive AND pragmatic d) heroic AND vulnerable. I am in a work-in-progress situation with respect to many of these, but the more I use this framework, the more am I able to deliver better and be a better leader.

One aspect which I am working through to amplify is inspirational leadership. I believe the ability to connect strongly and get the collective going is an opportunity area. The ability to engage and personalize the experience regardless of the size of the group, be it five or 50, can move mountains.

So, the way I really look at it is about trying to be a little better each day as these small actions will make a big difference.

Which is the most memorable day you recollect as a phenomenally great day?

Like I mentioned before, it is the business and people which really matter to me. Let me start by first talking about the people aspect. The adage goes, 'leaders create leaders', and I think I have been fortunate to work with some wonderful leaders. D. Sundaram used to be the CFO of HUL when I was recruited. He led the function for over 10 years, and played a phenomenal role in building a lot of great talent. Many of these people have gone on to do big roles and jobs in Unilever and elsewhere. So recently, when I got an opportunity to address a room full of finance professionals in a shared services forum, where he was the keynote speaker, I was absolutely thrilled. It was a very special day because I got an opportunity to present to Mr Sundaram how we are taking his legacy forward, building on everything he taught us and leading the function into the future. Even though I was addressing more than 50 finance professionals in the room, secretly, I was only presenting to him. It was my ode to my master, and I cherish that moment.

From a business standpoint, it has to be the day we announced our proposed merger with GSK Consumers Limited, one of the largest mergers in the Indian FMCG sector. This proposed merger not only makes HUL the lead player in the foods and refreshments category, but also gets us some transformational brands to meet the daily requirements of the consumer in the nutrition category. This business has a significant potential to grow, and we expect to do so by growing it in double digits into the foreseeable future, to create value which comes through sizeable margin expansion. The proposed merger has also given us a very new and different source of energy, since the business comes along with some very good capabilities in terms of chemist and pharmacy channels. It's a win-win acquisition. Therefore, playing a key role in enabling and making that acquisition happen is another memorable moment.

Can you talk to us about a day you want to erase from your memory?

Like everyone else, I have had my share of ups and downs in life. When the going is tough and you are really down, you wish for many different things and a very different outcome. But honestly, if I were to live my life again, I would not change a single thing in my career or life. I would possibly live through everything that has happened to me. I have learnt and enjoyed all the good things; equally, I have learnt and become stronger when things have not been great.

In 2003, I was handling forex and the treasury. I had a huge position running on dollar–rupee exchange rates. We all took a particular view, and did not take into account how it could be an event risk. We got it wrong and there was loss. But that's not the point. My vice president (VP), finance, came and asked me if it was going to affect the quarter results. Without thinking, I said, 'It won't.' Soon I realized that I had blurted out a blunder, and immediately went and owned up to my boss. He went and spoke to the CFO, who was very upset by it. Since my line manager was not in town, I was called in for the reprimand. That was an unforgettable moment and taught me a lesson. But it doesn't mean I want to erase that day from my life because what I learnt that day has remained, and will remain, with me for the rest of my life. What matters is learning from mistakes and to ensure not to repeat that mistake again. Reflecting back, these situations have made me a better human being and a better professional. And, I don't think I really want to erase anything from my life.

Anything you would do differently, if you were able to wind the clock back? We're not referring to bad things or good things, just something you would do differently.

It is an interesting question and I know one is always wise in wisdom and hindsight. But I think after a point in time, it isn't very helpful. If I were to really look to redo something, I would probably look at my academic background and knowledge very differently. I got into finance and commerce right after school. Perhaps, it would have been better if I could have explored some other distinct areas such as science or mathematics or arts, music and culture, before pursuing my interest in finance. Finance was, and continues to be, my passion. But I think the diversity of knowledge in some areas would have been helpful. As someone wise once said, 'It is never too late.' So, I am now picking on some of these aspects to add richness and aroma to my own experiences.

The other things I think I could have done better was to be more available to my family and friends. There were times when work took precedence, and I was unable to give time and attention despite being physically there. I wish I was 100 per cent there then, but I know I can't go back in time and relive those moments. Hence, for a few years, I have been consciously practising to be 100 per cent present and available in the moments that matter with the people who matter to me.

Thank you so much for your time!

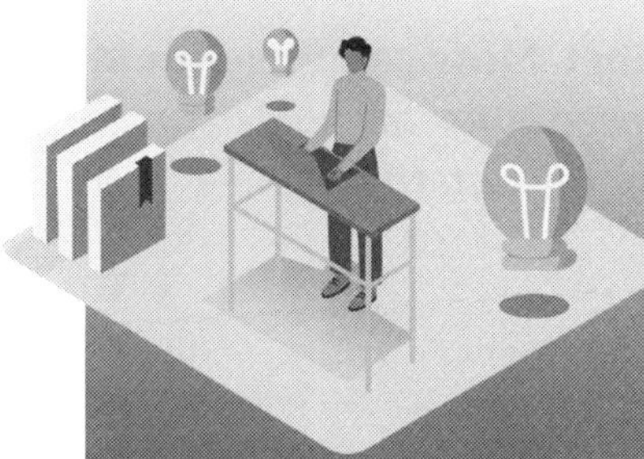

Key Takeaways

SRINIVAS PHATAK

Take 1: It takes time to find your purpose and realize your potential. Stay patient.

Take 2: The right outlook towards failure paves the way to success.

Take 3: The only opportunity you have is the one in front of you, so make the most of it.

Take 4: Have the resilience, self-belief and courage of conviction to make hard choices.

Take 5: Get a little better at what you do every day. Small actions will make a big difference.

Take 6: Get your 'personal board of directors' and make it work for you.

Take 7: Three dimensions of managing personal self are to manage energy, emotions and time.

Take 8: Organizational success = (Ambition>Resources) x Resilience.

Take 9: Never waste a crisis. It is an opportunity to reshape.

Take 10: Think big, dream big and achieve big.

Key takeaways that inspired me most. How can I use them to change my perspective? (*This space is for the reader to jot down the lessons that they learned from this interview*)

During the Treasury days

With wife Sumita

Cricket with the finance team

With the Shared Services Team at Unilever Accounting & Controls Olympiad in London

With the Finance Leadership Team

HUL Management Committee during Diwali celebrations

HUL Board at Bengaluru Shared Services Centre

HUL finance alumni meeting

Receiving ICAI's Best CFO–FMCG Category Award

Speaking at a Citi event

CLSA Event 2018 Gurgaon

Extra Shots

Srinivas Phatak

Do you have a personal board of directors?

When we reached out to Mr Phatak, he had just started on the CFO's journey in Hindustan Unilever. We had some very specific questions lined up for him, such as: What is the selection process for making it to the CFO's office? What are the first 100 days like? How to settle down in the CFO's office when you take on the reins?

The HUL office is very near the airport and we arrived ahead of time. As expected, all arrangements were lined up for the interview. While waiting for Mr Phatak, we had a quick look around the office. You instantly notice the power of the brand at the HUL headquarters. Everything in the office had a brand presence, including the washrooms. It was a very impressive set-up with the range of shampoos, soaps and other products displayed prominently. You could not be in that office for 10 minutes and not use at least one HUL product.

Mr Phatak has had a very unusual journey to the CFO's role, and that is a reflection of his personality. He is a risk-taker by nature, open-minded to all possibilities, and someone who focuses on the potential positives of each situation. As Mr Phatak likes to say, 'Never waste a crisis.' If someone were to take away only two learnings from his personality, they would be: 1) Look at every crisis as an opportunity. 2) Look for a way to continuously reinvent yourself by saying yes more often than no.

We could not finish the interview in one meeting and asked for more time the following Saturday. When we arrived at the HUL office at 10 a.m., we found him waiting for us, alone in the entire campus, although he had a temperature of 102 degrees. He could have called and cancelled the meeting, but he knew that we had travelled from different locations, so he came to office just to meet us even when unwell. This level of professionalism in an interaction with almost strangers defines the quintessential qualities that our CFOs stand for.

Learnings in Action

'*You cannot control the way the day ends but can certainly control how the day begins*' was simple yet very powerful. We have had much fewer grumpy starts to the day as we began seeing *each sunrise as a new opportunity to make an impact.*

We constituted our own *personal board of directors,* our confidants and mentors who we could reach out to when needed. Not all of them should have the same relationship with you because your needs vary at different times. Most importantly, they need to know their role as it requires them not to be a support group, but those who can help resolve conflicts, make decisions and move forward. The personal board of directors has suddenly expanded our span of skills and abilities. We understood that our resources no longer define our ambitions.

Do you have a personal board of directors? How will you use this board to grow beyond your capabilities? Where will you be if you can bet on yourself without fear, without constraints?

Sushil Agarwal

GROUP CHIEF FINANCIAL OFFICER
ADITYA BIRLA GROUP

The Aditya Birla Group is one of India's largest and most prestigious private sector conglomerates, with over $46 billion in revenues in the fiscal year 2020 (FY 20). Mr Sushil Agarwal is the Group CFO of this conglomerate and also serves as a director in Aditya Birla Management Corporation Private Limited—an apex body of the group—and in various other listed and unlisted entities of the group. A veteran with the group, Mr Agarwal has traversed one of the most exciting growth journeys we have come across. He joined Grasim (one of the group companies) in December 1988 as an officer in the projects division. He served in diverse roles, such as an executive assistant, CFO, COO and CEO for 27 years before he formally took over the role of Group CFO in 2016.

In his own words, Mr Agarwal likes to do different things and do things differently. His role in multiple capacities before he took over the Group CFO mantle, helped him create an appreciation for building a strategic perspective of the CFO function. He is widely acknowledged in the industry for his financial acumen, analytical skills and the ability to break down complex problems into simpler and manageable components. He loves to mentor and spend time with career aspirants.

In September 2018, Mr Agarwal was awarded India's Greatest CFO 2017-18 in the 3rd edition of 'Asia

One' India's Greatest Brands and Leaders Awards 2017-18 & Summit. In recognition of his stellar contribution, he was awarded 'Business Leader Corporate CFO' at the 11th ICAI Awards 2017. He has also been honoured with the Chairman's Exceptional Contributor Award in 2000 and Chairman's Outstanding Leadership Award in 2014.

Mr Agarwal is a Chartered Accountant by qualification.

Fireside Chat

Mr Agarwal, we were talking to a senior colleague in the Group and he mentioned that you consistently take out time to coach a lot of young professionals at Aditya Birla. Is that right?

I try to. It is very important, and I think the senior people in the system have a lot of responsibility towards the younger generation. We need to guide the next generation of leaders and help them identify their skills. Hopefully, your book will be another step in that direction.

Let us start with your early days then.

I was born in Jodhpur, and come from a very humble background. I grew up in Sri Ganganagar, Rajasthan, near the India-Pakistan border. My father was in government service and had a transferable job. This gave me the privilege to live in different cities all through my childhood. I completed my Master's degree in commerce from Rajasthan University and moved to Delhi to pursue chartered accountancy. I did my articleship in a CA firm in Delhi called T.R. Chadha & Company, where I got the opportunity to audit large public sector undertakings (PSUs), such as Steel Authority of India Limited (SAIL), National Thermal Power Corporation Limited (NTPC), IFCI (previously called Industrial Finance Corporation of India) and Bank of India, among others. These audits meant that I had to travel a lot to Bombay (now Mumbai), and somehow I got fascinated by the city, truly a city of dreams. As my stars conspired, I joined Grasim's projects division in Bombay. I moved to Bombay from Delhi, and lived in Juhu as a paying guest with a roommate from Jodhpur. He was also a CA and worked for Blowplast. There were no mobile phones at the time. I used to travel in the local train. Bombay trains and monsoon rains are something I will never forget.

In school, did you like academics or did you focus on sports?

I do not think sports was a great strength area for me. I knew I had to do reasonably well in education, and sports took a back seat. I would not say I was engrossed only in education. I loved watching cricket like other teenagers. Sri Ganganagar is near the Pakistan border, and I had a lot of friends in the Border Security Force (BSF) who made it possible for me to watch live cricket. This privilege wasn't available to most people at that time. I always had a flair for making friends, across age groups, and I believe this helped me in my career as well.

Were you always clear that you wanted to work in finance? If not, what did you aspire for early on in your life/career?

Honestly, in my childhood I never wished to restrict myself to a particular field. However, I always wanted to be in a place where I could make a difference. There is one thing I have always been clear about in my life—it is the urge to do things differently. Even today, I find myself questioning the expected, challenging the norms and doing things differently. As children, we are taught to follow norms and do things in a certain way. I have always questioned that 'certain way', and this approach cultivated my creative confidence.

In my early days, I was fascinated by the civil services after seeing the government officials in Sri Ganganagar.

But I didn't really take this option seriously. Another career that strangely attracted me was that of a fashion designer. People close to me know that had I not been a CA, I would have become a fashion designer (*laughs*).

When did you finally decide you wanted to study commerce?

I think it just happened. We are a huge joint family, and it had a significant influence on my life and ambitions. One of my paternal uncles was a CA, and another was a Bachelor in Engineering (BE) and MBA from IIM. Both of them were role models in the family and greatly influenced my thought process. While my uncle with the BE and MBA degrees inspired me towards the importance of a career, my uncle who was a CA influenced my choice of the career I decided to pursue. Initially, I wanted to go to Chandigarh for further studies because I had a few friends there and also loved the city. But my uncles asked me to come to Delhi instead. And, that's how I ended up going to Delhi from Sri Ganganagar.

It seems there was a lot of focus on studies in your family.

My family always believed education is the biggest asset one can have, and that it never depreciates. As a result, my family had postgraduates in an era where completing a pre-university degree was a herculean task in itself. This included even the women in the family. I have two sisters, and equal importance was given to their education as well. One of my sisters, Saloni, is a doctor and my other sister, Seema, stood fourth in the MSc examination in Rajasthan. We come from a humble background and never had the meaningful capital to grow our grandfather's retail business. Education was the best bet we had.

My grandfather ran a small shop. When we visited him during summer vacations, he would say, 'Sit in the shop for three hours, and you get 10 paisa; sit for the whole day, and I will give you 50 paisa.' I loved sitting in the shop and interacting with the customers. It made me realize the importance of money and hard work at an early age.

Out of context, referring back to the joint family, I think those vacations were some of the most fun days I can remember. All the siblings would come together at the same time for vacations. We used to sleep on mattresses laid on the floor, unlike today, when we stick to our personal hotel rooms during social functions. I used to wait for summer holidays because I could meet and play with my cousins. This led to such strong bonds within the family that even today we laugh remembering those days. It created a sense of bonding I take to every relationship, and try to respect people's emotions.

I believe that family bonding goes a long way in shaping a person's approach towards life and the personality as a whole.

You did your CA in Delhi and then moved to Bombay for your first job.

After qualifying as a CA, I continued to work with T.R. Chadha & Company, where I did my articleship. The partners gave an offer to stay on. As I was unsure of how to proceed further, I continued there for about a year. But soon I was in a dilemma about whether to remain in Delhi or go elsewhere; whether to practise or get a job. While I loved Delhi, I preferred Bombay over it in terms of the place of work, and applied to a few places for a job. Consequently, I met Mr Vinod Saraf, who was the head of the projects division at Grasim, the flagship company of the Aditya Birla Group, and also the managing director (MD) at Mangalore Refinery (the Aditya Birla Group had a joint venture with Hindustan Petroleum [HP]). The company was putting up a three-million-tonne oil refinery. Mr Saraf offered me a job and asked me to join in Delhi. He tried to persuade me a lot saying, 'You already have a set-up in Delhi and your uncle lives here. It would be a hassle to find a place to live in Bombay.' When I kind of stood adamant on the job location, he finally relented and allowed me to join in Bombay. I effectively started on 28 December 1988. I spent around 15 months in that division with Mr Saraf and Mr R.K. Saraswat. I had an excellent time as the projects division had plenty of exciting things going on.

So, how did your transition from the project role to Mr Aditya Vikram Birla's office happen?

Mr Saraf reported to Mr Mahesh C. Bagrodia, one of the stalwarts in the Birla set-up in those times who was responsible for various businesses, including new projects, cement, chemicals and lots of other areas. One day Mr Saraf called me to inform me that Mr Bagrodia wanted to meet me. He took me to Mr Aditya Birla, the chairman of the group. I was nervous, but I still went and met him. He offered me two options—to either join his office or move abroad for an overseas assignment.

When we came out of the office, and I told Mr Bagrodia, *'Sir, mere ko tho dono hi suit nahin karta hain.'* (Sir, neither works for me). He was a bit surprised, but gave me some leeway because of my young age—he asked me to think over it again and come back. I went back to work and thought the matter had ended there. A month and a half later, he called up again and asked me to meet him. This time he sat down with me and said, 'You must understand both these assignments are very rarely offered, unless the organization felt very confident in your abilities. It is a mark of recognition.' I definitely didn't want to go abroad. So, the only choice left was to join Mr Birla's office. I was a bit hesitant, but finally, I went on to join his office. So you can say, in a way, I was forced to join Mr Birla's office. But today, when I look back, I think it was the best opportunity I ever got. Mr Aditya Vikram Birla was an exceptional leader not only within the Birla group but in the entire Indian industry.

We have seen a lot of brain drain in India over the past decades. How did your decision to stay back in India affect your career?

I think it was one of the most important choices that probably shaped my entire life. In those days, settling abroad was considered very fancy. But I turned that down and decided to stay back. Looking at that day and today, I am very happy I made that choice. India has been the epicentre of growth during the past two and a half decades since liberalization. During this period, the group has done more than 30 acquisitions, several corporate restructurings and new forays into business. All of this action took place in India. I have been fortunate to be associated with many of these actions that shaped my career much better than if I had been outside India.

How was the experience working directly with Mr Aditya Vikram Birla?

I couldn't have got a better place from an opportunity point of view. He was a tough taskmaster for sure, and we had some long days. We started very early, and he was one of the first ones to arrive. Before he got into the day's work, along with the members of the Chairman Cell, he would review the pending issues across the group and take a pulse check of the business operations. In the evening, before leaving, he wanted us to send home all the papers related to the pending work. We made sure we worked extra hours and sent him all the papers before leaving for the day. There were no mobile phones those days. I lived in Borivali. By the time I reached home, there would be a message that

Sir wanted to meet me at 8.45–9 a.m. the next day. He would set down remarks on almost every paper we sent.

I never thought industrialists functioned like that. It left a clear message that he may be the owner, but worked much harder than all of us. His attitude towards work taught us everything you own is just not given; you have to continue working hard for growth.

Another great thing he developed in the office was the acceptance of bad news. He always said, 'Don't surprise me, tell me the bad news immediately.' I remember once there was a plant shutdown. Seeing he was already stressed, I postponed the bad news. He got really upset so I explained, 'Sir, you were busy, and I was waiting for the right time.' His response was, 'You have all the freedom to knock and come in; never delay the bad news.'

> *One of the early learnings we got from Mr Birla was if there is bad news, always try to get it first. Encourage a culture where people are not afraid of giving bad news as it gives you a slightly longer time to resolve the problem.*

I keep encouraging my colleagues not to be scared of bad news. We should not fret about what is not in our control, but work on what is in our control. This is the same with the board and the investors. The investors always ask us to give the bad news upfront and to never surprise them. If someone is a long-term investor, they would appreciate our belief and conviction. You have to reflect the conviction that you are fair, honest and right in all your actions because it is something in your control.

You had a fast-paced career growth at the Birla group. What advice would you have for young professionals who want a similar trajectory?

No one will give you important work or recognition just like that. You have to work and have the fire in your belly throughout your career to extract more responsibilities from your bosses and better performance from your colleagues. This comes from your own hunger. You have to show the strength and desire to work. I have served nine different bosses in my career, and have drawn varied learning experiences from them.

> *There is no standard recipe for growth. It will depend on your craving, and reflects from your daily behaviour. As a group, we have a formal appraisal system where we appraise every employee twice a year. However, I would say we actually get appraised daily. Right or wrong, whatever you do gets noticed daily. Sometimes the recognition can take a little longer, but it always comes.*

Tell us a little more about your work with Mr Aditya Vikram Birla.

Coming back to my early days at Mr Birla's office, he would always tell me to take notes (Sushil, *likh lo*) and at times, I would get mildly irritated about this. But then, gradually, I realized the importance of writing things on a piece of paper as it forces you to think systematically and explore all angles of the problem. There are several such small learnings I could talk about for hours. The most fortunate thing was he took time to teach me the basics of the corporate world and ways to operate more efficiently.

Let me give you another example. One day when Mr A.V. Birla was talking to his father Mr B.K. Birla over the phone, I happened to be in his room. Mr B.K. Birla had his own empire of companies that included Century Textiles, among others. Century Textiles had a pulp unit and Indian Rayon (a major Aditya Birla Group company) used to buy pulp from it. They were negotiating hard on the pricing of this commodity. To me, it appeared very strange. After the call ended, I asked him in my own way about why he was haggling with his father. At the end of the day, the business was all part of the same family. I still remember every bit of his answer. He pushed himself back on his chair and said, 'Both of us are doing our part of the job. He is responsible for a separate set of shareholders and I am responsible for a separate set. We have to be true to our responsibilities.' Can you believe it? The word 'Corporate Governance' did not even exist in those days, and yet the Birlas were practising it in the 1990s, rather, even earlier.

Was this kind of culture prevalent throughout the family?

Yes, throughout. Mr B.K. Birla would never take decisions on behalf of Mr Aditya Birla or Mr K.M. Birla, even if he could. Mr B.K. Birla would tell us, 'Go and talk to your boss, and let me know what decision is amenable to him.' I remember a very peculiar situation. I was part of Aditya Birla Nuvo, the company of the group with a range of business interests such as financial services and manufacturing, when it was running a rights issue. Mr B.K. Birla was a part-owner through a group company. He called me and said, 'I have no money to spare for the rights issue as I have other priorities in the business. So, I won't be applying for your rights issue,' and told me the rate in the market for renunciation. The point I am making is the difference between a family relationship and an organizational relationship. He did not talk to Mr K.M. Birla directly to avoid influencing his decision; he went through me and offered the benchmark price. He gave us 48 hours to execute the process, in case we would be interested; else, he would sell the rights renunciation in the market. These are just a few of the many examples of corporate governance being practised in this company a lot earlier than when it became a necessity for other organizations.

Did you have the independence of operations you desired even though it is a family-owned business?

Yes, 100 per cent. As long as you articulated your plan correctly and it made business sense, there was nothing that could not be discussed and debated. Let me tell you about another incident. During the early days, when K.M. Birla had just taken over, he called me and said he had been told our returns on surplus funds were lower than some of the other companies. There were no mutual funds those days, so we used to place surplus cash into the intercorporate deposits. I told him it might be true because we had our norms for risk management, which may not be the same as other companies. Our primary formula was based on SLR—safety, liquidity and returns. Our main objective was to run the manufacturing business. Management of the surplus cash was driven by the objective to drive the core business in the best way, where safety and liquidity was a priority and the treasury income incidental. If the business needed money on short notice, it had to be available. I told him clearly that returns were a lower priority than liquidity and safety, and it may be the reason for the lower returns. It wasn't like we were losing money. In fact, our returns were better than our borrowing costs; therefore, it was the right approach. He understood, and we continued to follow our original approach. About a year later, Mr B.K. Birla came back and told him our thought process on treasury management was correct as his money had got stuck in certain illiquid investments. I do not recall if we ever had a challenge in ensuring cash liquidity across businesses because we continue to follow this approach.

We have had our own asset management company (AMC) for the last 20 years. But, there is no compulsion for us to go and invest in our mutual fund. All our treasury managers have absolute freedom to take their own call, although we interact at regular intervals to share best practices and make sure the overall group risk profile is managed prudently.

From a family business perspective, you have closely seen the promoters' ethos and values and have imbibed them. Given that you are such a large organization, how do you make sure they percolate into the entire organization? Is it codified into something concrete? How does the lowest-level employee know how to behave in a certain situation?

We have successfully managed to codify our values, and percolate them to not only our organization but also the companies we have acquired over the years. In the last two decades, we have done over 30 acquisitions, and all of them have been very successful. Globally, the success ratio of acquisitions is, maybe, a quarter or somewhere around that.

Why have we been so successful? To me, all our ethos and all these group-level values are key drivers for success. When you become such a large organization, and your revenue grows from $2 billion to $48 billion, you must have a common value system. Today, we are present in 35 countries with more than 130 plants. Two things worked for us—a clearly laid out non-negotiable value system and our exposure to the open global economy very early in our life cycle. We took the best practices we could find, and implemented them across the group.

CFO Office Demystified

In your view, what are the top priorities for a new-age CFO?

Increased disclosure requirements, transparency and regulatory compliances have enhanced the criticality in the role of a CFO. With the pace at which technology is making things redundant, it has become very critical for a CFO to assess a risk and devise a risk mitigation plan. As I had mentioned before, the role of a CFO has evolved from being just a finance custodian or controller to a value creator. Their responsibilities are no more restricted to regular accounts, audits, taxes and compliance. It has gone much beyond.

CFOs are now equal business partners and responsible for the performance of the company. As the way of doing business evolves, the CFO's role has also become broader and more complex. They are now playing a strategic role in transformations. Performance management has become the top priority. There is a lot of focus to improve reporting and dashboards using more data visualization and data analytics. CFOs must streamline their efforts in tackling technological disruption and leveraging the digital revolution, including the use of robotics, artificial intelligence and so on. CFOs must strive to create long-term value for their shareholders through innovative fundraising, restructuring solutions, evaluating mergers and acquisitions (M&A) opportunities and driving operational efficiency through rigorous forecasting and benchmarking exercises. Meeting investor expectations should also be among the top priorities for a

CFO, which includes active engagement with the investors for their queries, concerns and grievances.

There is a lot of buzz around transformation and digital finance. How do you see that shaping your industry/ company?

Data management will no longer be an aggregation of performance data. Tasks will be handled by automated technology and finance will, instead, lead strategy by using the data to drive deeper prescriptive insights. Cloud technologies, robotics, machine learning, natural language processing and mobiles will push organizations towards extreme automation. Integrating these technologies will become essential to unlock their full potential.

This means moving beyond descriptive and diagnostic analysis to predictive and prescriptive analysis. CFOs must equip their teams with the right tools, skills and capabilities to provide leading insights and analytics as well as answers to critical questions.

At Aditya Birla Group (ABG), we have undertaken various digital transformation initiatives, such as enabling the approval of business documents on mobile devices; daily reports of all vital processes, such as production, quality and dispatches are sent on mobiles for all stakeholders.

We have also implemented smart manufacturing solutions which provide real-time plant performance by aggregating data from the manufacturing execution systems (MES) at plants to show their real-time key performance indicators (KPIs). Also, we have done a pilot roll-out of fully digitized contract staff security system for real-time tracking of labour inside confined spaces.

Currently, we are using artificial intelligence-enabled systems on customer-facing and internal employee websites. Further, we use augmented or virtual reality for the induction of new joiners.

Is there a different kind of finance shaping the future?

In a disruptive and technological age, CFOs and finance teams have the opportunity to support innovation, embrace automation, leverage data, lead strategy and recruit differently, thus, preparing their organizations for anything. Disruption can no longer be seen as an abstract concept. These business disruptors are changing the demands of finance, and with this, the strategic importance of the CFO's role is increasing.

Finance—which used to help businesses develop a capital plan, administer that plan, prioritize where the money is spent, and then police that spent capital—would need to think 'more like venture capitalists'. They would have to drive evaluation, allocation and monitoring of strategic investments in new platforms, customers and products.

While maintaining the traditional functions of control and increased process efficiency, finance functions will be responsible for leveraging digital technologies and data. They would have to embrace robotic process automation and artificial intelligence, own enterprise performance management data and analytics, deploy predictive tools and build business-partnering skills.

Do you see a changing talent landscape with this disruption in finance? How are you handling that change?

The impact of extreme automation and increased data availability will see a shift in organizational structures. Also, these changing responsibilities will create new roles in finance for people who will leverage threats and opportunities into strategic directions.

Data scientists would be those enacting the most critical roles that would advise the businesses on the impact of different scenarios. They would be people who have to work across multiple groups and functions—marketing, operations, finance, and production—to collaborate on business planning. Financial and regulatory accountants, innovation and investment strategists and business solutions architects would be among the few emerging roles.

At ABG, we have been proactive. We launched the Group Data Analytics Cell, which is closely working with businesses on digital transformation projects. Before we implement any transformation initiative, we conduct a 'Go live' session, where we train and create awareness of the technology being implemented. Currently, we are encouraging people to attend workshops we are conducting on data analytics and emerging technologies.

How do you retain talented people and keep them motivated?

There is a very thin line of difference between organizational success and failure, and that thin line is 'people'. People are the most important assets of an organization; therefore, it is very crucial for any organization to attract and retain the best talent. Competitors can imitate products and acquire tangible assets and technology, but they cannot replicate an effective and committed workforce.

It is equally important for an organization to retain talent and keep these employees motivated. It should respect their desires and aspirations and align them with its goals. It should ensure that an ample amount of freedom is given to its employees, even while keeping a watchful eye.

Besides attracting new talent, organizations should also consider training and developing their talent. According to me, job satisfaction is key to extracting the best out of employees. I encourage employees to take up higher responsibilities, which help in enhanced job satisfaction and creating the second line of managers.

For instance, post the Grasim–ABNL merger, we ensured people moved to bigger roles. The CFO of ABNL, at the corporate level, moved as the CFO of Aditya Birla Capital Limited (ABCL); the head of treasury and banking for the Grasim corporate level moved as the head of accounts and treasury of ABCL; the vice president (corporate finance) for ABNL moved as the function head of finance and commercial for one of the units of UltraTech Cement, the subsidiary of ABG.

At ABG, we have succession planning at the group level and most of our positions are filled internally. This helps create attractive growth opportunities continuously.

How do you interact with other CFOs/finance professionals?

I interact with other CFOs/finance professional colleagues, but not always in a very structured way. I keep myself available to them, just a phone call away in case of any exigency or help needed on any day-to-day affair. In a structured manner, we meet every quarter during reviews and board meetings to discuss business performance.

However, I make it a point to spend at least a few minutes to interact with trainees and young professionals working with us. Also, I tend to have semi-annual meetings with my mentees from ABG's leadership programme.

As a CFO, how much do you interact with other functions and your customers? How often? How has it evolved over time?

Today, most of the functions of an organization are well-knitted with a lot of interdependencies, and finance is omnipresent. I frequently interact with various people performing different functions. While I was the CFO at Grasim, we had weekly team review meetings, involving the respective heads of the accounts, tax, risk, legal and treasury functions.

Finance professionals are equal business partners. We have a monthly meeting where business CXOs meet to discuss progress, sustainability, long-term and short-term goals, key business risks and challenges. At the time of our planning and budgeting exercise, we closely work with all these business functions.

In the capacity of my role as Group CFO, I closely work with various business teams across our group companies on strategic projects. I head the Finance Talent Council for the group, and am actively involved with the group's human resources (HR) to draw the career path of the group's finance talent. I also happen to mentor FLPs (CA rank holders) from the ABG's leadership programmes, and enjoy every bit of it.

In my case, my customers are also my investors, who have invested billions of dollars across our group companies. I spend a lot of time engaging with them, addressing their concerns, answering their queries and explaining our winning business strategy.

This is quite interesting. It looks like there have been quite a few changes you've observed in finance and talent from the day you started till today. Are there any areas handled by finance professionals beyond finance?

There has been a significant shift from what finance used to be years ago. Over the course of time, disclosure and transparency requirements have increased momentously, and so has the accountability and regulatory responsibilities of the finance professionals. Of late, the role of finance professionals has evolved from that of custodians or controllers to value creators. Today, finance personnel are equal partners of growth. Their areas of operations have expanded from accounts, taxes and audits to commercial and financial planning, business IT, operations, investor relations, treasury, risk management, corporate strategy and business development.

At ABG, we have over 1,500 CAs, and more than one-third of them are working in diverse non-finance business roles.

We also see that in your career. We understand that you were involved in the insurance brokerage business as a CEO, and then later in a lot of other areas as well. Can you take us through your progression to the CFO's role, and how things evolved after Mr K.M. Birla took over?

As I said, I started with the Grasim's project division, and was soon moved to the chairman's office. The norm was to transfer to an operational role after the completion of five to six years. It was 1995, and I was due for a role change. That year, we faced the unfortunate demise of Mr Aditya Vikram Birla, and Mr Kumar Mangalam Birla took over as the chairman of the group. I went on to continue on my stint at the chairman's office for another few years.

Under Mr K.M. Birla, the whole group got a completely different shape. Predominantly, we were a manufacturing player. However, he saw very early that the services sector would be the next leg of growth from an organizational as well as the country's point of view. We entered various growth businesses from financial services to telecom to retail. I saw the transition from a completely manufacturing mindset to a service mindset. It was amazing to see how much we had to adapt to the new set-up.

Within these new businesses, it was in financial services that I was a lot more engaged. Although I was at the chairman's office, I started multitasking to grow our financial services' business. We entered into a partnership with Sun Life, the financial services company in Canada, for two of our businesses. We created an executive committee for the financial services' business at the shareholder level. It included some representatives from both Sun Life and Birla group. I, along with the then CEO Mr S.K. Mitra and business head Mr Puranmalka, joined the Birla group's side. We saw the entire growth phase of the asset management company (AMC) business, and then that of the insurance business once we were granted a licence. In early 2000, I moved from the chairman's office into more specific responsibilities within the financial services business. I ran the non-banking financial company (NBFC) and the insurance broking entity before I joined Aditya Birla Nuvo as the full-time CFO. So, it was a gradual transition from the Chairman's office to the CFO's role.

There have been significant changes in the overall organization of the ABG group driven by the chairman's vision. How did that play out in the context of your role at Nuvo?

Mr K.M. Birla had two clear objectives—to create leadership businesses and simplify the overall group structure by reducing cross-holdings and create pure-play companies as far as possible. He wanted to consolidate similar kinds of businesses and create an industry leadership.

Initially, the financial services business was outside Nuvo. Later, we merged the entire financial services business into Nuvo. It, crudely, had three growth businesses—financial services, Madura Garments, and our business processing outsourcing (BPO) business, Minacs. Nuvo was also the largest shareholder of Idea (telecom company), which was the fastest-growing company in those days. These were challenging times as the balance sheet was relatively smaller, and we had to support the growth businesses.

Thus, we came to a decision and spun off the carbon black business to use the money for other growth businesses. The carbon black business got consolidated at one place in the group and to date, we are the second-largest carbon black player in the world.

In 2012, we acquired Pantaloons, which filled up some gaps for Nuvo. It gave us entry into newer market segments such as womenswear and kidswear (Nuvo was predominantly a menswear company), expanded our presence in the value segment (Nuvo primarily catered to the premium segment) and gave us a strong market positioning in the east and north (Nuvo already had strong presence in the south). Again, with the same objective of consolidating similar businesses to create a pure-play market leader, we merged our other existing branded businesses such as Louis Phillipe, Van Heusen, Allen Solly and others into Pantaloons. Today, Aditya Birla Fashion and Retail is the country's largest fashion retail company.

Was the recent merger of Aditya Birla Nuvo into Grasim in accordance with the same strategy?

The Aditya Birla Group had two conglomerates—Aditya Birla Nuvo and Grasim. Both of them not only had a presence in similar businesses (textiles and chemicals), but were also holding stakes in group companies. The majority of Nuvo's earnings and valuation were driven by its fast-growing financial services business under Aditya Birla Capital Limited (ABCL). Considering its leveraged balance sheet, Nuvo needed a stronger parentage for ABCL to fund its growth capital and strengthen its competitive position. Grasim, a net debt-free, AAA-rated company, on the other hand, was eyeing growth opportunities.

Working on the possible answers for the strategic needs of both the companies, we chalked out the merger of Nuvo and Grasim, and the demerger of the financial services business by the listing of ABCL. This move not only consolidated similar businesses and scattered group holdings under one roof, but also provided ABCL with a strong parentage, and Grasim with a fast-growing business. The listing of ABCL unlocked value for both sets of shareholders.

You were the CFO of Nuvo for six years when all of this happened, and then as it merged with Grasim you became the CFO of...?

I actually moved ahead of that merger. I moved to Grasim in 2015, and this merger took place later.

As the Group CFO, you wear multiple hats and get several things done. Suppose the Chairman comes and says 'Can you please help with this as well?', what is your initial reaction? Don't you feel burdened?

I never felt burdened, to be sure. I keep saying this all the time: 'As long as you enjoy what you do, there is no burden on your mind or body.' Obviously, there were many pressure situations as we grew from $2 billion to over $48 billion today and expanded all over the world. But, trust me, I enjoyed every moment of it.

> *I believe that when we love and enjoy what we do, we never feel the burden. This is a principle I advocate to my juniors also. I try to find happiness in every deed, and that helps me overcome any obstacles in life. I embrace my role with open arms. Having said that, I am not very structured when it comes to priorities. I go by the need of the hour.*

This is a slightly controversial question. In your entire career, has there been a role which you didn't associate with and didn't like? Or someone you did not like to work with? What did you do in that case?

It does happen, especially in such a large group. In such cases, I think one should prioritize the value creation the task brings. If I have the belief and conviction that a given task will bring/add a lot of value to me and the organization, my priority would be to complete that task. If I understand the purpose of what I do, then life is simple because my purpose is not to deal with an individual. My purpose is to achieve that particular task which brings me satisfaction and creates value for the organization at large. I may or may not like you as a person, but I am fine with that because we have to accomplish the larger game plan. This approach makes things simple.

Managing one's personal ego is very important in corporate life. The clearer you are in your mind about your priorities, the less conflict will you have—internally and externally.

Are you a positive thinker?

I believe negativity hinders progress. If we are stuck at our personal likes and dislikes, it will affect the organization. At the end of the day, the objective of every organization is business. If we focus on personal perceptions, we will not be doing justice to the role we are conferred with.

Very interesting—a related question to that then. As a Group CFO, you manage the needs of several businesses, let's say in capital allocation. All of them believe they are value creating; all of them think their need is supreme. How do you manage when multiple CEOs come to you for capital allocation? How not to hurt egos?

Every resource is scarce in life. You have to see which one would help more, both from a larger value creation point of view and the long-term strategic objective of the organization. Start with this framework and break the situation into simpler sub-parts. If it doesn't fit the value creation framework, it cannot be prioritized. For example, in our case it was Minacs, the Canada-based BPO firm that we sold to a group of strategic financial investors.

You sold it at a very good profit?

It is not what we sold it for. It was an international business worth $450 million. It was not a bad business in any manner. We felt, given our key objective of establishing our leadership in growth businesses, it might not create the value which possibly financial services could, given the underpenetration in India. You have to think about where you are strong, and we had a lot of strength in the financial services business. That business needed a strong brand, which we already had. Comparing the two businesses, it made sense to let one go, and focus on the one with more growth potential.

But it is always a tough decision, right?

It is definitely tough, but that's what business is all about. It is even tougher for the person heading the business that is to be exited. However, if the person values and believes in the group's larger objectives of value creation and sustainability, it will definitely mean that the decision will be accepted wholeheartedly.

Can you talk about a business situation that didn't work out as planned? You don't have to name the specifics, just the situation.

All our actions are clearly and transparently geared towards shareholder maximization. However, at times, we have had gaps in communicating the same effectively to our shareholders. In the case of the Grasim–Nuvo merger, I think we didn't do a good job of communicating our intentions to the investor community. They possibly misunderstood the whole restructuring process. The moment we announced it, big chaos ensued. We reached out to the various sets of stakeholders, and it took a little longer for us to convince them. It was a superlative success, and we were, eventually, able to prove to the investor community the value of the merger. If you have a growth business, you need a strong balance sheet and a strong parent. ABG was the parent in both companies, but Nuvo had a slightly weaker balance sheet compared to Grasim. It was beneficial for the NBFC to be part of the stronger parent and grow on the back of an AAA-rated company. The stock price recovered eventually, and it went up. The restructuring alone unlocked $10 billion for the shareholders.

Getting Personal

Let us switch gears a bit and talk about a few personal questions. Who is your ideal/inspiration? How has the person impacted you?

Mr K.M. Birla. His thoughts, his words and his actions have inspired and influenced me, and changed my perception towards life. He always says that if we have rightfully performed our duties, sooner or later, they will bear fruits.

He believes in doing the right things the right way, and owning responsibility for those decisions with conviction. He respects individuality and believes in empowering people. His simplicity and compassionate nature enable him to touch the hearts of his people. Mr Birla is the epitome of patience. It has been more than 20 years working with him, but I have never seen him lose his cool, irrespective of his state of mind or the hardship of the situation. These qualities of him as a leader inspire me the most.

Besides his business acumen, another thing that inspires me is the caring nature, especially when he shows this side of him to his people. A few years ago, I was travelling to Delhi with Mr Birla. This was the time when he was extremely engrossed with a few ongoing projects. It was winter, and really cold. I had planned for a one-day trip, but we had to stay back for a few days. The next day, I was pleasantly surprised when he got me some winter clothes of my favourite brand. This incident touched my heart. The way he takes care of his people, even when he himself is fighting against the odds, makes him an inspirational figure.

Do you get inspiration from anything else? Movies, plays, paintings, travel, etc.? Can you share some experiences?

I believe everything has some good things for us to learn from. Like Shri Rabindranath Tagore's 'Where the mind is without fear' inspires my organizational vision and Sohan Lal Dwivedi Ji's *'Koshish karne walo ki kabhi haar nahi hoti'* (Those who try never fail) keeps me motivated. I even draw inspiration from travelling and the different cultures across the world. Every culture, every organization, every country that has become successful has had its own distinct way of looking at things. I like to observe and take inspiration from these. How can my organization and I learn and do things differently to grow better and better?

What is the role of a mentor in one's career? Can you share few of the life lessons instilled in you by your mentors?

A mentor plays an important and the most critical role in the formation of one's career. I am lucky to have been mentored by the late Mr Aditya Birla and Mr K.M. Birla, whose mentorship gave me the eternal lessons of governance, trusteeship and people management, among others. It also played a vital role in the formation of my career. I have already spoken of multiple learning moments from my years of experience.

It is essential for a mentor to help their mentees identify their strengths. Once, I was constantly following up with Mr K.M. Birla to look into certain accounts. I thought he must be really tied up, and hence was deferring it. One day, I thought I would push him really hard to review the same. He responded, 'Sushil, I will go through it. But I know I could not have done any better than you.' It was a million-dollar moment for me, knowing that he had entrusted me with a higher degree of responsibility. This trait of his personality also made me realize the importance of putting faith in the team and building a sense of ownership.

Tell us a little bit about what your normal day looks like.

I am up by 5 a.m. It is the best time of the day, when I sit in peace and stimulate my creative cells. After that, I clean up my emails and messages, and then re-energize myself with 45 minutes of yoga and brisk walking.

I am not sure if God exists or not. But, I believe some power constantly guides and fills us with energy. I devote a few minutes every day to prayer, praying to have the power to make me capable enough to help others. These few minutes I spend praying strengthens my body and soul.

Owing to the nature of my role, most of my day is unplanned. However, as they say, 'The best things in life happen unplanned' (*laughs*). My normal day is full of meetings, and I keep shuffling between priorities.

I try and push off to sleep by 11.30 p.m. after updating myself on the day's news highlights, and some time on reading a book. I firmly believe and recommend one should maintain consistency in sleeping time for a healthy body and mind.

Keeping on the reading topic, can you please share the top five books that shaped your thinking? What are you reading now?

1) *The Monk Who Sold His Ferrari* by Robin Sharma
2) *Jack: Straight from the Gut* by Jack Welch
3) *The High-Speed Company: Creating Urgency and Growth in a Nanosecond Culture* by Jason Jennings
4) *Nobody is Perfect* by David Elliott

I am currently reading *The Art of Thinking Clearly* by Rolf Dobelli.

How do you define work–life balance? How do you find that balance as a CFO?

Good question. But I believe no one has got it right. A work–life balance is a state of mind and differs from person to person. For me, if I am comfortable doing my work and can be available to my family when needed while performing my duties, then I have met my work–life balance goals.

I believe the family plays the most important role in one's work–life balance. My wife, Anita, almost single-handedly raised our children, managed our family and home, yet never complained. Rather, she supported me throughout as I performed my duties. I totally agree when they say, 'Behind every successful man there is a woman.' My children, Tanushree and Anshul, always understood what I was doing was critical and important, and I would always be there whenever they needed me.

On my part, I make sure when I am with family, I am 100 per cent with them. In this tech world, we have forgotten to live in the moment. I often see families sitting together to spend 'family time', but each individual is occupied with their phones.

> *Cell phones bring you closer to the person who is far from you, but takes you away from the person sitting next to you. The people present with you either chose to be with you, or you wanted them to be around. So, don't disrespect them.*

What are your hobbies? How do you find time to pursue them?

I am a great fan of cricket. I love nature and am fond of travelling. Depending on work, if I see a holiday bucket, I try and accommodate a quick family vacation. I even find a lot of joy in sitting with friends, chatting and remembering the good old days.

As a need and also a preference, wherever I am, I like to pamper myself and take care of my body. Just like machines, even the body requires regular maintenance. Over the weekends, I try and run myself through a series of body rejuvenation exercises.

How do you stay updated on current events/trends/ academics?

As I had mentioned, I spend a few minutes daily to update myself on the latest news and developments. I also get to learn more about the latest trends and developments during my interactions with bankers and industry colleagues.

To keep ourselves updated with the latest academic developments, between friends in the industry and subject matter experts, we have formed a friends' study group. All of us meet periodically to discuss the latest changes and share the best practices. At times, we also call an external speaker to deliver dialogues on some specific trending areas of interest.

Being a member of the Confederation of Indian Industry (CII), the Federation of Indian Chambers of Commerce and Industry (FICCI), the National Advisory Committee on Accounting Standards (NACAS) and other industry bodies, also provides me with an opportunity to stay abreast with the current events and developments.

Take us through a life-changing experience in your career.

I clearly remember one incident. It was during the early days of Mr K.M. Birla joining the group as the chairman. We had sought some legal opinion from a reputed law firm involving a listed firm and a private company of the group. The firm raised the invoice in the listed company's name, and I sent it to Mr Birla for his go-ahead. One day, while I was discussing some other matter with him, I asked him about the invoice. Very calmly, he said he wanted to speak to me about the invoice. And then he asked, 'Which company has benefitted the most from the opinion?'

I took a few moments and figured out it was the private company. I got my answer and debited the invoice to the private company. This was one of the very early incidents of my career, which refined my thoughts and made me understand the spirit of trusteeship, and strengthened my conviction regarding good corporate governance.

By virtue of my role as the group CFO, I often come across conflicting situations, involving various group companies; till today, this incident acts as a guiding light in doing what is right.

Was there an event in which things did not go as planned? How did you cope with it and overcome it? What was the learning?

Let me talk again about the most talked about restructuring in the history of corporate India—the merger of Aditya Birla Nuvo with Grasim Industries Limited, and the subsequent listing of the financial services business.

Initially, the restructuring was completely misinterpreted. Early reactions from media and proxy advisors further created odds against the deal. Investors were made to believe that funding of the telecom business was the primary motive.

From day one, our objective was very clear—we wanted the transaction to get approved by all the shareholders without adding any sweetener. We drew a detailed road map on how to reach out to institutional investors, analysts, proxy advisors, media and retail shareholders, and explain the long-term benefits of the transaction and address their concerns. We developed a special management information system (MIS) report for regular analysis of various voting outcome scenarios based on investor interactions. It was a real test of patience to deal with the investors who were not aligned.

Finally, the shareholders of ABNL and Grasim approved the scheme (more than 83 per cent of the minority shareholders voted in favour in the case of ABNL and over 93 per cent in the case of Grasim) without any changes. The retail shareholders' participation is generally very low as they abstain from voting. In some of the recent schemes, less than 0.50 per cent of the total retail shareholders voted. In the case of ABNL and Grasim, we had 130,000 and 150,000 shareholders, respectively, and 3–4 per cent of the non-institutional shareholders voted compared with an industry norm of 0.5 per cent. It is uncommon to have such large retail voting participation for a merger approval.

This entire episode gave me a lesson of communication with consistency, clarity and candour. If we look at the history of the most contentious situation between activists and companies, the problems arose mostly because the management declined to engage in a frank and open discussion. The mistake most companies make is to ignore activist shareholders, which gives an impression of stonewalling. Instead, we should engage with them to understand how they perceive the company and acknowledge their concerns. We should always remember the people on the other side of the table are those who have invested billions of dollars in our company, and it is very important they have conviction.

In hindsight, what are the things you could have done differently?

I think there is scope to do much more on my time-management skills. This is one skill set that probably we can keep on perfecting.

The other thing I want to develop is the ability or the courage to say 'No'. At times, this habit of not being able to say 'No' disturbs my other priorities and distracts me from things which could be relatively more important.

What are the top qualities you recommend for youth who aspire to have a successful career?

Keep your work simple and short. Everything around us is very simple, but we overthink, overdo and make things complicated. My advice to finance aspirants would be to work on sharpening their analytical skills and be able to differentiate between letter and spirit, or as they say substance over form. It is important to stay up to date and abreast of the latest developments as we stay in a VUCA—volatile, uncertain, complex and ambiguous—world.

As we talk about building a successful career, a person should equally focus on developing people skills, and remember that a successful leader stands on the foundation of a highly effective team.

One should be sensitive to emotions and think from others' perspectives before making conclusions. Learning should be a continuous process; one must always be open to suggestions and have the courage to accept failures.

Any specific advice you have for a young finance professional who is serious about a career in finance?

My advice to a young finance professional who is serious about a career in finance would be to focus on concepts. It is essential to get the basics correct and the roots strong to build the entire pillar of finance. The future belongs to those who prepare for it today.

> *One should be confident of one's actions and ensure it passes the 'Headline test'. When one has the courage to stand up before a crowd and take ownership of the things done, and has acted to one's best ability based on the circumstances prevailing at the time of action, then one has passed the 'Headline test'.*

As one progresses towards a professional career, one should keep in mind the following things:

a) When you see abnormal gains or loss, it is time to dig deeper.
b) Develop a wider perspective to evaluate long-term ramifications.

c) Don't complicate things. Keep them simple and short.
d) One should be courageous enough to speak up when needed.
e) One should work freely, without any kind of fear.
f) Focus on soft skills.
g) Trust can be either zero or 100 per cent (it cannot be in between).

That sounds just about right, Mr Agarwal. It has been an amazing journey. Thanks a lot for your time.

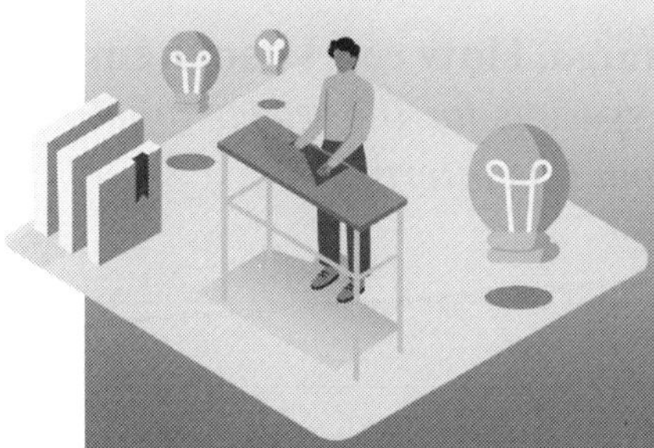

Key Takeaways

SUSHIL AGARWAL

Take 1: Everything around us is very simple—do not overthink and make your life and work complicated.

Take 2: Trust can be either 0 per cent or 100 per cent. There is nothing in between.

Take 3: Never delay communicating bad news.

Take 4: Enjoy what you do; work will then never be a burden.

Take 5: Communicate with consistency, clarity and candour.

Take 6: Be confident of your actions—ensure that it passes the 'Headline test'.

Take 7: When you see abnormal gains or loss, it is time to dig deeper.

Take 8: Be able to differentiate between letter and spirit.

Take 9: A leader stands on the foundation of a highly effective team.

Take 10: If we have rightfully performed our duties, sooner or later, they will bear fruits.

Key takeaways that inspired me most. How can I use them to change my perspective? (*This space is for the reader to jot down the lessons that they learned from this interview*)

With family

Enjoying life to the fullest

With few of the world's best cricketers — Brian Lara, Brett Lee and Sachin Tendulkar

With former Chairman Mr Aditya Vikram Birla and current Chairman Mr Kumar Mangalam Birla (1994)

Receiving the Chairman's Award from Mr Kumar Mangalam Birla for exceptional contribution at the ABG Awards function (2000)

With colleagues from the Chairman Cell, Mr K. M. Birla and other senior executives (2001)

With Mr Basant Kumar Birla (Chairman of the B.K. Birla Group) and his wife Mrs Sarla Birla (2003)

With the Financial Services business team on an offsite in Jodhpur

Receiving the National Award from Hon'ble President Smt. Pratibha Patil for the movie 'Black', produced by Applause Entertainment, in New Delhi (2007)

Receiving the ICAI Business Leader Corporate CFO Award from Union Minister Shri Suresh Prabhu in 2018

With his team post the merger of Aditya Birla Nuvo and Grasim in 2018

With colleagues during his farewell event at Grasim in 2019

Extra Shots

Sushil Agarwal

Keep it simple. Never delay communicating bad news. Try until you succeed.

Mr Agarwal's passion for helping students and youngsters is well known and it was no surprise that he was very excited about contributing to this book. He started by saying that he sees this sharing as an opportunity to connect with a large number of students, finance professionals and other finance enthusiasts, who he otherwise would not have been able to reach. *Give before you receive,* and *senior people have a responsibility to the younger generation* is what Mr Agarwal stands for.

How often do we consciously take the effort to do this?

As we started the interview, a few details about his dressing sense caught our attention. He wore nothing ostentatious, just very well placed details of his attire. We came to know later that his alternate career ambition was to be a fashion designer. He has been able to live that dream through multiple group companies that own all the fashion brands he loves. This shows in his CFO acumen wrapped up with passion and deep industry insight.

Mr Agarwal comes across as an extremely grounded, affable, and likeable person. He restructured his daily schedule to give us three hours instead of the asked for 90 minutes and stayed back in the office to make sure we covered all the content. Another thing we noticed was the clear devotion that his staff has for him. He takes care of them beyond the normal course of work, and the feeling is reciprocated.

Learnings in Action

Both of us are consultants and we have applied so many of his principles on a day-to-day basis. 'Keeping things simple' when solving a complex business issue; 'Never delay communicating bad news' when we knew the likelihood of a loss; Taking the 'Headline test' as we grappled with business versus ethics choices—all became integral to the way we conduct our affairs. These small changes have helped improve the overall perception other people have about us.

During the past 24 months, we also made changes to our personal finance choices. His guidance on corporate investments is so relevant, even for personal investments. SLR—safety, liquidity and returns in that order. And the logic is simple, the company's primary business is not treasury management. How often do we get confused about our primary goal or purpose?

Try out the 'Headline test' next time you are faced with an ethical crisis. Maybe it would help make your decision a lot easier.

FINAL THOUGHTS

As we reflect on the past 24 months, many of the important decisions and choices in our personal and professional lives have been influenced by our conversations and the life lessons we were fortunate to have early access to, as we started putting this work together. Both of us have very different careers today from 24 months ago. A large part of the changes we made was driven by some very specific conversations we had with the CFOs who became our mentors.

As we put together our thoughts here, there are some very specific areas we wanted to cover:

- Are there any common behavioural patterns we noticed as we interacted with the CFOs?
- Is there a more probabilistic career path or professional qualification that an aspirant can take to make it to this coveted office?

In behavioural patterns, it was surprising how different they were in some areas, such as different factors that motivated individual CFOs and yet how similar they were in some other areas, primarily on the 'human' side.

There were very small things we noted, most of which have been captured in the conversations you read but some were subtle aspects we picked up during our discussions. We have summarized the key takeaways at the end of each interview based on the conversations we had. Let us bring you the subtle ones:

- All of them, without exceptions, loved conversations and instantly put us at ease. Given their larger-than-life image each of them had, we were quite nervous, to say the least. But 10 minutes into the conversation, we were made to feel at home
- They made us feel important and gave us all the possible indications that the conversation was important for them. We visited them over weekdays and weekends based on their schedules, but regardless of when the meetings took place, they were *with us* completely. Mobiles were switched off even though days later we found that they could have been in the middle of important transactions. When we asked Mr Shankar Raman what would be the outcome if there was an urgent call while his mobile was switched off, he replied, 'I have committed my time to you. It is important I give it completely; people know where to find me if it is something very important.' We still are struggling to get to that level of personal engagement in our lives but were often nudged towards it with the conversations echoing in our minds when we picked up our phones during a meeting.
- They had a different paradigm of commitment in all their actions—personal or professional—and did not like to give any excuses. We still recollect the Saturday when we met Mr Srinivas Phatak for the second time. We went through the interview and noticed he was not looking comfortable. It was only when we enquired if everything was fine that he mentioned he was running a high fever. When we said that we could have 'postponed the interview', he just said that we had travelled far and he did not want to disappoint us. This shows that these mentors remained committed to a choice.

- They all had an aura of positivity and they took away the option of negativity from their lives. We did take long flights at odd hours to be there for these meetings sometimes. Whenever we had a hectic day and were very tired, wondering how we would see the meeting through, we were energized by them. On all occasions, five minutes into the conversation, we had a high positivity dose injected into our mind and spirit. Not only during the meeting but also for a lot of time after the meeting ended, we felt deeply refreshed. Both of us had many interesting discussions on how the conversation for the day was directly relevant to a life situation we were currently handling.
- They all had a deeply ingrained motive of *being human.* The respect that they showed to their subordinates in all these conversations, the art of effectively delegating authority, and the human aspect of any decision that was taken into consideration were greatly visible. We do believe that both of us were certainly inspired to become better people.
- They all believe deeply in *action*. They did not indulge in overthinking and always took the plunge if it aligned with their perspectives. They took a *chance* with themselves, and we started doing this more often after meeting them. They frequently picked up new opportunities and did not feel comfortable with comfort. If there was an option available to take on a challenging role with high risks, you can bet that these CFOs would raise their hand first.
- They all mastered the art of delegation and had trusted people around them. They exercised the choice to be available for decisions that would have a high impact.

- They had a regimented *morning routine*. They faced each day head-on to make it count.
- They had a deep sense of *giving* which far outweighed the receiving. This work, where they opened their lives for all, stands as a living testament to their commitment to give positive guidance to all of us.

They, of course, had their unique ways in certain areas:

- Some of them were introverts and others were extroverts in their personal space. However, all of them led large teams with ease and adapted to the societal requirements of the role. They did rationalize their interactions at different levels, but never avoided connecting with people.
- They had different ways of acquiring knowledge. Their patterns of reading and absorbing knowledge were very different. Yet all of them stayed at the top of the game and were prolific *learners for life.*

Now we come to the more probabilistic path to the CFO's office, with different choices for roles or professional qualifications, if any. Interestingly, you would have noted that they all have different qualifications but we did note some patterns in underlying education and roles:

- They all had *early access to the seat at the table* with the senior leadership. If you were given a choice between two roles and one of them had such early access, the access will be a more probabilistic ticket if you want to make it to the CFO's chair faster. With this early access, they had the exposure as well as visibility, which counted in the process as they got selected for the role. It also allowed them to pick up the tenets exhibited by senior leaders early on, which would have acted as an invisible force as they made their choices.

- They all had qualifications that set their *early romance with numbers.* They were at ease with numbers and numbers found their natural companion in them. All of them have either a chartered accountant and/or an MBA (Finance) degree, and without exception, all of them had a high numerical quotient as required by their professional qualification.
- They all had picked up roles that allowed them to have higher *business and people impact.* They always participated in large transformational projects and that had lasting impacts on their business and people. They took a larger view of their roles, always behaving like business leaders rather than finance experts, which gave them an edge.
- They, at some point in their career, handled *cash.* It could have been either to raise funds or deploy funds or as a trading desk leader, they all had their exposure to roles that required them to deal with *capital.* You will be an outlier if you make it to this office by just being on the controlling side.

We were fortunate to have witnessed such learning in our lives from these teachers. We do hope that you, too, can take advantage of their learnings and further develop your professional and personal lives. We hope that this engagement with you through this book is the beginning of our new relationship.

Please reach out to us with your feedback.

Pramod and Sandeep
prasan@cfoniti.com